Cashing In on a Second Home in Central America

How to Buy, Rent and Profit in the World's Bargain Zone

by Tom Kelly, Mitch Creekmore and Jeff Hornberger

Crabman Publishing • Rolling Bay, WA

Cashing In on a Second Home in Central America
How to Buy, Rent and Profit in the World's Bargain Zone

Produced by Crabman Publishing, Rolling Bay, Washington, U.S.A
Copyright © 2007 Crabman Publishing

ISBN 978-0-9770920-1-7

Kelly, Tom, 1950 Oct. 8-
    Cashing in on a second home in Central America : how to buy, rent and profit in the world's bargain zone / Tom Kelly, Mitch Creekmore, Jeff Hornberger.
        p. cm.
    Includes bibliographical references and index.

    LCCN 2007922459
    ISBN-13: 978-0-9770920-1-7

    1. Real estate investment—Central America. 2. Real property —Central America—Foreign ownership.
    I. Creekmore, Mitch. II. Hornberger, Jeff. III. Title.

HD333.K45 2007   332.63'24'0928
                                  QBI07-600067

Cover and interior design © 2007 TLC Graphics, *www.TLCGraphics.com*

Cover photo: Hacienda Pinilla, Santa Cruz, Guanacaste, Costa Rica. H.G. Pattillo, owner; Agroganadera Pinilla S.A., developer and builder. Photo courtesy of Stewart Title, Costa Rica.

Sales and distribution to the book trade facilitated by Biblio Distribution, Inc., a National Book Network Company, 4501 Forbes Blvd., Lanham, MD 20706. (301) 459-3366; (301) 429-5745 Fax

Printed in the United States of America

Table of Contents

PART TWO: PREPARING, PLANNING AND RENTING

PART THREE: THE MONEY PICTURE

PART FOUR: HELPFUL SOURCES

About the Authors

Tom Kelly is a nationally syndicated newspaper columnist and radio talk show host. He served *The Seattle Times* readers for 20 years—several as real estate editor—and his work now appears in the *Los Angeles Times, The Houston Chronicle, The St. Louis Post-Dispatch, The Portland Oregonian, The Miami Herald, The Rocky Mountain News, The Des Moines Register, The Tacoma News Tribune, The Reno Gazette-Journal, The Louisville Courier-Journal,* plus more than two dozen other newspapers.

Tom's award-winning radio show, "Real Estate Today," recently began its 16th year on 710 KIRO-AM, the CBS affiliate in Seattle and the state's largest station. The show is syndicated by Business Talk Radio to approximately 40 domestic markets and airs on 450 stations in 160 foreign countries via American Forces Radio.

He is the author of *The New Reverse Mortgage Formula* (John Wiley & Sons), *Real Estate for Boomers and Beyond* (Kaplan Publishing), and co-author of *How a Second Home Can Be Your Best Investment* (McGraw-Hill).

Tom was president of the Santa Clara University Class of 1972. He and his wife, Dr. Jodi Kelly, an associate dean and professor at Seattle University, have four children and live on Bainbridge Island, Washington.

Mitch Creekmore is senior vice president and director of international business development for Stewart International, a world leader in title insurance and other real estate information services. He joined Stewart Title Guaranty Company in 1994 and has been responsible for the development of the company's marketing strategy with implementation of the business plan for Stewart-Mexico. His primary effort has been to enlighten the international legal and real estate community about the availability and benefit of title insurance. He has been a licensed real estate broker for more than 20 years.

In 2003, he was appointed by Arizona Governor Janet Napolitano as co-chairman of the Real Estate Task Force on Mexico in participation with the Arizona-Mexico Commission. He gained approval from the State Bar of Texas and the Texas Real Estate Commission, as well as the Arizona Department of Real Estate and the California Department of Real Estate, to provide a mandatory continuing education course for attorneys and real estate agents entitled "Acquiring Property South of the Border." He has authored numerous articles on real estate conveyance, foreign ownership requirements (including land title matters) subdivision development procedures, escrow and tax considerations.

Mitch graduated from Louisiana State University in 1976. He has served as a captain on the Houston Livestock Show & Rodeo's International Committee, on the board of directors of the Houston Racquet Club and as an officer of Stewart Title Guaranty Company. He is a licensed private airplane pilot. Mitch has four children and lives in Houston.

Jeff Hornberger is the National Association of Realtors' International Market Development Manager, with a specific focus on Latin American and European markets.

Prior to joining NAR, Jeff worked for a United Kingdom-based global manufacturer where he was responsible for developing distribution channels throughout Latin America and creating/implementing individual country marketing plans. Jeff holds a M.S. in Business Management from United States International University in San Diego, and B.A.s in Economics, Latin America Area Studies and Spanish from the University of Wisconsin.

Jeff has lived in Argentina, Spain, and Mexico and is fluent in Portuguese and Spanish. Based at NAR's Chicago headquarters, Jeff is responsible for managing NAR's programming in Latin America and Europe. He directs new international market opportunities for members as well as other business development projects, including a focus on the international second homes market.

Jeff has visited Central America dozens of times and is quoted in numerous publications about Central America real estate issues, including *The New York Times,* the *International Herald Tribune,* and *Business Week.* He has invested in real estate in Central America (Panama) and resides in Chicago with his wife, Paulina, and two daughters, Julia and Megan.

Acknowledgements

This book is dedicated to my six siblings — Mike, Bill, Pat, Kate, Maureen and John — for decades of insights, laughs and genuine support. I could not have asked for better young-life housemates and true friends. All of them have made the world a better place.

My genuine thanks to all the Realtors, developers, mortgage lenders and many individuals from tax and accounting, printing, editing and distributing who have aided me for years in my newspaper writing and radio work, and who also provided creative insights and useful information for this book. I have called upon them often and their patience, interest and kindness have been extraordinary. Leading this list are Linda Owens, CJ Yeoman, Heidi Henning, Tami Dever, Erin Stark, Monica Thomas, Laura Shelley, Dennis Dahlin, Joanne Elizabeth Kelly, Rob Keasal, John Tuccillo, Omar Ayales and Kevin Hawkins. I also am grateful to the numerous second home buyers and renters for sharing their stories.

— *Tom Kelly*

I would like to thank my associates at Stewart Title Latin America for their kind contributions to this book: Lic. Carlos Gonzalez, Lic. Orlando Lopez and Christopher Hill. Thanks also to Mike Skalka, chairman and chief executive of Stewart International; and Rebecca Rice, counsel, and Julie

Kleine, vice president, and Mandy Johnson, copy writer, for their continued support and assistance in our efforts.

A special thanks to Margo Taylor, our kids Megan and Ashton; and the rest of my children, Courtney, April and Tanner. I also wish to thank my wonderful mother, Leslie, and my siblings, Gary, Denise and Kevin, and family members, Candy and Ric. They're great fun and provide tremendous encouragement. I'm thankful to have them all.

—*Mitch Creekmore*

Thanks to all the volunteer leaders of the National Association of Realtors in Central America, including Jorge Cantero, Deborah Valledor and Carlos Fuentes for bringing things to the next level in the region. Also, special thanks to Lucia Sacasa for the help in Nicaragua, Patrick Crowley for the input on Honduras; Sara Siegel for the assistance with Guatemala; Linda Gray and Mercedes Castro for Costa Rica, and Luis Dominguez for El Salvador. I also wish to thank leaders of the Panama Real Estate Association, Prima Panama, and especially Jose Boyd for showing me Panama. A special thanks to Gail Geerling, Jocelyn Carnegie, Grupo del Sol and Frontier Property Group for their efforts in bringing knowledge of the emerging Nicaragua real estate market to this book.

Finally, thanks to my family, Paulina, Julia and Megan, for their support in my endeavors and their patience while I was away on so many trips.

—*Jeff Hornberger*

Why Central America?

Boomers seek adventure ... and a place in the sun

Ian Richardson, a southern California mortgage broker, was burned out. It was time for more than a vacation – it was time for a full-scale review of how, and where, he spent his time.

"I stood on a piece of property in Malibu that was absolutely gorgeous," said Richardson, 52, a husband and father of two teenage girls. "I thought that maybe I could slide out of the pressure cooker and work out on the deck of this place with my computer. The trouble was, I would be creating more pressure for myself just trying to pay for the property."

Three years ago, the millions that Richardson would have borrowed, sweated and spent on the Malibu piece turned into a $180,000 waterfront lot in Costa Rica. He did not have to pay cash because the seller was willing to carry the mortgage, but Richardson had enough savings in the bank and bought the parcel free and clear. He plans to build a second home in a few months.

"There was no way I was going to put one nickel into Central America real estate," Richardson said. "I also didn't want to purchase in Mexico because I didn't really understand the Mexican trust. If I bought in another country, I thought I would fear for my life every day, the agents would try to take me to the cleaners and all the governments would be corrupt with standing armies."

One visit not only eliminated his anxiety and questions, it rejuvenated his resolve to spend more time with his family and telecommute as much as possible.

"I wish I had done it five years sooner," Richardson said. "Not only has the property appreciated like crazy, but my family loves being there. Besides, with an Internet connection, I can do a ton of work from just about anywhere."

Why Central America? There are so many places to start … yet Ian Richardson provides a prime example. Let's check his reasons for making a second-home move to Central America. Topping the list are affordability, weather, increased airlift by major carriers and the rapid growth of the Internet, which has made the international market accessible to millions of consumers. More dreamers have become active second-home players because once-difficult-to-gather data is now at their fingertips.

In addition, there is more political and economic stability in the region than in years past; the U.S. dollar goes a long way; improved, inexpensive health care is available; homes and amenities often resemble what boomers retirees find in the

States; and most Central American countries are rolling out the red carpet with appealing tax incentives.

While Europe has also been a popular destination for U.S. consumers to purchase second homes (were you part of the group ready to jump on a plane after reading *Under the Tuscan Sun?*), the dollar has been weak against the euro for several years and air travel tends to be more costly and lengthy to European destinations. Couple that with the number of first-generation Latino residents in the U.S. who have a particular interest in staying connected to their homeland and you have an entirely new category of potential second-home buyers.

But the wildcard in the boomer deck is adventure – it is part of their hardwiring. Not only is this the largest, healthiest and wealthiest group ever to come down the U.S. pipeline, but boomers also seek the thrill of the exotic and are very willing to borrow to obtain that experience.

An overview of a diverse, fascinating region

Central America is as different as the readers of this book. The region is an absolute paradox. It may be all that you imagine, but surprisingly, it is much more than one could ever embrace. It is more than the long and winding territory that connects North and South America. To the typical North American, the area conjures up vivid and varied images. On the geographical side, a mountainous area with volcanoes, colonial cities, jungles and, of course, bananas and coffee. On the political front, turmoil, dictatorships and instability. On the economic front, rich versus poor, agriculture-based economies and sweatshops where United States garments are manufactured and exported.

It is a complex and fascinating place, home to 41 million people with a total gross domestic product of about $88 billion.

How do you begin to categorize such a dramatic and extraordinary place? For starters, this region geographically encompasses seven countries: Belize, Costa Rica, El Salvador, Guatemala, Honduras, Nicaragua and Panama. These countries have many mysterious cities and fascinating destinations that you could only hope to place on the map in your mind. Where, exactly, are those exotic places on the flight boards at the Miami, Los Angeles and Houston airports? Cities such as Tegucigalpa (Honduras), Liberia (Costa Rica), Belmopan (Belize) and Colon (Panama) … Once you learn where to place the countries on a map, then you'll realize the geographic diversity that these countries present. Striking and picturesque volcanoes line El Salvador, Guatemala, and Costa Rica. Coastlines range from remarkable and mountainous (Costa Rica) to black volcanic (El Salvador and Guatemala) to low-lying Caribbean. Culturally, Central America is extremely diverse. Guatemala has a strong history of native American Mayan cultures where much of the population is mixed, or *mestizo*. Some countries, such as Costa Rica, have over 90 percent European ancestry with nearly no *mestizo* influence. The slave migration from Africa to the Americas resulted in English-speaking areas of African ancestry along the eastern coasts called *garifunas*. Panama is a true melting pot, with Asian, European and Latin American cultures meeting at a true crossroads of the world.

The economies also differ. Nearly every country has its own currency (El Salvador and Panama utilize the dollar) and relies on agricultural exports such as coffee, bananas and other natural resources. Others have heavy manufacturing *maquiladora* bases (El Salvador and Honduras) and other countries are discovering tourism as a major source of income (Panama and Costa Rica). Some countries have a stable middle class (Costa Rica and Panama) while others have dramatic differences between rich and poor (nearly every other country in the region).

Once you can recognize differences between countries (if you can tell the difference between each country's flags and currencies and can point to the location on a map, it's a good start!), then you need to sift through these markets and make a decision. Where would you buy a second home . . . and why?

Who is buying second homes . . . and why?

According to the U.S. State Department, more than four million Americans live abroad, excluding military and government personnel. Mexico has the largest percentage at 25 percent, or 1 million American transplants, followed by Canada with more than 688,000. Central America is not far behind. In fact, an Urban Land Institute study on tourism developments estimated that up to 100,000 Americans live in Costa Rica alone. What does all this mean? As a North American, you will be in good company in Central America. There are many, many Americans living there full time as well as locals who have spent some time in the United States, either studying or working.

Geography also plays a factor. Major Central American destinations are a mere three-hour flight from international airports in the southern United States, including major hubs such as Miami, Atlanta, Dallas and Houston. All of these cities offer numerous direct flights to Central American places that you can't pronounce or quite place on the map. The "U.S. connection," both culturally and geographically, also points to a reason why Central America is so exciting: it feels close to home.

These countries are in the same time zone as many U.S. departure points, making it easy to get to and from home. Network news is broadcast on television via satellite live at the same time as it is in New Orleans or Houston. And it is also comforting to know that you can actually drive to all cities in Central America in a four- or five-day period from the southern United States. (Granted … it's a long, windy, and bumpy trip and not highly recommended for a variety of reasons we'll outline later.)

While buying a second home in a foreign land may lead you to initially consider places such as Europe, the South Pacific or Australia, practically speaking, Central America makes sense from a geographic, cultural, and economic standpoint that we'll explore in later chapters. This proximity has also resulted in Central American countries being a haven for U.S. companies and franchises. Drive in any Central American city and it may resemble a typical U.S. suburb, with every fast food franchise imaginable, warehouse/membership clubs, hotel franchises, rental car agencies, malls and other comforts of home. You can buy peanut butter in Central America and get U.S. brand products at prices similar to what you would find at home! The recent passage of the Central American Free Trade Agreement (CAFTA) means that more products than ever will be available from the United States.

What is driving second-home investment in the region is price. Central America, considered by many to be the "third world," offers real estate at a fraction of the price found in the United States. Better yet, the geography presents opportunities to own property in beach and mountain locations at prices that haven't been seen in the United States in more than 30 years. A low cost of living allows you to live like a millionaire on a modest retirement income. Thousands of foreigners are buying second homes because they have found Central America is a place where their dreams can come true—along with a live-in maid, cook, gardener and chauffer.

Low purchase price is not the only factor driving the second-home boom in the region Many Americans are drawn to Central America because it is an appealing alternative to Mexico or the Caribbean. Mexico, a much larger international second-home market, is an obvious and popular choice for North American citizens buying abroad. (For more information on Mexico, check out the first edition of this series, *Cashing In on a Second Home in Mexico*). Second-home buyers are oftentimes drawn to Central America because Mexico, for whatever reason, didn't make their list. While Mexico hotspots such as Los Cabos, San Miguel de Allende, and Ajijic have reached a "critical mass" of North American second-home communities, Central America is just beginning. It's "the next frontier" in international real estate investment. Some people are simply finding lives that they could not have in Mexico by finding their perfect getaway, or opening small businesses, operating farms or growing crops. Some have been able to integrate more easily into the culture of these countries since they are smaller and more manageable—and it's just not about money. It's true that many foreign buyers of second homes are enjoying excellent appreciation rates and are finding the region is a good investment. But many others are learning that Central America is a unique place and are drawn there because it is *not* Mexico.

In a capsule, Central America is an exotic place. It is different. The risks can be greater because the region is so atypical. Decisions are less obvious and more choices need to be made.

Second homes of any type, taste, and budget are available in Central America. Great urban high-rise developments are common in Panama City and Guatemala City. Attractive beachfront developments are in every market. Inviting subdivisions are tucked away in mountain retreats and numerous farms and agricultural properties offer distinctive opportunities. Local, charming homes offer unusual tile work, living areas and access to wonderful local culture that you could never find in Florida. However, if you want your second home to resemble a sprawling Florida manor, then numerous master-planned communities offer aesthetics, lifestyle and security that is familiar and comfortable. There are prices to match every taste and budget.

Central America is not for everyone. Despite a promising future and improving economies, these are third-world countries. They are not immune from natural disasters such as hurricanes and earthquakes. There is extreme wealth and poverty as well as crime. The region has become more stable over the years but governments are fragile and corruption is real. Getting around from country to country is painfully slow and the roads are terrible. The rainy season (North America's summer) is a bit long.

But, by and large, the region is changing dramatically and has a very promising future, one filled with tourist dollars and partnerships with the United States and other foreign countries. Gone are the days of CIA intervention, communist struggles and military rulers. Dictatorships have dissolved and democratic governments are in place. The region as a whole is friendly to North Americans and Americans are viewed relatively favorably here, unlike in many areas of the world. Visitors will not find graffiti declaring "Yankee, Go Home!"

The United States returned the Canal to Panama and the Panamanians have done an outstanding job managing it. Multinational corporations are discovering the healthy work ethic and are launching major manufacturing and service operations in once-taboo areas such as El Salvador. Newly discovered retreats such as the Bay Islands of Honduras, Guanacaste (Costa Rica) and Antigua, Guatemala, are booming with tourism. The economies are irreversibly tied to the U.S. dollar. The region is changing dramatically with new construction and modern conveniences—no longer the stereotypical "banana republics." Most importantly, every government in the region recognizes the magnitude of the international second-home market and the multiplier effect it has on jobs, economic development, and international relations. By buying a second home in the region, investors become important contributors to the economic development of a rapidly emerging region.

The goal of this book is to provide an educational adventure to a vastly undiscovered region. It will not require riding on old U.S. school buses with musical hits from the 1970s blasting in the background as you drive along bumpy roads with hairpin curves. You won't have to change currencies or wait hours to cross borders in front of guards with machine guns. But have a seat and imagine yourself in a thatched hut *palapa* with a cool drink, fresh food and sunshine along a deserted beach. Or, imagine yourself hiking through a misty rainforest with a view of a volcano in the distance while counting exotic birds. All of this unfolds a few hours' flight from the predictability of life at home. Stay with this book and discover why buying a second home in Central America may change *your* life, economically, mentally and spiritually. Where is the most activity? Sure ... there's plenty of information about Panama and Costa Rica but we'll provide you some intriguing content on the new-look

Nicaragua, the cayes of Belize, the colonial magnet of Guatemala, the islands of Honduras and a few unknown beaches of El Salvador approximately 20 minutes from one of the most efficient airports on any continent. What are the most important rules of buying real estate in the region? Be open, flexible, cautious, a bit adventurous and most importantly, *diviértete! (have fun!)*.

In Part I, we explore the countries and explain where and how second-home buyers—real people—have purchased property in Central America. There are simply too many cool hideaways and gorgeous towns to chronicle, yet let's investigate some of the most intriguing locations of a terrific region. Some of the stops already have been discovered, yet others are just appearing on the radar screen. First up, that booming country of Panama.

PART ONE

Exploring the Possibilities of a Dynamic Area

CHAPTER ONE

The Lure of Panama

U.S. efficiency ... with a Latin soul

If you have traveled abroad, you know the routine ... Get off the plane, hot and restless, dump your bags in the room and then check with a local—perhaps a cab driver or a hotel clerk—about his favorite place to grab a bite to eat. You discover this wonderful, cool refuge tucked away in a back alley and immediately request ... bottled water! The initial inquiry in any faroff place is for that prized, sealed-top liquid that not only satisfies a thirst but provides a sense of security and reliability at the same time. In most places in Panama, your waiter or host will enthusiastically interject that you absolutely can drink the water that flows from the Chagres River, a key tributary of the Panama Canal watershed. A popular old saying is often repeated: "Once you drink water from the Chagres, you will return to Panama."

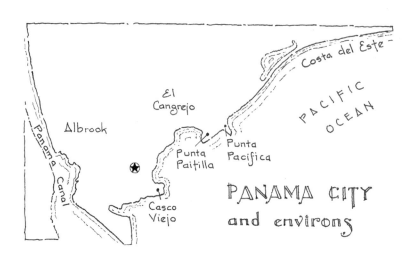

PANAMA CITY
and environs

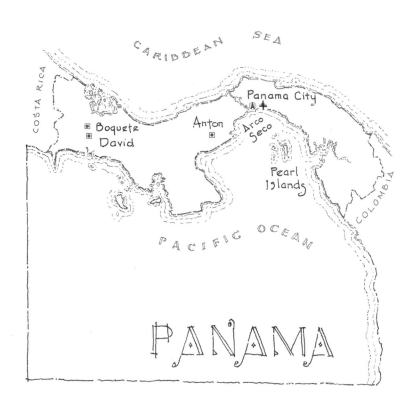

PANAMA

For many second-home seekers who have toured this intriguing country, a new saying has surfaced: "Once you see the variety of affordable real estate, you will run back to Panama."

The Panamanians are a proud people, and the fact that the water is drinkable is a fitting metaphor for their country. This small, Central American nation feels comfortable to foreigners, especially North Americans, who seem more preoccupied with the quality of drinking water than visitors from other parts of the world. In fact, Panama is perhaps the only Latin American country where you can indeed drink the water and not worry about a negative outcome. The nearly 100-year presence of the United States in the "canal country" has produced many dividends, including an excellent water purification system that is the envy of neighboring countries.

As a second-home market, Panama is appealing for individuals looking for a hybrid of U.S. efficiency and a Latin soul, combined in an intriguing mix that offers both comfort and adventure. From the moment you step off the plane at the modern, bustling Tocumen International Airport, located approximately 30 minutes from Panama City, you know that you've arrived in a region that is unique in Latin America. A divided four-lane highway whisks you into the suburban sprawl of Panama City, complete with freeway exits, strip malls, high-rise buildings housing a variety of corporate regional headquarters and expansive manicured homes and gated communities that resemble Miami more than any other city in Central America. Panama City's dramatic skyline appears along the coastline, with construction cranes everywhere. The familiar feel of the U.S. permeates the infrastructure, yet with a distinctive Latin American flair that is carried by the culture and its people. For example, you will pay your taxi driver in U.S. dollars—and your change will be delivered in U.S. paper dollars by an instructive driver eager to point out how closely the local coins, called *balboas*, resemble U.S. currency and carry the same value (but won't work in soda machines back home).

The buzz about Panama—an inexpensive, fascinating second-home market—has turned to boom. North Americans are visiting in droves and buying property. The buying interest has expanded outside of Panama City, to what is called the "interior" that includes mountain highlands, colonial towns, beachfront developments, islands, gated communities, and suburban-style developments. There are now developments, properties and estates to match any taste or budget, from an affordable view condo ($100,000 in 2007) in downtown Panama City to multimillion-dollar homes on the beach.

All properties have one common denominator: they can be purchased at a fraction of the cost you would expect to pay in the U.S. The cost often is the prime reason for rationalizing a Panama purchase, however, the ultimate decision to buy is bolstered by the stable government, a dollar-based economy, impressive government incentives, friendly Panamanians who are accepting of Americans, the low cost of living, a lack of natural disasters such as hurricanes and a country that truly offers (along with Costa Rica) the most "U.S. style living" in Central America.

Paul McBride, chairman of the real estate committee for the American Chamber of Commerce in Panama (*www.panam cham.com*), was educated at the University of California-Berkeley and then spent 12 years in Alaska. He first visited Panama more than a decade ago and immediately fell in love with the country because it reminded him of a "tropical Alaska" with beautiful coastal mountains, fertile waters teeming with fish, abundant wildlife and lush rain forests ... and better weather.

"Having witnessed Alaska blossom during my stay there, I immediately saw that Panama had the same, if not more, potential," McBride said. "More than anything, it was the business opportunities that intrigued me most about the country."

McBride is now director of Prima Panama, a research and marketing company that helps investors and consumers better understand the nuances of buying and living in the country. The company completed an extensive survey of its members to determine their motivations, attitudes and preferences detailing the process of considering Panama as a place to buy or invest. He is also part-owner of a tour company, Panama Travel Experts (*www.panamatravelexperts.com*).

"The overwhelming majority of people looking for real estate in Panama have one primary motivating factor—the low cost of living here," McBride said. "This motivation transcends all economic and demographic categories. Everyone is seeking a less expensive place to buy and to live. Fortunately, Panama does truly offer a much lower cost of living and the quality of life is as high as I've ever experienced. Although real estate prices have risen significantly over the past two years, they are still a bargain compared to the U.S. or Canada. When you combine the cost of living, the great lifestyle, a U.S. dollar-based economy, a stable government, low crime rates and fabulous weather, you have a country that offers a lot to North Americans seeking an alternative to their home country."

According to Prima Panama's research, the motivations vary for North Americans buying in Panama. The survey revealed that the market can be divided into three groups: primary residents, second-home buyers and investors. Each category has different objectives and, curiously, each category buys in different areas of the country. For example, primary residents tend to cluster in the mountain areas near the border of Costa Rica, where the climate is mild and larger numbers of foreigners reside. Second-home buyers generally look to the beach areas, where they can get an oceanfront condo with rental potential. Investors concentrate almost exclusively in Panama City where an unprecedented construction boom is under way.

"If I were to give any single piece of advice to someone looking to buy or invest in Panama, it would be to remind them that Panama is a developing country and it's not just the U.S. or Canada in the tropics," McBride said. "Things do not operate the same way here as they do in the U.S. and Canada and you can't expect the same safeguards as you have in those countries. I often tell people that Panama has one of the highest levels of personal freedom in the world. However, with that freedom comes personal responsibility. If you do something stupid, don't expect anyone to bail you out.

"We believe that if provided enough information, most people will make a rational and informed decision. However, information can be a precious commodity in Panama and it's up to the individual to seek out as much as possible before they make their decision. The advice, then, is to do your research, trust but verify and be prepared to take life slowly. But in the end, isn't the slow pace of life what we're really after?"

History of the second-home market in Panama

Although Panama is just emerging as an international second-home destination, the country has always had a market with a foreign presence. After the failure of the French to build the

Canal, the Americans stepped in and finished the project in an astonishingly short period of time. From 1908 to 1999, the U.S. military administered the Canal Zone, which cut right across the middle of the country. It was a controversial territory in the eyes of many Panamanians, who were prohibited from entering the Canal Zone because it was deemed a U.S. sovereign territory.

Thousands of soldiers and workers who were stationed in the Canal Zone spawned a U.S. lifestyle in the region, and they easily mixed with locals. The Americans who grew up there, called "zonians," did not even need a passport to enter into the zone from the United States. Zonians who returned to the mainland U.S. often grew homesick for the Canal Zone because it offered a lifestyle unlike anywhere in the States. A beautiful tropical climate, stunning scenery, friendly locals and a low cost of living were just some of the magnetic factors.

Other than for the select individuals who were exposed to the Canal Zone, Panama was never considered to be a second-home destination. The country was seen merely as a port of call where cruise ships carried curious passengers eager to see how the passage between two great oceans with a difference in height was engineered. Rarely did passengers even leave the decks of the huge vessels that squeezed through the narrow passage. While military personnel often darted away to enjoy a weekend of nightlife in Panama City, only the most adventurous of people ventured to the beaches or interior for a vacation.

In 1977, the Torrijos/Carter accord (signed by President Jimmy Carter and Panamanian leader General Omar Torrijos) initiated the process that would relinquish control of the Canal Zone to Panama. Under the terms of the agreement, the U.S. would give control of the Canal Zone to Panama in 1979 and give complete authority over the operation of the Canal and former U.S. military bases effective December 31, 1999. The treaty also stated that U.S. military intervention in Panama would be justified if free transit through the Canal was ever threatened.

During this period, several incidents produced a doom-and-gloom picture of Panama. The United States military intervened in 1989 to overthrow the military dictatorship of Manuel Noriega, who was accused of narcotics trafficking and endangering U.S. citizens and interests. Noriega, who was removed and jailed in Miami, had a profound impact in creating a negative image of Panama. As the 1999 handover date loomed, uncertainty revolved around whether or not Panama would be able to rise to the challenge of securely managing the Canal. Economic questions surfaced, including how much would a mass exodus of United States citizens depress the real estate market?

More than 10,000 U.S. troops had been stationed in Panama through the mid-1990s. (Troop presence was highest during World War II, when about 65,000 U.S. military personnel were based in the country.) The Canal, and the adjacent Colon Free Zone, generate major economic activity and draw businesses from around the globe. The Free Zone, which began operation in 1948, is the second-largest free-trade area in the world. Companies located within the walled zone area may import goods free from duties and they pay very low taxes. Companies also obtain favorable immigration benefits for executives and other employees.

When the Canal was peacefully turned over in late 1999, Panama began to actively market its so-called "reverted areas," which were U.S. government properties sitting on valuable real estate. Sales of reverted lands initially were sluggish. But as

Panama began to reinvent itself in the years following the Canal turnover, an important economic tool was discovered: residential tourism. Promotions filtered into North America and Europe proclaiming the wonders of vacation spots on two different coasts with miles of available, affordable beachfront for sale.

The boom took hold in 2003, when the first serious buyers came on the scene, mainly as a result of rising property prices in Costa Rica. Speculation now is fueling demand and prices are on the rise. While Panama is poised to become what many call "the next Costa Rica," its neighbor to the north was developed slowly over dozens of years on a smaller scale and by "word of mouth" of vacationers who turned into homebuyers. Panama's second-home expansion is a more organized effort on a grander scale with big-time builders and huge government support and incentives. Panama is betting on the international second-home industry. The biggest factors are the increasing number of foreign visitors arriving to vacation and buy, and the expected Canal Zone expansion. An estimated 13,000 new homes are anticipated before 2015—a staggering number given a nation of three million inhabitants. The housing industry is expected to bring more than $15 billion in foreign investment and become one of the largest income generators in Panama.

According to the National Association of Realtors' report titled *Profile of Second Home Buyers, 2005,* nearly 40 percent of all residential sales in the United States were for second homes (recreation and investment), up 10 percent from 2003. Fueling the demand are baby boomers, who are turning 50 at a rate of 13,000 every day, or one every seven seconds. According to the survey, the majority prefers to drive to their second home, yet others are not opposed to jumping on a plane to markets such as Panama and trading miles for less expensive real estate. Boomers crave adventure, much more so than previous generations, and don't mind going the extra mile to find it. The United States Embassy in Panama estimates that more than 30,000 Americans are living in Panama, but no accurate figures are available for the actual number of second-home owners there. These numbers are expected to multiply in the coming years. The Canal expansion is expected to cost an estimated $6 billion and create thousands over the next decade—and a roaring real estate market. Investors in international realty claim it would be better to buy sooner than later.

Drilling deeper to understand migration

According to *America's Emigrants—U.S. Retirement Migration to Mexico and Panama*, a 2006 study conducted by Washington, D.C.-based Migration Policy Institute (MPI), an independent, nonpartisan, nonprofit think tank dedicated to the study of the movement of people worldwide, the size of the U.S.-born senior population (those aged 55 or older) grew 136 percent in Panama between 1990 and 2000. At sites in Panama, real estate agents, developers, attorneys and insurance brokers pointed out repeatedly that this growth had continued locally in the post 2000 years, reaching what one called a "frenzy" in this country. Visa statistics from Panama, likely to capture only a subset of people who live there part-time or year-round, showed that the number of U.S. citizens obtaining pensioner visas more than tripled between 2003 and 2005.

A few key components of the MPI study are helpful in understanding the deeper motivations behind Panama's popularity and the bigger picture of Americans' interest in other countries.

Four significant trends were described in the subsection, "Why Is Retirement Abroad Important?" First and foremost, the large baby boom generation is on the cusp of retirement, meaning that the retirement-age U.S. population will grow at unprecedented rates, and its proportion to the economically active population will rise dramatically. As this demographic shift occurs, the retiree "market share" will grow. Business and government interest in this segment of the population will intensify in the US and abroad.

Second, the skyrocketing cost of medical and nursing care paired with increasing life expectancies have led to growing doubts that Medicare, Social Security, and private retirement plans will be sufficient for a decent retirement living for all but the most fortunate of retirees. According to a recent Gallup poll, 40 percent of U.S. residents are somewhat or very worried about not having enough money during retirement. These doubts have already begun to push some retirees to "shop around" for a more affordable spot to retire. Some of the retirees interviewed in the MPI study mentioned that covering their medical expenses in the United States or sustaining a comfortable lifestyle in the United States with only their retirement benefits and savings was not feasible, and they found moving abroad to be a solution to their economic quandaries.

Third, advances in communications technology and cheap direct transportation have lowered the social and economic costs of living abroad and have paved the way for retirees to look to other countries as alternatives. A lower cost of living in another country allows retirees to enjoy amenities that would be nearly impossible to afford in the United States, while communications technology and increasingly efficient air travel allow them to stay in touch with family and friends in the United States.

Finally, international retirement migration streams can affect the economies and communities of favored retirement destinations, sometimes profoundly so. Retirement abroad, much like tourism, can be a powerful form of direct foreign investment and thus contribute to development efforts in other countries. Retirees buy or rent homes. They provide employment for local workers, consume goods and services, and may attract greater investment and more foreign visitors to retirement areas.

While research on the economic impacts of U.S. retirees in Latin America remains quite sparse, research on interstate migration in the United States has found that such migratory streams play a large role in redistributing wealth among states. At the same time, some evidence suggests that retiree flows tend to inflate housing prices, which can push some native residents out of areas in which foreign retirees settle, the MPI study revealed.

Popular areas with potential return

Think of Panama, approximately the size of South Carolina, as a country shaped like an "S" on its side. In some locations, the sunrise is on the Pacific and the sunset is on the Caribbean Sea, causing confusion and disorientation (and lost wagers) for many visitors. At its narrowest point, only 30 miles separates the Caribbean Sea and the Pacific oceans. About half of the country's population lives in Panama City, located on the west side of the country on the Gulf of Panama, with the remainder living in the interior areas. All international flights arrive at Tocumen International Airport, with domestic flights leaving from nearby Albrook Airport on puddle jumpers. Most domestic flights average about 60 minutes.

Roads are generally in good condition, with much of the highway from Panama City to David (about 50 miles from the Costa Rican border) divided into four-lanes. The Interamerican Highway traverses most of the country, but the road ends about 60 miles from the Colombian border. It takes approximately five hours to drive to the northwest Chiriqui province from Panama City and about six hours to Bocas del Toro in the northeast.

Panama City

Panama City is the only city in Central America with a true skyline. Parts of it have a first-world look and feel and its variety of buildings is impressive. It is a melting pot, reflecting the various cultures in its history, from Asian immigrants who labored to build the canal to Latin Americans who call Panama their second home. Thriving Muslim, Jewish and American communities live peacefully. The dozens of international bank headquarters make for a true international finance center.

The city is densely populated which gives it a Manhattan flavor but also gives it Manhattan-style traffic jams during rush hours. To alleviate congestion and flow, two toll roads the *Corredor Norte* and *Corredor Sur,* traverse the city to more efficiently move traffic, but several choke-points still back up during rush hour. The government plans to expand the Corredor across the Bay of Panama near Punta Pacifica and near the Old Quarter (*Casco Viejo*), which will move traffic more efficiently but change the ocean views from nearby new condominium towers.

Due to the presence of the U.S. military on lands adjacent to the Canal, Panama City was landlocked for years. Now the "reverted lands" have opened up brand new areas of the city, most notably the Punta Pacifica area, an old airport where highrises and cranes are sprouting up like weeds.

This thriving metropolitan area has something for everyone and U.S. visitors will feel at home. Two shopping centers, *Multi-Plaza* and *Multi-Centro,* feature department stores, cinemas, food courts and many US restaurant and retail chains. Existing and new highrises meld together nicely with older buildings and homes. Housing alternatives range from U.S. suburban-style homes to highrise oceanfront condos to restored and funky colonial neighborhoods. Here are some popular areas in metropolitan Panama City that offer opportunities for value appreciation.

Unique urban environments:
Casco Viejo and Amador Causeway

One neighborhood of particular interest and charm is the *Casco Viejo* (Old Quarter), a neighborhood once neglected and run-down that is now being lovingly restored by both Panamanians and foreigners. Cobblestone streets and quiet plazas with churches and colonial buildings resemble San Juan (Puerto Rico) in early stages of redevelopment. The neighborhood, which is surrounded on three sides by ocean, is truly an historical and colonial oasis in a sea of modernity. Panama's tourism minister calls this neighborhood home. Americans and other international second-home owners are renovating properties. Buyers here should be interested in the project of restoring an old building rather than flipping a property. The neighborhood is still a work in progress, so don't expect to have a sanitized look and feel. Besides the charm, the major benefit is location. The *Casco Viejo* is in the middle of Panama City, with easy access to almost anywhere, and breathtaking vistas of the evolving skyline on one side and ships entering the Canal on the other.

The Amador Causeway is a narrow strip of land connecting several islands built on material dredged from the Canal during construction. The causeway was previously "off limits" to Panamanians when the Canal was under U.S. control but is now prized real estate. It's a recreational hotspot during the weekend, with outdoor cafes, discos and shopping. The one highway that goes along the causeway is studded with palm trees and pedestrian walkways, providing breathtaking vistas of the city and canal. Land is limited in this area, but several new construction projects are under way there and offer views in all directions.

Urban living: Punta Pacifica and surrounding central-city areas

Punta Pacifica (a former airport) is new, with every square inch of land under construction. It offers new highrise developments from major and well-known multinational developers, with spas, marinas, penthouses and other amenities that make it seem like a mini South Beach in Miami. The newer projects offer parking and high levels of security. The buildings are all striking and the area has an exclusive feel to it, although it is short on sidewalk and street life. But it has easy access to nearby downtown and entertainment, health care, restaurants and anything else you can imagine. Prices tend to be steep in this neighborhood, with many of these condos pricing out at the top luxury level. It remains to be seen how this neighborhood will look and feel when completed; but it appears to be on the rise—in more ways than one.

Buyers who want to be near *Punta Pacifica* but seek a more established neighborhood may opt for nearby *Punta Paitilla*, where buildings are older and the area is more established, with tree-lined streets and more affordable prices.

Another main artery with easy access to *Punta Pacifica* is Balboa Avenue, which is Panama's version of Michigan Avenue (Chicago), Sunset Boulevard (Los Angeles) or Park Avenue (New York). It's the city's main drag, with the ocean on one side and highrises on the other. It connects *Punta Pacifica* with *Casco Viejo* and all points beyond. Several parks line the waterfront with a nice walking area. Parts of Balboa Avenue might look run down with old warehouses and buildings—but looks can be deceiving. These vacant and under-utilized properties will soon transform into modern and attractive highrises, with oceanfront views of ships and boats and a world-class skyline within walking distance to nearly every possible amenity. This high-profile area is also definitely worth a look.

Costa del Este:
Suburban living in the middle of it all

The stretch of road from Tocumen Airport to downtown Panama City is a well-planned area with a U.S. suburban-style feel. The showcase neighborhood, *Costa del Este*, which is the brainchild of a prominent Panamanian business family, can be reached via a couple of exits clearly marked from the *Corredor Sur*. It is split down the middle by the toll road (*Corredor Sur*).

This neighborhood contains subdivisions with attractive tract-style homes, complete with garages, yards, sidewalks and pools. It could be in Anywhere, U.S.A. Several multinational businesses have set up headquarters in this area, with expansive office parks and parking lots. Several private international schools catering to a variety of ages are nearby. A large park is centrally located with many other adjacent green spaces.

Costa del Este also offers highrise living, for folks who want ocean views and accessibility but not the congestion of other areas closer to Panama City. The new highrises, nearly all of which are under construction or in planning stages, line up along a nice stretch of ocean called *Paseo del Mar*—the area is being dubbed as Panama's Ocean Drive. When complete, this will be an attractive area that will be lively and convenient but with a suburban feel to it.

The area has strict zoning for commercial, residential, industrial and high/low density. New projects are selling fast. *Costa del Este* will be built out in the near future, but plans exist to build new neighborhoods nearby that include more single-family homes, golf courses and other amenities that will satisfy buyers who want the "U.S. suburban" feel. As *Costa del Este* expands and prices escalate, development will stretch all the way to the international airport along the Corredor Expressway. The next hotspot in the region is the highly publicized *Costa Sur*.

Downsides of Panama City—"reality check"

Not all is perfect in Panama City, nor are we out to paint an unrealistically ideal picture of Panama City (or anywhere in Central America). Here are a few things to consider. These observations are not meant to take the wind out of your sails, but rather to serve as a "reality check."

While it is easy to find properties with an ocean view or ocean front, keep in mind that, by and large, the water surrounding Panama City is not safe for swimming and tends to be polluted. Although plans are under way to clean up the Bay of Panama, you will find that the dramatic tides that occur in the afternoons and evenings expose unsightly expanses of rock and mud that produce an unpleasant smell. You will soon realize that the Bay of Panama is by no means Miami Beach.

Panama City is inspiring and has a modern feel to it, but bear in mind that Panama City is *not* a U.S. city, and you will find some distasteful trappings associated with the third world, including blaring horns; cars badly needing mufflers; buses, trucks and taxis that belch noxious fumes; potholes; and occasional slums. Lack of zoning can sometimes create a hodgepodge that is unsightly and makes you realize that Panama is not the paradise you may have been led to believe. Some parts of town look and feel like any other third world country.

Panama City is large and fast-paced, but things can move slowly and are unpredictable. Rush hour can triple or quadruple your travel times. In general, service tends to be slow in Panama City (and all over the country for that matter). Simple errands can take what seems to be an eternity. We offer the disclaimer that Panama—like most places in Central America—is not for the "faint of heart." An adventuresome spirit is needed, along with some flexibility and understanding that despite similarities, it is not America.

Outlying areas of Panama City

While Panama City is surrounded on all sides by water, there are no real beaches. This is due in part to tides and pollution (which will be addressed by a multimillion-dollar clean-up effort in the future by the government of Panama). If you want to live on the beach and still make day trips to Panama City, the area prime for development is the Pacific beach corridor 60 to 90 miles west from Coronado to the former Rio Hato Air Force Base. This region is referred to by some as the *Costa Blanca* and by others as the *Arco Seco*, or Dry Arc of Panama, named for its infrequent rains in the summer months that can pour on nearby Panama City. This coastal area begins at Coronado, an upscale beach area popular with Panama City residents, which is built up with single-family residences, condos and other services.

Further up the coast, several new projects on the ocean offer anything to match taste and budget. This is an area that is still a work in progress, so don't expect to find the amenities that you would find in Panama City (two hours away via divided highway). The ocean here is cleaner than in Panama City, but it comes with often treacherous waves and periodic dramatic tides.

A few all-inclusive resorts cater to tourists, and the masterplanned communities are spectacular for anyone looking for oceanfront living. Developments such as Vista Mar and Buenaventura boast world-class golf courses, oceanfront homes at amazing prices, and landscaping, ambience and development that give them an upscale feel. As in many locations in Panama, the heat and humidity can be intense, but this is your best bet for oceanfront living within a manageable drive to Panama City. The surrounding topography is varied and diverse, with interesting small villages tucked away in the mountains. A drive up the mountains takes you to a cooler climate, with several developments taking shape that cater to second-home buyers. An area called *Valle de Anton* is especially interesting and charming. It features a weekend craft market that draws in day trippers and tourists from Panama City. This area offers outstanding beauty in a mountain setting with easy access to the beach and Panama City. The 2-hour drive to Panama City is the downside. In the coming years, this region will have more ample shopping and services but, in the meantime, it is limited.

Island living close to Panama City

Within an inexpensive 10- to 20-minute plane ride or two- to three-hour boat ride from Panama City, there are over 90 islands that make up a chain called the Pearl Islands archipelago, made famous by the television show *Survivor* that was filmed there. These islands all feature exclusivity and remoteness, yet they are a stone's throw from Panama City. The most famous of the islands is *Contadora*, an exclusive enclave 50 miles from Panama City that is home to famous leaders, writers, entertainers and businessmen and where the Shah of Iran lived in exile. Several hotels, restaurants and other services make it an ideal hub for exploring the rest of the islands. *Taboga*, or "Island of Flowers," is also a well-known island only 45 minutes by boat from a marina on the Amador Causeway (there is frequent daily commercial service to this island).

These islands are the stuff of travel-magazine cover photos: beautiful waters, white-sand beaches with secluded coves, reefs, tropical flowers and boats passing by on their way to or from the Canal. While *Contadora* and *Taboga* are the most famous, development is happening on other islands, such as *Saboga*, which boasts a second-home development that resembles eco-friendly treehouses. Golf carts replace cars. Folks leave their doors open. You get to know your neighbors. The beaches contain reefs and protected swimming waters, a rarity on the Pacific side of Panama. These are places truly to get away from it all. Due to their proximity to Panama City and beautiful settings that feel a world away, this is an area to watch. It is truly a unique second-home destination. Think of it as living in Hawaii within a stone's throw of a small, tropical Manhattan.

Boquete and Chiriqui highlands

Any and all of the Panamanian stereotypes will go out the window from the moment you arrive in Boquete in the province of Chiriqui. Dubbed by a local American developer as the Aspen of Latin America, Boquete sits nestled in the cool higher elevations at 3,500 feet, where daytime temperatures never rise above 85 degrees and nighttime temperatures dip into the 50s. Neither heat nor air conditioning is necessary here. The sun makes a dramatic appearance daily, but cool and frequent showers called *bajareques* sweep this valley, resulting in dramatic foliage of all flower types, which would be sold at a premium at a local U.S. nursery but grow wild here. Exotic species of birds live in these elevations, and every kind of food imaginable grows in the fertile lands. For many it truly is paradise with an eternal spring-like climate.

Boquete is an escape from the sometimes oppressive heat found in other regions of Panama. This sleepy pueblo was relatively unknown and had the reputation of a coffee-growing village with backward ways. But this all changed when an American developer moved there with his Panamanian wife to relax and enjoy life. While on a horseback ride in the mountains, he discovered a beautiful valley on the edge of town and began to ponder why Americans didn't live there. Sam Taliaferro, a U.S. technology entrepreneur, built an American-style master planned community called *Valle Escondido*, complete with a pedestrian-oriented town center, golf course, town homes, single-family homes and other amenities along side a raging river that can be heard from all parts of the valley. One of the first gated communities in Panama, it became an idyllic place with a Disneyland-like atmosphere. It is a captivating area that somehow seems to fit on the outskirts of a charming Panama mountain village.

Valle Escondido began the Boquete revolution that has inspired dozens of other developments in and around Boquete. Thousands of homes designed for foreign second-home buyers will be under development in the coming years, complete with golf courses, hiking trails, community centers and other amenities, prompting this region to become a tourist mecca. Within a few hours' drive, you can hike a volcano, experience a jungle canopy tour, explore coffee plantations or relax in Boquete. The entire area is banking its future on residential tourism and the economic benefits that it brings. Prices are jaw-dropping in this somewhat remote area of Panama. There are only a small number of foreigners living here (a future boom will bring many more) so now is the time to discover this corner of Panama, before it gets uncovered.

Boquete, which is sprouting new restaurants and hangouts, is only a short drive from the border of higher-priced Costa Rica, and a six-hour drive from Panama City. Its charm and remoteness is also its liability. To arrive in Boquete from the United States is a travel odyssey, requiring a flight to Panama's Tocumen International Airport, then a transfer to the domestic airport (Albrook), a 30-minute taxi ride away (without traffic). From there you must take a puddle jumper, which has baggage weight restrictions, for a one-hour flight to Chiriqui's capitol, David. But wait—you aren't there just yet ... an additional 45-minute drive up the mountain is required from the uninviting town of David to Boquete. In other words, the remoteness of Boquete will never result in it becoming a jet-set location like Aspen. Nonetheless, many Americans are finding their retirement and second-home dreams come true here. The American Association of Retired Persons (AARP) magazine *Modern Maturity* and *Money Magazine* have recognized Boquete, and you should check it out too.

Master-planned communities offer single-family homes here at very attractive prices and with all the amenities. Some of the largest include *Hacienda de los Molinos*, *Cielo Paraiso*, and *Montanas de Caldera*. Developments are mainly spread out

THE LURE OF PANAMA

along the David-to-Boquete highway. The closer you get to David, the closer you are to sea level, and as you get up to Boquete it gets cooler; so you can choose the development that fits your microclimate! Some developments sell homes and lots overlooking steep canyons. Other offer space for horses. It is recommended that you fully explore all developments in order to find the choice that fits you best. Keep in mind distance to Boquete versus David. Boquete tends to be charming, quaint, touristy, whereas David is more practical with the regional airport, small mall, U.S. retail and fast food chains, and health care; but David definitely lacks the charm of Boquete. The cost of living is dramatically lower in the province of Chiriqui than in Panama City (which is already low). Your money will stretch very far for restaurants, services and labor.

Within an hour's drive of Boquete, yet still in the province of Chiriqui, is an expansive, yet undeveloped, strip of the Pacific Ocean, with some smaller hotels and developments popping up. This area looks promising in the future but currently, access remains a problem. The beaches on this stretch of coast are expansive and dramatic, but the black, volcanic-like sand may not be appealing to some consumers. But many inlets and bays make it ideal for boating and the construction of waterfront communities. The area is not yet on developers' radar screens and definitely a region to watch.

Chiriqui definitely has variety, with mountains, beaches and a range of microclimates. Nearly every crop imaginable grows, so food is abundant, fresh and inexpensive. People in Chiriqui are known nationwide as being kind and laidback. As is the case elsewhere in Panama, you will find a foreign presence welcome and will be made to feel "at home." Perhaps the biggest downside to Chiriqui is its accessibility to international flights.

25

If there are ever direct flights from the United States to Chiriqui province, the region will more than likely explode with second-home development similar to the Guanacaste province in Costa Rica.

Bocas del Toro

Bocas del Toro, or "mouth of the bull," has a funky and laid-back, almost bohemian feel to it. Lying in the extreme northwest corner of Panama, this place is for water and nature lovers. If you are looking for upscale, cosmopolitan living, "Bocas" is not for you. If the lyrics to Jimmy Buffett's "Margaritaville" put you in the proper frame of mind, then you may have found your ideal place to settle. Bocas is a collection of nine islands and more than 200 keys sprinkled about 25 miles off the coast near the Costa Rican border. Christopher Columbus named the archipelago, which today counts 10,000 residents.

A short description of Boca's natural environment includes luxurious rain forests, sunny islands, beaches that rival the best in all of the Caribbean with coral reefs and crystal water, mangrove islets in what appears to be lakes, Indian villages and government-protected lands dedicated to preserving nature, including the huge Bastimentos National Marine Park. It all makes up an incredible, natural archipelago tucked away in the corner of Panama. If you were disappointed in the Pacific coast, then Bocas will make up for your disappointment. To really know Bocas, you must take a boat tour (in fact, the roads to Bocas Town are only connected to the mainland by a ferry at the town of Almirante). It is a stunning archipelago with small homes, bars and restaurants only accessible by water and beautiful nature scenes—don't be surprised when dolphins follow your boat and jump in the wake you leave behind. The water is crystal clear, and the area remains unspoiled despite its status as a development hotspot.

Bocas Town, the main village of fewer than 5,000 people, is the hub of activity. It is a laid-back town that is densely packed, with many curious streets and some stray chickens vying for the road with the relatively few vehicles. Businesses, homes and other establishments made out of wood and tin sit on stilts over the calm waters alongside thatched huts. The town is surrounded on nearly all sides by water, thus earning its nickname the "Venice of the Caribbean." For a small town off the beaten path, it has a lively restaurant and entertainment scene with Lebanese, Mexican and Thai restaurants. A mixture of European and U.S. tourists gives it a true international appeal. English is widely spoken and understood. While Bocas is off the beaten path, you'll be surprised that cell phones and email work just fine, thanks to Panama's excellent telecommunications infrastructure. You are only a 50-minute flight to Panama City and Costa Rica is 20 miles away. Bocas has many paved streets, treated water and sewer systems, electricity, telephones, cable TV, a hospital and ambulance service and a fire department. As is the case in all of Panama, there are no hurricanes in Bocas, giving it a big leg up on other destinations in the Caribbean. All signs point to Bocas being a boom place, but things don't happen overnight in Central America. Investors need to always keep this in mind.

Bocas del Toro is an ideal place to build the single-family home of your dreams where waterfront properties are plentiful and affordable. Several large-scale developments are under construction, such as Red Frog Beach Club, which will have single-family homes and condos spaced over several dozen acres. Special consideration of the environment has been taken, and it will feel like a luxurious Jurassic Park when completed. As is the case in all of Panama, title insurance is a must. There have been several publicized incidents of problem claims in the area, but research and due diligence usually take care of most problems. Unlike David and Chiriqui, there are no plans for an international airport. So the tranquil, remote area should remain popular for years to come.

Tips on buying real estate in Panama

So, you've decided to buy a second home in Panama, either for investment, retirement or vacation reasons, and you want to get in on the boom. What do you need to know?

Panama has a surprisingly sophisticated real estate market. Salespersons must be licensed to sell real estate in Panama, and the country has approximately 1,000 licensees. When working with Panamanian agents, first confirm that they are members of the local real estate association, or ACOBIR (*www.acobir.com*). Members of ACOBIR are some of the best in the country; they utilize a Multiple Listing Service and must adhere to a code of ethics similar to the code honored by the National Association of Realtors. ACOBIR also participates in the International Consortium of Real Estate Associations (ICREA), where all properties are also listed. A U.S.-based broker should be able to locate a reputable broker in Panama. It's always advisable to work with agents who hold the Certified International Property Specialist (CIPS) designation (see appendix). These professionals are fully trained and have the knowledge and expertise needed to guide you through the transaction.

Some differences and other tips in buying real estate in Panama:

- Appliances are traditionally not included. These are negotiated separately and understand that you will pay extra for these. This must be factored into the home price. Appliances can be purchased at rates similar to those in the United States.

- The rental market tends to be weak in Panama due to high home ownership levels. Do not buy property in Panama with the expectation that you will make a decent rental income—yet.

- Financing is widely available for local and international clients. There are more than 70 banks operating in Panama, and most offer long-term mortgages. For foreigners, the usual terms call for a down payment of 30 percent, sometimes less, with mortgage terms of 30 years. Interest rates vary from bank to bank, yet Panama will come closer to equaling U.S. rates than any country in Central America—another benefit of the long-time American presence.

- Lenders will require a full application form, a copy of your passport, a letter of reference from your bank, an income statement or job letter with proof of income, the last three years of your personal tax return statements, and fire and life insurance (also known as mortgage-life insurance) for 100 percent of the mortgage. Shop around for the best mortgage. While financing in Panama is readily available to foreigners, the process can be different.

- Several companies offer travel to Panama at deeply discounted rates. And, if you purchase a property, you are rebated a percentage of the trip. This is a low-risk way of fully exploring the country and looking at the variety of real estate available. The pressure level is low and not what you would find on a timeshare presentation trip. One firm offering the service is Prima Panama, Panama's premier real estate and travel company. This company sells special "passports" that entitle you to "2-for-1" hotel deals, rental cars and other discounts. A VIP service at the airport makes you feel comfortable upon arrival and a 24-hour hotline ensures that English-speaking help is close at hand. This is an outstanding way to explore Panama's real estate opportunities. (Visit *www.primapanama.com*. Realtors can enroll in a special program via *www.primapanamaprogram.com*).

Capital gains tax

Taxpayers can choose how the capital gains resulting from the sale of Panamanian real estate are taxed. There are two options, and both can be confusing:

1. 5 percent of the sum of the following:

   a. The property's cadastral value (public-record value, similar to a county assessment)

   b. Improvement costs

   c. 10 percent of the property's cadastral value for each year of owning the property

This method of taxation consolidates the transfer tax and the capital gains tax, meaning the taxpayer choosing this option is not liable for the 2 percent transfer tax. Taxpayers choosing this option also are not subject to any more tax on capital gains arising from the sale.

2. 2 percent of the higher value between:

   d. The sales price

   e. The sum of the property's cadastral value at the time of acquisition, improvement costs effected at the time of ownership and 5 percent of the cadastral value of the property (including the improvement costs) for each year the property was held

Taxpayers choosing the second option are subject to a further tax on the capital gain. The taxable gain is the selling or transfer price less the following: the acquisition cost or the cadastral value, transfer costs and 10 percent of the acquisition cost for each year the property was held. The gain is then divided by the number of years the property was owned by the seller. The resulting amount is then taxed at the standard income tax rates.

In the second option, the 2 percent initial tax on the selling price can be credited as real estate transfer tax. In computing the capital gains tax liability for the same property, this tax can therefore be deducted from the selling price as a cost of transferring ownership.

Reasons Behind the Purchase

Ron Acker is a fairly typical second-home buyer in Panama. He is a baby boomer within 10 years of retirement and is thinking of where he would like to spend his leisure time while diversifying real estate investments. Acker is also an Orlando, Florida-based Realtor who bought property in Panama primarily as an investment and secondly as a possible place to retire. This is a combination not typically found in other Central American markets. While someone moving to Honduras or Nicaragua probably is focused on an alternative lifestyle, Acker bought in Panama with an eye toward gaining equity via property appreciation while not discounting the possibility of living there. As an investor, salesperson and baby boomer, Acker provided helpful information about buying property in Panama.

Q: What made you decide to buy property in Panama?

A: I have traveled to many areas on behalf of international real estate, including eastern and western Europe and some Latin American countries. What I saw in Panama was amazing. There aren't many places within a few hours' flight of south Florida where construction is priced as favorably as Panama. I was impressed at the quality of construction, too, and the first-world feel to this hot market.

Q: Are there any risks involved in buying in Panama?

A: Risks are inherent in any international real estate investment, but I bought in Panama for a variety of reasons. Firstly, I like what I see there economically. A referendum on expanding the Canal is expected to pass, which will create jobs and economic activity. Americans are moving there in large numbers and the lifestyle appeals to them. I can make it from my home (in Orlando) by leaving in the morning and arriving to Panama at lunchtime. I will either keep my unit in Panama or resell. In any case, I'll collect rental income while it appreciates in value. Several Realtors also bought real estate while I attended a conference there. We know good value and appreciation when we see it. Panama's risks are low (at this point in time).

Q: Where did you buy and why?

A: I bought a condominium in a new construction building called Green Bay Plaza, which is in a neigh-

borhood called Costa del Este. Costa del Este lies halfway between the international airport and downtown Panama City on a key artery highway called the Corridor. The look and feel reminded me of Florida. Efficient zoning creates good aesthetics. It is close to employment centers, which translates into rental income. And it would also make a great second home. From my unit, I get an excellent skyline and ocean view. Low monthly maintenance fees include parking, pool and security. Prices were unbelievable and you can get in on the ground floor (literally) with new construction developments there.

Q: How is the buying process different than in the United States?

A: I've learned that things operate on a different time frame. The developer reserved my unit with a minimal down payment—but completing the contract took months, which is different than in the United States. There is negotiation in everything but the buying process and contract process are remarkably similar to the United States. Documents are fully translated into English.

Q: There seems to be a lot of new construction developments in Panama City. Is it recommended to buy new construction or resales?

A: New construction is where the action is right now, and those who buy early have the potential of good appreciation. New construction projects have a 20-year exemption on taxes. The building designs and construction quality improve dramatically year after year. But resales are also a viable option in Panama. What is challenging is the lack of a multiple listing system (MLS) like one would find in the United States; this makes it hard to determine the true market value. But this will change in the future. As is the case with any property purchase in Latin America, you need to make sure you are dealing with a reputable agent and/or developer with solid credentials and a good track record.

Q: Would you retire in Panama?

A: I would absolutely consider retiring there. The low cost of living, lifestyle and proximity to the United States are primary reasons. Not only is real estate well priced, but you can go out to dinner at high-quality restaurants at a fraction of the cost. Everything from health care to entertainment is cheaper. But the lifestyle is also very comfortable, especially for Americans. The close proximity to the United States means that I could live there for a few months of the year—possibly during hurricane season in the U.S.—and rent it out at other times and/or lend it to family and friends. What I really like about buying (in Panama) is that I've got a variety of options.

Government incentives
for second-home purchasers

It's no longer the best-kept secret in second-home possibilities. Publications such as *Modern Maturity, International Living, The Wall Street Journal* and *The New York Times* have published stories explaining why Panama has finally hit the radar screen as a retirement and second-home location. However, the benefits and rationale go beyond the gorgeous landscapes and bargain-basement prices. The Panamanian government is very keen on increasing second-home ownership and has outlined several programs through which investment in the country is rewarded with economic incentives. The most significant incentives are exemption of property taxes on new construction properties for up to 20 years plus one of the most generous pensioner/retiree programs in the world.

While the plan is aimed at retirees, anyone over the age of 18 may apply and can qualify as a *pensionado* in Panama. All that is required is a guaranteed pension income of $500 per month ($600 for a couple). It must be a pension from a government agency (e.g., Social Security, disability, Armed Forces, etc.) or a defined-benefit pension from a private company. An immediate, fixed annuity doesn't qualify.

As a qualified *pensionado*/retiree, you are entitled to a one-time exemption from duties on the importation of household goods (up to $10,000) and an exemption every two years from duties on the importation or local purchase of a car (only sales tax and luxury tax would still apply).

In a capsule, Panama has two visas—the *pensionado* and *rentista*—that specifically target retirees. In addition, some retirees may qualify for economic self-sufficiency visas. Panama's *pen-*

What Are Panama's Real Estate Taxes?

- There is an annual Land Tax and an Improvements Tax

- Land Tax is exempt for the first $30,000 of value. Amounts greater than $30,000 are taxed at approximately 2 percent of value. For example, on a lot worth $100,000 you will pay a yearly tax of $1,400 ($100,000 − $30,000 = $70,000 X 2 percent)

- Improvements Tax is exempt for 20 years. After 20 years, the tax is approximately 2 percent of value. As of September 2007, the tax break will vary depending on the value of property as shown below: Under $100,000 – 15 years; $100,000 to $250,000 – 10 years; greater than $250,000 – 5 years

- Tax benefit on improvements transfers from one owner to the next. For example, if you buy in 2008 a property that was built in 2000, you will still have a tax benefit of 12 years.

sionado visa was modeled on that of Costa Rica, which implemented policies favorable to international retirees and drew large flows of foreign pensioners in the 1980s. (However, Costa Rica significantly scaled back the incentives associated with its *pensionado* visa). Applicants for a *pensionado* visa in Panama do not need to be of traditional "retirement age," but they must be retired (no longer employed, at least in Panama) and receive government or private pensions of $500 per month, or $600 per month for a couple. The *pensionado* visa allows retirees to remain in the country indefinitely, although they are not eligible for citizenship with this visa type.

Retirees who do not receive regular pensions may instead apply for Panama's *rentista* visa. *Rentista* applicants must place an amount of money—now hovering around $225,000—in a five-year certificate of deposit at the National Bank of Panama in order to yield at least $750 in interest per month. The *rentista* visa, unlike the *pensionado*, allows its holders to obtain a special Panamanian traveling passport, though like the *pensionado* it does not confer Panamanian nationality. The *rentista* visa must be renewed every five years.

As a qualified pensioner in Panama, you would be entitled to:

Travel and entertainment benefits

- 50 percent off the price of admission to movies, theaters, sporting events and other public events
- 30 percent off fares for buses, trains, small boats and ships
- 25 percent off the fares of national airlines
- 50 percent off hotels and motels from Monday through Thursday, and 30 percent off from Friday through Sunday

---

- 25 percent off restaurant food and 15 percent off fast food chain restaurants

Health care benefits

- 15 percent off hospital and private clinic services, if you have no hospital insurance
- 10 percent off prescription medications
- 20 percent off medical consultations
- 15 percent off dental and optometry services

Professional fee discounts

- 20 percent off technical and professional service fees
- 50 percent off closing costs and commissions for loans
- 15 percent discount on loans
- 1 percent point reduction of mortgage interest rates

Utility expense discounts

- 25 percent discount on power bills of less than $50
- 25 percent off fixed cost of telephone service
- 25 percent off water charges below $10

Other Key Issues

Safety

According to the Pinkerton Intelligence Services, Panama has one of the highest ratings for safety in all of Latin America.

THE LURE OF PANAMA

While petty crime is common, kidnappings and violent crime are rare. Many citizens of nearby dangerous countries such as Colombia, Venezuela and Guatemala visit Panama as a vacation place or buy a second home due to the safety factor. It is safe and easy to rent a car in Panama and roads are also safe. The country's lone area of political instability is in Darien Province, which is isolated from the rest of the country—no roads connect it to Panama City and the more populated western provinces.

Health care

Panama boasts good health care, with many of its doctors educated in the United States. Health care costs are much less expensive than in the United States with similar quality. Major hospitals such as Johns Hopkins have affiliate facilities in Panama City's Punta Pacific neighborhood. Many U.S. citizens travel to Panama on "health tourism" and get dental, plastic and other surgeries at a fraction of U.S. costs.

Cost of living

One of the major advantages of living in Panama is the lower cost. There are no currency exchange risks that you would find in other markets. Panama boasts one of the lowest inflation rates in Latin America.

Education

Panamanians are educated, with many having studied in U.S. universities. Panama has a 90 percent literacy rate. Several U.S. universities have a presence in Panama, as do institutions such as the Smithsonian, which runs a research center there. The U.S. presence results in many U.S. organizations, clubs and other intellectual pursuits.

Families have a number of excellent schools from which to choose, and there are numerous American-accredited schools.

Weather

Panama experiences no major natural disasters such as hurricanes, tornadoes and snowstorms, and only minor earthquakes and tremors. Panama is marked by two major seasons: the dry season, which is from December through March; and the rainy season, which occurs during the rest of the year. But even during the rainy season, there is usually sunshine for at least a portion of the day. Panama's highland regions, such as Valle Anton and Boquete, have year-round spring climates for which neither air conditioning nor heating is required. The downside is the climate tends to get humid and muggy in the wet season.

Familiar conveniences

Thanks to the Canal Zone, Panama has every U.S. franchise and chain restaurant imaginable throughout the country. There are three North American-style shopping centers in Panama City alone, plus warehouse clubs, movies and restaurants. Inexpensive shipping prices are due to the presence of the Canal as a major freight point. Movies are released in Panama a short time after release in the United States. ATM machines are found throughout Panama since it is an international banking center with no foreign currency transaction fees.

Quality construction

Home seekers will be pleasantly surprised by the high quality of Panamanian construction. Homes are well built and tastefully designed. Panama architects attend U.S. construction-industry conventions to keep up to date on the latest in construction styles, floor plans and quality living. Some of the newer developments in Panama cater specifically to U.S. buyers by eliminating maid's quarters and designing open floor plans and kitchens and smaller formal areas.

Panama has jumped to a spot near the top of the charts for international second-home buyers and investors. There's waterfront on two of the world's great oceans, tropical-forest getaways and a very attractive downtown condo market where absentee owners have found responsible renters to help carry the monthly mortgage. And, many investors have seen double-digit appreciation over the past few years.

Now, let's take a look at the first real draw for second-home buyers in an area south of Mexico—Costa Rica.

CHAPTER TWO

Costa Rica: Once-Secret Paradise Found

Guanacaste region remains immensely popular

Costa Rica has been "found"—several times. First came the fishermen looking for the fighting billfish of the blue Pacific, followed by the surfers seeking secluded waves no longer available on the busy southern California coast, and lastly by second-home buyers hoping to lay claim to a cozy spot away from the chaos of their work-a-day routine.

Despite all the new arrivals, there's still plenty of room to find an isolated lifestyle—and future property appreciation.

Costa Rica now ranks at the top of international tourism destinations and is widely regarded as one of the safest and most popular markets for real estate investment in the world.

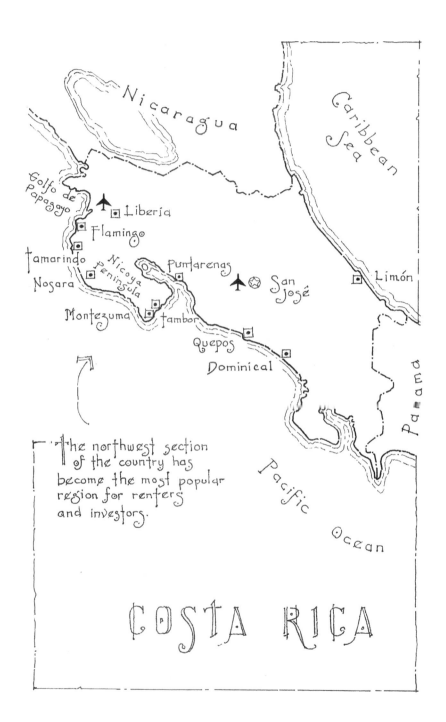

Nicaragua

Caribbean Sea

Golfo de Papagayo

✈ ▣ Liberia

▣ Flamingo

▣

Tamarindo

▣ Nicoya Peninsula

▣ Puntarenas

✈ ✪ San José

▣ Limón

Nosara

Montezuma ▣ Tambor

▣

Quepos

▣ Dominical

Panama

The northwest section of the country has become the most popular region for renters and investors.

Pacific Ocean

COSTA RICA

44

According to *The Wall Street Journal*, more than 83 percent of coastal developed property is owned by foreigners. A fair legal structure, democratic government, favorable tax laws, anonymous protection for banking transactions and equal rights for foreigners under the Political Constitution (property ownership rights) have made the country an example of success for its Latin American neighbors. The Instituto Costarricense de Turismo (ICT) reported that 1.6 million foreign tourists visited the country in 2005, generating about $1.589 billion.

Costa Rica, bordering both the Caribbean Sea and the Pacific Ocean between Nicaragua and Panama, is slightly smaller than West Virginia and, like most Central American countries, has two basic seasons: the rainy season runs from May through November and the dry season runs from December through April.

Yet one region, Guanacaste, has remained hot year-round for second-home buyers. Located in the country's northwest corner, it is known for its captivating shoreline and world-class surfing, snorkeling, bird watching and windsurfing. The region has not yet reached the development level of some retirement and vacation resort areas, but the high-end, master-planned, gated communities definitely have arrived. Yet laid-back beach getaways also can be found.

The key to Guanacaste (derived from the word *quahnacaztlan*, the native word for the guanacaste tree) has been the expansion of the Daniel Oduber International Airport near Liberia. Ask any developer, Realtor or second-home investor: the potential for buyers and renters is in direct proportion to the number of flights to a nearby, accessible airport. The facility, named after the country's president from 1974 to 1978 who launched the idea of an international airport in the northern portion of the country, features nonstop flights from Chicago, Miami,

Atlanta, Houston, Charlotte and Philadelphia, with more U.S. cities standing in line. Traffic to the airport increased 122 percent from 2005 to 2006. Before 2002, travelers to the region typically flew into San Jose's Juan Santamaria airport and either took a short flight or drove several hours via the Pan-American Highway.

Historically, Costa Rica has attracted retirees from the U.S. and Canada, but the boomers are now arriving along with a variety of age groups from Europe. Bob Davey, a long-time broker in Playa Flamingo (*www.century21costarica.net*), said about 70 percent of his clients are North Americans seeking single-family homes with an ocean view, 20 percent are Europeans, and the remainder come from Central and South America. Some of the most popular northern Guanacaste areas are Flamingo, Playa Grande, Playa Hermosa/Ocotal and Tamarindo.

"You have to have an open mind to the slow pace and slow service," Davey said. "The Costa Ricans are not a service type of culture like the North Americans. *Manana* definitely exists in Costa Rica. Be patient and pay attention and you can adapt well. Otherwise you will be very frustrated.

Tom McKenzie, a San Diego-area resident, knows all about the frustration that comes from the laid-back pace. In the long run, however, the frustration is worth it.

"The process is confusing and it just takes a long time," McKenzie said. "We probably made four trips down there just to complete the details. We had to meet with attorneys and decided to set up a corporation. It's not like buying a car … you have to watch everything."

McKenzie bought as close as he could to the beach because he felt it would have the most appeal as an investment. His family was not going to be able to make the house work without the rental income, so he tried to appeal to the biggest rental pool possible. He said he did not want to take the chance of speculating on vacant land because investing in the house was scary enough.

"We now have this five-bedroom beach house that has great waves right out in front and snorkeling around the corner," McKenzie said. "It broke even with rent the first year; we are now in our third year and making money. We get about 99 percent of our renters from the Internet, and we turn away people on a regular basis because it has become so popular."

Scott MacDougall, a residential broker who has focused on the area around Guantacaste's Playas de Coco for more than 15 years (*www.real-estate-costa-rica.com*), said almost everyone he meets wants to know about incorporating, buying property and obtaining residency. "We believe these three issues are the main components of what we would call the 'typical investment package,'" MacDougall said.

The area has been in desperate need for more hotel rooms and it seems more than enough help is on the way. Long-time and newcomer developers have been in discussions with at least 10 major hotel chains. The Hilton Hotels Corporation, Regent International Hotels, the Starwood Group's St. Regis Hotels, The Ritz-Carlton Hotel Company, Rosewood Hotels and Resorts, Hyatt Hotels and Resorts, Aman Resorts International and JW Marriott have been jockeying for waterfront property. Most are planning five-star resorts. Part of the space problem has been compounded by a constant concern — Guanacaste's deteriorating infrastructure. Some big-time investors have been reluctant to spend millions of dollars when many roads are crowded or in need of repair. Others are earmarking funds to do their own roadwork, knowing from experience that help from the government may not meet their requirements.

The Nosara factor

If there is an anchor for Americans outside of the Central Valley area of San Jose, it has to be the Nosara area on the Nicoya Peninsula in Guanacaste. Playas de Nosara is the oldest expatriate community in Costa Rica and was founded in 1968 by a U.S. investor group as the Nosara Civic Association (NCA) "American Project" or "Proyecto Americano."

The NCA development stretches along more than two miles of protected beaches and encompasses approximately 3,000 acres. Of these, 850 acres are held in trust as protected green zones—a national wildlife and nature preserve woven throughout the community. Among Nosara's other draws are the Lagarta Lodge sustainable hotel and wildlife refuge, Ostional Wildlife Refuge for the protection of turtles and Playa Guiones' consistent surf. The Nosara Yoga Institute and the Omega Institute's recent investment of $17 million in land acquisition for an exclusive yoga and healing resort have made the area a destination for holistic health and wellness.

Nosara's remote location, highlighted by boutique hotels and restaurants and nestled in a fertile river valley near the mouth of the Nosara River, has resulted in a family-friendly destination with a community feel. It has been a quiet, favorite stop for celebrities including singer Jackson Browne, actors Tim Robbins and Susan Sarandon and football coach Pete Carroll.

"What was originally planned as a golf course country club has now become an eco-community where residents live in harmony within the jungle surroundings," said Chip McGraw, a transplanted Florida surfer who is now owner/managing broker of Coldwell Banker Del Mar Realty, Nosara (*www.cbnosara.com*).

While resales of the original NCA lots comprise a large part of McGraw's business, he and partners are developing several new projects of built housing. These include Las Olas Nosara, The Palms at Palada, Centro Pelada (a mixed-use condo and commercial project), and Villa Pelada (a private, gated patio home community). A good example of the activity on the periphery of Nosara is the Miramar development (*www.miramarnosara.com*), a private residential project of 55 lots on 62 acres of lush hillside featuring panoramic ocean views. The location is less than a mile from the ocean and a short drive to the town of Nosara and its restaurants and services. The main compound, 15 minutes from Nosara's community airport, has a community clubhouse and lap pool.

McGraw has seen a shift in the type of buyers, from mostly investors, developers and retirees to younger "end-users" who are building their own homes. New buyers include the 35-to-55 age group, who like to stay active with surfing or hiking.

Central-Southern Pacific

Puntarenas is the largest province in Costa Rica and stretches along two-thirds of the country's Pacific Coast 75 miles west of the capital city San Jose. It encompasses the entire Central-Southern coastline. This province's main features are its friendly beaches and slow-paced lifestyle. Puntarenas (also the name of a city on the North Central Coast) meanders from the southern Nicoya Peninsula around the Golf de Nocoya and extends to Costa Rica's southern border with Panama. Playa Jaco, perhaps the country's most popular beach community and a second-home haven for residents of the San Jose area, is popular among the spring-break college set. Los Suenos Resort, just north of Playa Jaco, featuring a marina and a new Marriott beach hotel, golf course and residential development, has proven to be a great success as a top-quality master-planned resort community. There are also several private beaches that stretch down the coast. Hidden by patches of forestland, these beaches are paradise for those who want some peace and quiet. Available real estate here is in great demand and often is sold by word of mouth.

One of the more attractive areas—especially for view and oceanfront property buyers—is the Southern Zone, stretching approximately from Jaco to the Panama border. Long, vacant beaches and huge parcels of undeveloped land covered with lush rainforest attract savvy investors and second-home seekers. The dramatic coastline changes from the desolate shorelines near Matapalo and Hatillo, to rocky cliffs south of Playa Dominical, to the Terraba River deltas and then the dense Osa Peninsula jungles.

The Southern Zone includes the famous surfing beaches of Jaco and Playa Dominical, Uvita's Whale's Tail reef formation in the Ballena National Marine Park and the Corcovado National Park. These are a few of the lures that make areas in the Southern Zone one of the best potential investment areas in the country.

"Over the last five years, we have seen real estate investments appreciate 20 percent to 35 percent per year and occasionally 50 percent to 100 percent," said David Hollander, owner/broker of Coldwell Banker Dominical Realty. "Although our area is no longer a secret, it is relatively undeveloped, with unlimited and untapped opportunities."

Jason Fairchild, a computer communications specialist, saw those untapped opportunities when he came to the Dominical area a few years ago on vacation. Like many visitors, he was impressed by the property available and subsequently purchased a lot for investment. His purchase process not only pushed him into helping other non-nationals via his company Costa Rica Real Estate Service (*www.costaricarealestateservice.com*), but he now has a local development team in place working on five separate parcels. His site also includes properties for sale throughout the country.

"Everybody looking to buy asks about the wow factor," Fairchild said. "The wow factor, especially around Dominical, is the initial beauty of the land. You can find it in many areas of Costa Rica but you are going to pay a lot more for it in places like Nosara."

When the Quepos-to-Playa Dominical road improvements are completed, drive time from Quepos will be cut from 90 minutes to less than 30 minutes. Construction has started on the Osa Hospital near Palmar Sur. Daily commuter flights have increased from San Jose to Palmar Sur and, Costa Rican government has announced studies to determine the location for a new international airport serving the Southern Zone. Electricity service now covers formerly blacked-out areas south of Uvita. Phone and Internet service is available almost everywhere. New Internet cafes, banks, businesses, hardware stores and commercial office suites are surfacing, including a modern shopping plaza with a movie theater in San Isidro de El General (also known as Perez Zeledon), about 45 minutes south of Playa Dominical.

Hollander said there is no typical second-home customer. The Southern Zone is attracting everybody from adventurous young people and retirees seeking affordable house lots to developers looking for larger properties on which to build resorts, marinas, golf courses, condos and villas.

"This could well be the last place in Costa Rica that offers affordable properties with fantastic ocean and mountain views and beach access," Hollander said.

This coastal area also includes the Osa Peninsula and the Golfito area in the south plus ever-present fishing villages, world class surfing beaches, and Corcovado National Park, with over 103 acres that was reported by *National Geographic* as "the most biologically intense place on earth."

Dominical is casual, cool and laid back. It's a former fishing village now synonymous with surfing and an excellent take-off point for hiking or horseback riding. Nine miles south of Dominical is Uvita and the Brunca Coast, named after a local Indian group.

This area is still pretty much undeveloped and it offers a superb wildlife and marine refuge. Further south is the Osa Peninsula, a nature lover's paradise with abundant wildlife and rain-soaked forests, known for sport fishing, diving and wilderness lodges.

Inland from the Osa Peninsula is the Golfo Dulce (Sweet Gulf) and the Golfito, a town that came to life in 1938 when the United Fruit Company established plantations and Golfito became the banana capital of the region, as well as the main banana shipping port in Costa Rica. Today it's a favorite with yachters, sport fishermen and nature travelers. It is also home to a duty-free zone created for Costa Ricans, established to help the local economy after the demise of the banana plantations.

Central Valley

With beautiful mountains and a mild and dry climate all year round, it is no wonder that Costa Rica's Central Valley is where over two-thirds, or 70 percent, of its 4 million people reside. This valley lies at an altitude between 3,000 and 4,000 feet above sea level and offers a spring-like climate year-round. It is surrounded by mountains and is Costa Rica's primary agricultural region, as the rich volcanic soil makes it ideal for growing almost anything, including what is arguably the best coffee in the world. The capital city of San Jose is located here as well.

The Central Valley includes the cities of Alajuela and Heredia as well as Santa Ana and Escazu, which are extremely popular areas for new arrivals as well as seasoned residents. We will take a quick look at each of these neighborhoods. (For more information, many of the areas have individual websites, or visit *www.thecostaricaguide.com*)

Sabana—Rohrmoser—Pavas

La Sabana Park is a large city park with lakes, trails, museums, sports fields, a stadium, an olympic pool and many more amenities open to the general public. It is located just on the outskirts of the center of the city and has nice upscale neighborhoods to the north, south and west, also under the Sabana umbrella. Just west and north of Sabana is Rohrmoser, which is an established, impressive neighborhood made up of mostly traditional homes with some businesses along the main tree-lined road, Rohrmoser Boulevard. Many embassy homes are located in this area, as are some very nice neighborhood parks. Most residents here are middle- to upper-class, with a mixture of Costa Ricans and foreign nationals. There is excellent access to all major highways and to all types of services and amenities. Shopping in the area includes Plaza Mayor Mall, an English-language bookstore and movie theaters. Pavas is just west and south of La Sabana and is highly commercial with middle-class homes. The main road, Pavas

Boulevard, is home to the U.S. embassy along with banks, restaurants, shops, cafes and bakeries.

Escazu—Bello Horizonte—Trejos Montealegre

These are popular neighborhoods for North American residents and the main thoroughfare into Escazu is a clear indicator—Tony Roma's, TGIF, McDonald's, KFC, Blockbuster, Rooms to Go … You have to blink twice to make sure you're not in the U.S. Located here also are palatial estates, high-rise penthouses, luxury hotels such as Villas del Rio and ambassadors' homes that mix right in with simple local homes. Many of the finest homes in this area are owned by wealthy Costa Ricans who enjoy the beauty of the area and the convenience of having great restaurants, top-notch shopping malls, state-of-the-art medical facilities, office buildings and great nightlife and entertainment. Escazu is also home to the exclusive Costa Rica Country Club, which offers golf and tennis for its members. Many private, bilingual schools are also located here or nearby. Known as the Beverly Hills of Costa Rica, Escazu—along with Trejos Montealegre and Bello Horizonte—will continue to appreciate.

Santa Ana—Ciudad Colón

Just west of Escazu is Santa Ana and Ciudad Colón. This area has seen tremendous growth as the city of San Jose continues to expand. A big assist has come from the highway that begins at La Sabana and currently ends at Ciudad Colón. It will eventually continue on toward the Central Pacific beaches when the Ciudad Colón-Caldera highway project is completed in the next few years. This connection will put the ocean less than 30 minutes away for a majority of Central Valley residents. Santa Ana offers a warm, dry climate year-round and is near the CIMA Hospital and Medical Tower, Costa Rica's largest mall, the Intercontinental Hotel and the ultra-modern Plaza

Roble and Forum office complex. A good mixture of Costa Ricans and foreigners seems to share the area. Downtown Santa Ana retains its local small-town flavor and is very much like the majority of small towns in Costa Rica, featuring a small church opposite a park and soccer field at the center of town. Santa Ana also has an interesting variety of restaurants and some small boutique hotels nearby, including the popular. Definitely a boom area as the city grows to the west.

Ciudad Cariari—San Antonio de Belén

Known more commonly as Cariari and located approximately five miles north of San Jose, this high-end neighborhood has as its centerpiece the Cariari Country Club. Located just off the highway from Juan Santamaria International Airport, Cariari has many top hotels, including Melia Cariari, Herradura and the Residencias de Golf, as well as good restaurants and the American International School. Just across the highway is Real Cariari—a major shopping mall complete with a great kids carousel. Just to the west of Cariari is San Antonio de Belén, or simply Belén. This was generally a laid-back town yet has experienced rapid growth since Intel's huge microprocessor plant opened. A variety of housing is available.

San Pedro—Los Yoses—Barrio Dent—Curridabat

These neighborhoods, located to the east of downtown San Jose, are well established and have a mix of both new and older high-quality homes and businesses, especially Los Yoses. Curridabat is the farthest east and is an upscale area composed primarily of large residences and Costa Rica's first real mall—Plaza del Sol. Farther east is the University of Costa Rica campus—many surrounding restaurants and a variety of entertainment venues, all catering to the university crowd and the local residents. A newer

American mall and other shops line the main road, as do several language schools.

Heredia—Alajuela

These towns also are on the outskirts of San Jose and feature open green areas, views, local flavor and a variety of housing options, from inexpensive, simple homes to multimillion dollar mansions. Heredia is cooler because of its higher elevation and features attractive neighborhoods like El Castillo, home to the beautiful La Condesa Hotel and upscale residential developments San Rafael and Barva. This area is located 25 to 30 minutes from San Jose and offers a beautiful rural environment with plenty of homes and lots.

Alajuela is the second-largest city in Costa Rica. It is located about 30 minutes from San Jose and is home to Costa Rica's major airport. Heading east past downtown Alajuela you will very quickly encounter the rural feel of Costa Rica, with lots of coffee farms, an oxcart or two, horses and lots and lots of green areas and spectacular views. As in most of Costa Rica (outside of gated developments and a few communities), you will find that housing varies greatly, with expensive homes often built near more modest residences. Nobody seems to mind.

Caribbean Coast

With wild rainforests and lush landscapes, Costa Rica's Caribbean Coast, which lies inside the Limon province, consists of roughly 125 miles between the borders of Panama and Nicaragua. First discovered by Christopher Columbus who landed here in 1502, this province is one of the least traveled areas of the country. Normally hot and humid throughout the year, this part of Costa Rica receives the highest amount of rainfall, with major downpours taking place between May and August and, once again, between December and January. A diverse region with inland rainforests that stretch right up to the coastline, the Caribbean expanse of Costa Rica has beautiful swampy lagoons to the north and is bordered by the towering Talamanca Mountains to the south. Limon offers diving, surfing and exploring. It is home to the Tortuguero National Park, which is famous for its turtle nesting, and the Cahuita National Park. Limon has the last remaining indigenous Indian tribes of Costa Rica, namely the Bribri, Cocles and Talamanca Cabecarv communities.

Northern Plains

Scarcely populated, the cloud forests, rolling hills and one of the most active volcanoes in Central America make this a unique area of Costa Rica. A striking characteristic of this zone is the sharp contrast in topography with the Nicoya Peninsula found on the other side of the Tilaran mountain range. The Monteverde Cloud Forest Preserve provides an excellent chance to see many rare birds, such as the resplendent quetzal, one of the most beautiful birds of the tropics. Arenal volcano draws tourists from all over the globe. The nearby town of La Fortuna has several hotels and restaurants.

Real estate system and buying process

In foreign countries such as Costa Rica, the normal stress of the purchasing process can be compounded by other risk factors, such as language barriers and unfamiliarity with local laws and procedures. That said, foreigners can and do legally and successfully purchase property in Costa Rica including houses, condominiums, timeshares, farms, finished lots and beachfront property. However, understanding the various methods that are available for purchase is critical in the evaluation process, according to Omar Ayales, general manager of Stewart Title's Guanacaste office (*www.stewartcr.com*).

Fee simple

The most comprehensive form of property ownership in Costa Rica is fee simple ownership, which is the same in Costa Rica as in the U.S. Fortunately for foreigners, the conditions for this type of ownership are the same for Costa Rican nationals as they are for foreigners. Basically, fee simple ownership gives the owner of the property the absolute right to materially own the property, use it, enjoy it, sell it, lease it, improve it and so on, subject only to conditions outlined in the Costa Rican Laws. Fee simple also means that if the owner is obstructed from enjoying any of his/her rights to the property, he/she has the right to be made whole—in other words—have the property restored to its original condition. Buyers who purchase fee simple title have the most rights under the law to enjoy and use the property as they see fit.

Concessions in the Maritime Zone

Concession property is more commonly known as beachfront property. Approximately 95 percent of beachfront property is considered concession property and is governed by the Maritime Zone Law and other specific regulations including but not limited to special dispositions stated by municipalities and the ICT (Costa Rican Tourism Board). These legal dispositions set forth the conditions under which foreigners and local residents can own concession property. A concession in Costa Rica is defined as the right to use and enjoy a specific property located on the maritime zone for a pre-determined period of time. The state, through its respective municipality, grants this right. Note that the first 200 meters measured horizontally from the high-tide line defines the boundary of the maritime zone. This zone also includes islands, pinnacles of rock, mangroves, estuaries, small islands and any small natural formation that overcomes the level of the ocean. This 200-meter zone is divided into two areas:

Public Area: The first 50 meters measured horizontally from the high-tide line. This zone is not available for ownership of any kind. No kind of development is allowed except for constructions approved by governmental entities. Further, this area is deemed a public area and any individual wishing to utilize this area for enjoyment has the right to do so. In other words, there are no truly private beaches in the Maritime Zone.

Restricted/Concession Area: The next 150 meters. This area is available for concessions to be granted. A concession is, in essence, a "lease" on the property granted to the lessee for a specific period of time. Normally the concession period is granted for 20 years. An owner of a concession may build on that concession, subdivide the concession and perform other acts to the property. However, appropriate permits from the local municipality must be obtained.

Ownership Limitations

Unlike the scenario of fee simple property, foreigners do not have the same rights as citizens when it comes to purchasing concession property. The law establishes that foreigners cannot be majority owners of a concession property. A foreigner can, however, enter into a partnership with a Costa Rican citizen where the ownership is divided 49 percent/51 percent between the foreigner and Costa Rican respectively. One exception is if a foreigner has resided in Costa Rica for at least five years; in that case, he/she may be majority owner of a concession. Both foreigners and Costa Ricans alike are required to purchase all Maritime Zone property through concession.

Condominiums

When U.S. citizens think of condominiums, they normally think of large apartments or townhouses. In Costa Rica, however, there is a specific law called "Condominium Law" that provides certain benefits to developers of many different types of properties, including single-family residence projects, finished-lot projects, condos, etc. This set of laws allows a developer to restrict and regulate certain aspects of the development. Each condominium development has its own bylaws containing all of the restrictions, limitations and privileges that can be enjoyed by individuals who purchase a property in such a development. Ownership of property "in condominium" is fee simple ownership but usually carries with it a few additional restrictions set forth by the developer. It is advised that you require the owner of the property to give you a copy of the by-laws to check for architectural guidelines, land-use restrictions and other limitations that may be placed on your property. Most often, developers use the condominium laws to allow themselves to build private roads in a development and set architectural guidelines. For the most part, condominium laws are designed to protect the integrity of a development and maintain the "look and feel" of the project.

Untitled property

There are properties in Costa Rica that are not recorded at the Public Registry of Properties. Families have inhabited some properties of this type for generations, while others have never been occupied. In either case, it is possible that someone claims they "own" the property and puts it up for sale. They may even have fence lines or other boundary markers that separate "their" property from a neighbor's. Regardless of the time that an inhabitant has lived on the property or to what extent he/she has demonstrated ownership, unless that property is registered at the Public Registry, there is no official owner. The title is unclear. It is strongly recommended that this type of property be avoided at all costs because there is no way to prove that the "owner" has the right to transfer the property or, even worse, what the dimensions of the property really are.

The purchase process

A basic terminology

Feeling comfortable with the purchase process starts with understanding the most common terminology. While the purchase process may seem very simple, there are some keys ideas with which a buyer should be familiar. The following define the most common vocabulary used in real estate transactions in Costa Rica:

1. **Folio Real**: This is the "social security number" of properties. It is the unique number assigned to each property to identify it and distinguish it from other properties. This number is composed of three parts: the first number indi-

cates the province, the second group of six numbers is the number of the property itself and the last group of numbers indicates how many co-owners the property has had. All titled properties must have this number in order for clear title to be obtained.

2. **Transfer or Conveyance Deed** (*escritura de traspaso*): This document contains all of the stipulations regarding the transfer of real estate, including basic information about the buyer, seller, the property and any special terms of sale, such as easements or mortgages. An attorney who is also a Public Notary must prepare this document and the deed must be recorded in his/her Notary Book as well as at the Public Registry of Properties. Once the deed has been prepared and signed at the close, it is the attorney's responsibility to record the deed immediately at the Public Registry. The recording process consists of two phases. In the first phase, the Notary presents the deed to the public registry for its annotation; from this moment the property is protected against any third-party interest. After the registry verifies the deed is structurally correct, the second phase of registration begins and the property is recorded in the name of the new owner. Because Costa Rica operates on a "first in time, first in right" system, registering the deed immediately is critical to ensuring that the new buyer's rights to the property are ahead of any other claims by third parties.

3. **Public Notary**: Attorney licensed by law to perform legal acts with Public Faith. All transactions performed by a Notary are recorded in his/her Notary Book. A Public Notary is necessary in order to purchase a property. Most attorneys in Costa Rica are also Public Notaries.

4. **Power of Attorney** (*Poder*) This document authorizes a person to act on behalf of another to perform specific actions such as the purchase of a property. This tool is especially useful for clients who wish to close on their property without returning to Costa Rica. It is best to sign the power of attorney before leaving the country because the law requires that the power of attorney be signed in the presence of a Costa Rican Notary. Thus, a visit to a Costa Rican consulate in the U.S. is necessary. One exception to this rule, however, is if the property is being purchased through a corporation. In this case, a signed proxy letter will suffice and there is no need to visit a consulate.

Power of Attorney comes in two forms, general and special. General power of attorney allows a representative to sign on behalf of an individual for multiple transactions, and must be recorded at the Public Registry. A specific or special power of attorney allows the representative to sign only for the item specified in the power of attorney contract and under the conditions specified there. It is highly recommended that only a specific power of attorney be granted for property purchases to limit the rights of the representative to sign only for the property in question and nothing else. Additionally, the specific power of attorney does not have to be recorded at the Public Registry. However, it should be granted before a Public Notary.

5. **Survey Plan** (Cadastral Department): In addition to the Public Registry of Properties, which holds all property deeds, Costa Rica also has a Cadastral Office that holds all of the property surveys. In order to transfer, mortgage or acquire a property, one must record a survey at the Public Registry. When dealing with property segregations, a municipality

authorization is also required to be inserted on the survey. The official drawing of the property is validated through an approval process by the Public Registry of Properties as well as by the municipality where the property is located. Because the Public Registry and Cadastral Office are separate entities, it is not uncommon for old property surveys to be on file at the Cadastral Office. If this is the case, it is recommended that a new survey plan be registered with the Cadastral Office so that there can be no dispute over boundary lines.

Purchasing methodologies

There are two basic ways to purchase property.

1. **Acquiring properties through direct transfer:** A purchase process whereby one or more individuals acquire a property in their personal names.

2. **Acquiring properties through corporations:** A common practice in Costa Rica is to acquire properties through a new corporation or through an existing corporation that currently owns the property of interest. The process of setting up a corporation is not complicated but does require a knowledgeable attorney who understands the exact protocols and procedures necessary to properly set up the corporation. The advantage of this system is that it allows a buyer to protect his/her asset anonymously.

Further, if a purchaser acquires a property through an existing corporation that already owns the property, there are no government transfer taxes and stamps to pay, which usually must be paid anytime there is a change in the ownership of the property. If a buyer acquires the shares of an existing corporation, technically there is no change in the recorded owner of the property (i.e. the corporation still owns the property). However, if a property is acquired through forming a new corporation to buy the property, the transfer taxes and stamps must be paid because the name of the property owner has changed. The risk for the buyer in acquiring an existing corporation is that the corporation might have other liabilities, and there is no way to verify 100 percent that the corporation is clean. When buying a Costa Rican corporation, it is important to keep in mind that there are other obligations and responsibilities that must be addressed. Examples include yearly tax declarations (even if the corporation is inactive), payment of income taxes, if any, and keeping the legal books of the corporation up to date and in order.

Using title guaranty and escrow services

Once a buyer has seen a property of interest, the next step is to understand what the process of acquiring the property may entail. The following are the basic steps that a purchaser follows when buying a property:

- Step 1: Sign an Option to Purchase/Sale with seller

- Step 2: Deposit funds into escrow

- Step 3: Title research performed and Title Commitment issued (review if property is free and clear of defects)

- Step 4: Closing—Execution of Transfer Deed, Endorsement of Shares and/or Mortgage Deed and disburse funds

- Step 5: Register new owner with Public Registry

- Step 6: Receive official Title Guaranty

Fee structure

1. **Transfer taxes, stamps and other charges:** In order to record the transfer of the property, the government charges 1.5 percent of the purchase price. An additional 1 percent is charged for other stamps at the Public Registry.

2. **Notary fees:** Notaries are required by law to charge 1.25 percent as their legal fees.

3. **Survey fees:** If you require or demand a new survey for your property, there are qualified surveyors available to perform this function. Pricing depends on the location and size of the property.

4. **Mortgage registration fees:** The government charges .6 percent of the mortgage value to register the mortgage deed on the property.

5. **Title Guaranty fees:** Guaranty fees are typically based on a sliding scale depending on the purchase price.

6. **Escrow fees:** Fees are dependent on the escrow provider.

7. **Incorporation:** Fees for purchasing a corporation typically run $500 to $1,000.

A look at taxes

Income tax

(Impuesto sobre las remesas al exterior) Income earned by non-residents in Costa Rica is subject to a final withholding tax on the gross amount. The standard tax rate, which is applicable to rental income, is 30 percent. Husband and wife are treated

separately for the purposes of assessing income tax on the non-employment sourced income of residents.

Real estate/habitation tax

(Impuesto sobre bienes inmuebles) Property taxes are levied on the cadastral value (similar to county assessment) of the property as assessed by the tax authorities. Property taxes are levied by the municipalities at the flat rate of 0.25 percent. The real estate tax is calculated on a calendar-year basis and must be paid annually, semiannually or quarterly, depending on the municipality.

Capital gains tax

Capital gains are not taxed in Costa Rica unless they are derived from constant or consistent deals, known as habitual transactions. Capital gains derived from habitual transactions are taxed at the standard income tax rate.

Protecting the real estate investment

One of the greatest concerns of foreigners purchasing real estate in a foreign country is to ensure that the transaction will be executed legally and that the system can ensure a lifetime of enjoyment of the property. The Costa Rican legal system, if followed correctly, does give ample protection to investors, but if the transaction is not executed properly, loss can and does occur. To guarantee the security of any real estate investment, there are three tools that should be present in any real estate transaction:

1. **Adequate legal representation and an experienced Notary:** While a Notary's primary duty is to provide Public Faith to a transaction, his/her job is also to act as the legal representative of the buyer, providing legal advice and representation throughout the process.

2. **Title guaranty:** As in the U.S., the title guaranty serves as a contract by which a third party (guaranty company) commits to indemnify losses due to legal situations that could affect the property, minus any exceptions or exclusions from the coverage. This legal document grants the buyer the security and peace of mind that the property has free and clear title and is protected in the event of defect. The process of issuing a title guaranty includes the issuance of a title commitment before the closing to allow the buyer time to examine the legal status of the property and evaluate if the property is in proper condition for purchase. The final title guaranty is issued after the close and is based on the title commitment. The title guaranty is a new concept in Costa Rica and Latin America in general, but it has already proven to add value to initial real estate purchases and resales. It has also encouraged transparency and increased liquidity in the real estate process. See Chapter 12.

3. **Escrow:** Most buyers from the U.S. understand escrow service to include not only the managing of funds for a property purchase, but all of the administrative work required to execute a closing. In fact, in states where an attorney is not required for a real estate purchase, the escrow agent becomes the central party responsible for ensuring that all documentation is in order before the close. In Costa Rica, the escrow agent performs many of the same duties. The primary function is the financial service to prevent manipulation or mishandling of funds prior to closing. The escrow agent is a neutral third party with responsibility for issuing checks and executing payments. This system gives confidence to all interested parties (i.e., attorneys, brokers, seller, buyer) that funds are protected during the buying process and that all funds will be disbursed appropriately to all parties at closing.

Squatters

The greatest potential danger for land ownership in absentia—typically in large, rural settings away from the ocean—is the problem of squatters. Knowledge of the legal procedures along with due diligence is necessary to maintain one's property rights. Numerous passages are written into the Civil Code that deal with the rights of possession that are reminiscent of the earlier days of agricultural reform.

Technically, squatters can only attempt to gain legal rights to a non-maritime property by peacefully occupying non-cultivated, unimproved agrarian land over an extended period of time. The difficulty of maintaining one's rights over those of the squatters is due to the nebulous nature of the law and what legally passes as "non-cultivated" or "unimproved" land.

There are legal steps that can be taken to rid one's land of squatters. Procedurally, the eviction process is divided into three phases. The first phase is the eviction of squatters during the first three months of occupation. Such early discovery is key, as during this period one need not go to court. Theoretically, one need only alert the local police, who are then obliged to evict the squatters. The catch is that it can be extremely difficult to get the police to carry out their duty, and if one is not in the country, actual eviction is very difficult to verify. Even though eviction within the first three months is a rather straightforward procedure, at least in principle, early recognition can prove to be difficult if one is not residing on the property.

The second phase is after the initial three months of occupation but before one year. If squatters are "allowed" to squat on property for this duration of time, one must go to the courts and start the process of "administrative eviction." The third phase is continued occupation for more than one year. According to the law, squatters have then achieved a "legal assumption," and the owners must go through an ordinary lawsuit process. In order for the court to grant the property rights to squatters, they must prove that they have been on the land "uninterrupted," "non-challenged" and "peacefully" for 10 years.

Incorporating in Costa Rica

The typical limited liability company (*Sociedad Anónima* or *S.A.*) must be incorporated by at least two people before a Costa Rican Notary Public. After such incorporation, the shares may be transferred and it is legally feasible to have a corporation in which one person is the owner of all shares. The incorporators must choose a name (which must not be similar to any existing corporate name); appoint a Board of Directors (which, by law, must have a minimum of three members, President, Treasurer and Secretary); and appoint a Comptroller. Each one of these positions must be occupied by a different person; however, the initial incorporators may occupy them.

Other crucial issues to be decided include:

- **The capital of the corporation.** The higher the capital, the more registration taxes are to be paid.

- **The number of shares composing such capital.** A share cannot be divided according to Costa Rican Law—fractions of shares are not acceptable. Therefore, it is advisable to have a number of shares that would permit future distributions of the participation in the company.

- **The representation of the newly formed company.** There must be at least one representative of the company with power of attorney to act on its behalf. However, at the time of incorporation or later on, the powers of the company's representatives may be limited—for example, to specific actions or amounts.

Costa Rica has what we call a "hybrid" corporate system. The incorporation deed, as well as all changes to the company's by-Laws, are recorded in the Public Registry, where any person has access to them. All transfers of the company's shares, however, are recorded in the Shareholders Registry Book, which is kept by the corporation and is only available to company shareholders and officials; all other parties can review it only with a Court order.

When purchasing real estate, it is advisable to do it in a corporation's name. In this case, transfers could be made easier and the structure may be more flexible for other transactions and for organizational matters.

Before you buy

Most properties in Costa Rica are registered in a computer system called Folio Real. This system is centralized at the offices of the Public Registry in San Jose. Before buying land (or even before seriously considering an offer to buy land), you should perform a title search in Folio Real. Such a title search shows all data on the property, including area, ownership, boundaries, location, mortgages and other liens. A few properties have not been incorporated into the Folio Real system yet. They are registered in special books kept in the Public Registry, where they may also be accurately title searched. When considering buying land, the first question you should ask is if you are being offered ownership rights (*derecho de propiedad*) or occupation rights (*derechos de ocupación*). In the case of occupation, you would be dealing with land that has not been registered, cannot be title searched and must go through a long process in order to be registered. Ownership rights, on the contrary, are registered and are equivalent to the concept of owning land in the United States or Canada.

Another situation regarding land, especially in beach areas, is the concession option. As mentioned later in this chapter, the government gives a private party the right to use the land for a specific period of time. In general terms, the concession may be considered a lease. The concessions registration system is different than the one for regular land and has particular requirements regarding zoning, terms, occupation, etc. So, before buying, before offering or even before seriously considering a piece of land, inquire about its status and perform a title search. These simple steps could save you a lot of money and effort, and will definitely ensure that your Costa Rican investment is worthwhile.

General residency rules

Costa Rican immigration laws allow foreign citizens to become residents in specific cases that range from having a family relationship with a local citizen (marrying a Costa Rican, having Costa Rican children) to demonstrating to the government that the applicant will not be a burden for the country—mainly showing sound resources to become established in Costa Rica and, in some cases, to create a business there. Two categories are recommended: the *resident pensioner* and the *resident annuitant*. They are both administered by the ICT (Costa Rican Tourism Board). The resident pensioner status is used for foreign citizens who have retired from government service or from selected private entities and receive from them a permanent life-retirement income of no less than $600 U.S. per month. Such amount must be transferred periodically to Costa Rica, and its reception and conversion into *colones* (Costa Rican currency) at designated institutions has to be demonstrated. The resident annuitant regime is applicable to all foreign nationals, regardless of age, receiving a fixed monthly income of no less than $1,000 U.S. The funds of the deposit can come locally or from abroad and their conversion into *colones* at designated institutions has to be demonstrated.

Financing

Mortgages are now available to foreign buyers but interest rates typically are higher than in the U.S. Not all banks offer mortgages to non-residents, but a few do, including Scotiabank (*www.scotiabank.com*) and Banco Banex (*www.banex.com*). Typically, loans to non-residents require a down payment of at least 25 percent, though that figure is often 40 percent for land-only mortgages. There usually are no prepayment penalties.

The process is somewhat more cumbersome than that of the U.S. but the concept is relatively new to the country. More information on financing is available in Chapter 13.

Remember, any foreigner is able to purchase, own and receive full rights to property in Costa Rica, and the country's constitution fully protects that ownership. It's best to start your search with a competent, licensed real estate agent affiliated with the U.S.-based National Association of Realtors. In Costa Rica, the Costa Rica Global Association of Realtors (CRGAR) has a bilateral agreement with NAR. Despite Costa Rica's popularity, many wonderful getaways can still be purchased at bargain prices. Speaking of bargains, have you considered Honduras? Let's head there next.

CHAPTER THREE

Getting a Handle
on Honduras

*Huge barrier reef brings curious buyers
to Caribbean coast*

P hil Weir is a sucker for clear, warm water and tropical fish. He has taken dive trips all over the globe, and he so loved an area in the western Caribbean approximately 40 miles off the northeast coast of Honduras and about 200 miles south of Cancun that in 1991 he bought a place on the island of Roatan, the largest of 50 islands and keys that are collectively known as *Islas de la Bahia*, or Bay Islands.

"I had always been in the diving business in one form or another," Weir said. "But in 2001, I thought I would open a real estate office and then 9/11 happened. We got it going in 2002, nearly starved for a year and half and then were amazed

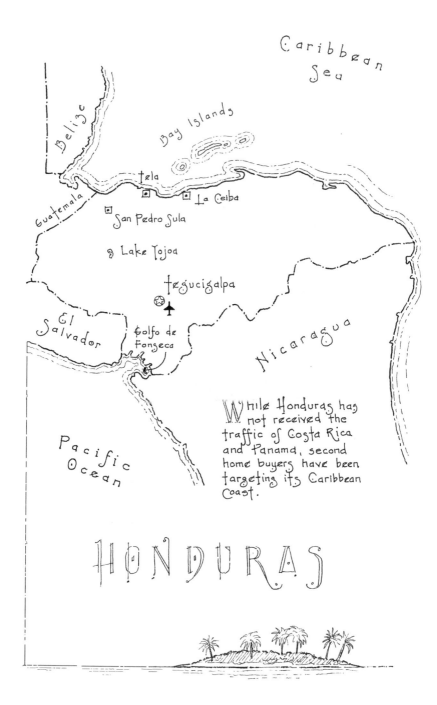

Caribbean Sea

Belize

Bay Islands

Guatemala

Tela

La Ceiba

San Pedro Sula

Lake Yojoa

Tegucigalpa

El Salvador

Golfo de Fonseca

Nicaragua

Pacific Ocean

While Honduras has not received the traffic of Costa Rica and Panama, second home buyers have been targeting its Caribbean Coast.

HONDURAS

when we did $20 million in sales in 2005. It seems the divers told more divers ... who then told their snorkeling buddies."

First Costa Rica, then Panama, and now the world has discovered the beauty of Honduras, for a variety of reasons—not the least of which is the Barrier Reef of Roatán, second-largest in the world. More than 10,000 U.S. citizens live in Honduras full time. Most live in the capital city of Tegucigalpa and the manufacturing center of San Pedro Sula with its large industrial parks and tax benefits. The second-home center of the country is the Bay Islands of Roatán, Utila and Guanaja plus the mainland beach areas near the fruit towns of La Ceiba, Tela and Trujillo, where the green forests behind the deserted beaches feature waterfalls and clear mountain rivers. Like several Central American getaways, most of Honduras is still off the mainstream, second-home radar screen, with beachfront condos readily available for less than $200,000.

The lure of Roatán, about 32 miles long and two miles wide, is its extensive barrier reef system that offers some of the clearest saltwater swimming in the world. It is the largest of the chain's six main islands and can be reached by nonstop flights from Houston, Miami and Atlanta. While Roatán is still in the early stages of development as a tourist destination and the overall level of development is still modest on an international scale, the last few years have seen a substantial increase in real estate activity and the number and quality of new developments. More people are simply auditioning the Jimmy Buffett island lifestyle and/or investment opportunities. The island is better known for its decompression chamber for divers than it is for its several clinics, two hospitals, American-trained doctors and state-of-the-art medical equipment. And it's no longer a sleepy little island waiting for people to show up so the locals can survive—nearly one million cruise ship passengers visit each year.

Marci Wiersma, a Pacific Northwest native, moved to Roatán in 1999 in search of slower, warmer days. She juggles the chores of her real estate brokerage with the responsibilities of raising two young daughters. "The real estate market has really moved along the past three years but I think it has a long way to go before it caps out," Wiersma said.

T.J. Lynch, broker-owner of RE/MAX Bay Islands Real Estate, sold his Vancouver, B.C.-area property company more than 10 years ago to head south to the sun and sand. "I would estimate that business is going up by more than 100 percent every year," said Lynch, one of eight agents in the office. "But 2006 was really off the charts. We sold more property in January and February than we did in all of 2005."

Ownership and financing

The ability of non-nationals to buy property in Honduras is a relatively new development. The Honduran Constitution prohibited foreign ownership until 1990, when a decree was passed allowing foreigners to purchase properties in designated tourism zones established by the Ministry of Tourism. In a capsule, foreigners can own up to three-quarters of an acre subject to certain building requirements. Construction must begin on vacant lots within 36 months of purchase. Larger parcels may be purchased by forming a Honduran corporation.

Financing is available, but it is not common in Honduras. Offshore bank financing has begun to trickle in as U.S. and European lenders and fund managers look to assist the equity-rich baby boomers who are fueling the rapid second-home growth and appreciation. Traditionally, local banks have charged 10 to 11 percent interest while requesting reams of unrelated loan documents. As an alternative to the red tape and high loan rates, home buyers have paid cash—usually via a home equity loan on their primary residence—or obtained financing from the seller or developer.

While every seller-financed situation is different, buyers usually pay 30 percent down, with the balance payable within five years. Now, some local banks, like Banco B.G.A. (*www.bancobga.com*), are making loans on approved properties with 10-year payback periods. The buyer typically is responsible for transfer taxes and some closing costs amounting to approximately 6.5 percent of the price of the property. Real estate agents charge five to ten percent commission, usually paid by the seller. Property taxes are extremely low and usually run one-third of one percent of the value of the property. While U.S. dollars are common, the official currency is the lempira (HNL).

Transaction costs		Who pays?
Transfer Tax	1.50%	buyer
Notary Fees	3.00% – 5.00%	buyer
Registration Rights	0.15%	buyer
Agent's Fees	5.00%	seller
Costs paid by buyer		4.65% – 6.65%
Costs paid by seller		5.00%
Buy-sell costs		9.65% – 11.65%

This includes all costs of buying and then reselling a property—lawyers' fees, notary's fees, registration fees, taxes, agents' fees, etc.

A typical customer according to Wiersma (*www.aboutroatan realestate.com*) and Weir (*www.roatanlife.com*) is a 40- to 60-year-old American looking to retire in five years. Other common buyers include Canadians, other Central Americans and Europeans. Some U.S. buyers want to try out retirement by buying a second home now, using it a few weeks out of the year and renting it out for the remaining time. "The biggest mistake people tend to make is that they leave their brain at the airport," Wiersma said. "Everybody's so nice here and the island is so beautiful … but you have to work to get things done. If you are building a house, you have to have a plan and the right people to put that plan in place."

Weir suggests a week-long visit before customers decide on where to sink money into a Honduras getaway. "Most people come here dead-set on buying on the water but they usually end up buying on a hillside," Weir said. "I think if we sold them exactly what they thought they wanted to buy that they would be unhappy."

Other popular areas

La Ceiba

La Ceiba, the gateway to the Bay Islands, is the beach and eco-tourism center of mainland Honduras. Colorado native Kent Ownbey, who lived and worked in the Bay Islands during two different 10-year periods, decided to focus on developing second-home possibilities near La Ceiba in 2004 because he liked the idea of empty beaches and building homes with modest price tags. In the interim, he returned to the U.S. to pursue a banking career before the lure of full-time island life grabbed him once more.

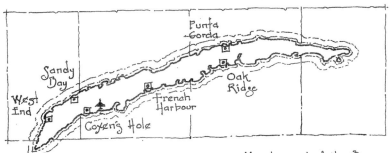

ROATÁN ISLAND

~ the largest of the Bay Islands, Roatán is approximately 34 miles long, and 4 miles wide. It is the chief draw for second home buyers.

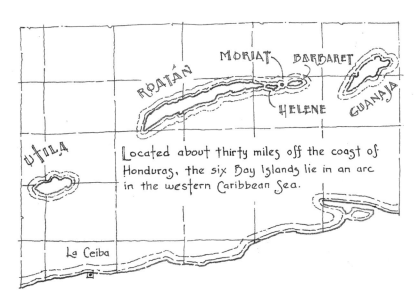

Located about thirty miles off the coast of Honduras, the six Bay Islands lie in an arc in the western Caribbean Sea.

BAY ISLANDS of HONDURAS

"I think Roatán is still great, but it's more of a luxury condo market now," says Ownbey, who first visited Roatán while in college in 1971 and stayed for 10 years. "In those days, there were four taxis on the entire island, beach land was $200 per acre, lobster crawled on the reef and there were conch by the thousands just 50 feet off shore. There have been lots of changes since then, some good and some sad. Saddest part of Roatán is that nobody in the governments ever wanted to enforce a true master plan that could have saved some of the most beautiful beaches in the world from becoming wall to wall condos."

La Ceiba is 14 minutes by air from the Bay Islands and 25 minutes by air from the economic capital of Honduras, San Pedro Sula. La Ceiba's international airport offers flights to all major cities in Central America, the Bay Islands, Miami, New Orleans, Atlanta, Houston and Los Angeles. It gained its early economic strength from the large fruit companies, including Standard Fruit Company with its pineapple, banana and coconut plantations. Because of ample rain and rich soils, the fruit production also has become famous for mangoes, limes, star fruit, avocado and an assortment of other exotic fruits. The area is also known for friendly people, great beaches, river rafting and kayaking, cloud forests and one of the most popular carnivals in Central America honoring its patron, San Isidro. La Ceiba has the potential to be the Honduran capital of ecotourism with its proximity to sites like the beautiful tropical forest Pico Bonito Park and the Cangrejal River, which is ideal for river rafting, as well as the Cayos Cochinos Marine National Park. There have been many recent developments, such as the Palma Real resort and the Water Jungle.

Ownbey's Mango Tree development (*www.honduras-real estate.com*) features single-family view homes, typically situated on half-acre lots with a community beach. The project, like several others led by long-time project managers, has arranged its own financing—a helpful step for North Americans who would rather not conduct the mortgage research from scratch. For example, Banco de Occidente (*www.bancodeoccidente.com.co*) and BAMER (*www.bamernet.hn*) offer financing to both lot and house purchasers in Mango Tree, with a 25 percent down payment and "market interest rates" that are generally two percentage points greater than 30-year, fixed-rate mortgages in the States. The loan is amortized over 10 years, but borrowers usually are offered a 15-year refinance program during the initial loan term.

"While the largest cities of the country have many North American business people, the U.S. buyers and French Canadians who come down here looking for second homes are looking to be close to the water," Ownbey said. "La Ceiba also has rivers that are easy to access and when you consider the cloud-mountain forests also are close by, it's easy to see why the area is quite a draw."

Tegucigalpa

The capital city of Honduras has grown from a small colonial mining town to a city of approximately 1 million people. It exhibits its deep Spanish colonial heritage in the architecture of the buildings. Several museums and parks are also located in the historical center and the national orchestra performs regularly, offering another interesting and enjoyable option for tourists. The Manuel Bonilla Theatre is an architectural jewel inspired by the Atenee de Paris Theatre and frequently presents plays for every taste. Besides an appealing cultural experience, this city also offers a vivid night life, with a great range of restaurants, bars and other social establishments. Tegucigalpa is also surrounded by beautiful forests and natural reserves like the National Park of La Tigra.

San Pedro Sula

San Pedro Sula has grown to become the most industrialized city in Honduras. It is located in a valley surrounded by beautiful tropical mountains. It is characterized by a very hospitable population experiencing rapid commercial and industrial growth. A strong Spanish influence is evident in the way the city is built, with an organized arrangement of blocks divided by streets and avenues. The Cathedral and many other buildings also show this influence in their colonial architecture. The city's proximity to the North Coast, its warm climate and its exciting night life attract high levels of tourism annually, which has been an important factor in the growth it is experiencing. San Pedro Sula is a great destination for newcomers looking for a fast-paced tropical city surrounded by natural beauties.

Lake Yojoa

At approximately 2,100 feet above sea level, this natural lake is located 80 miles northeast of Tegucigalpa and 50 miles south of San Pedro Sula. It is surrounded by beautiful mountains that reach up to 8,000 feet and is home to more than 350 different species of birds. The lake's coastlines and surrounding areas are ideal for the cultivation of different crops, especially coffee. Due to the high fishing productivity and the lure of water-sports enthusiasts, Lake Yojoa became a popular tourist site and has grown in popularity. Main highways and comfortable hotels have helped popularize its living communities.

Tela

Tela, a small port town propelled by the banana trade, is home to wonderful beaches, the beautiful Lancetilla botanical gardens, the Telamar Resort, which is one of the most popular hotels in the region, and a beautiful golf course attracting local and foreign golfers throughout the year. The tropical Garifuna culture has a strong presence in Tela, giving it a vibrant cultural heritage and a gracious atmosphere. A variety of new real estate developments are under way due to its convenient location.

Buying process

Most of the time, North Americans buying property in a foreign country have a greater level of comfort when dealing with an agent who is a member of the National Association of Realtors or one of NAR's associate organizations. In Honduras, that group is ANABIR (*Asociacion Nacional de Agencias de Bienes Raices de Honduras*/The Honduras National Real Estate Association), which represents more than 60 companies throughout the nation. ANABIR was founded in 1997, is headquartered in Tegucigalpa and has two regional branches.

After choosing an agent and a specific property, the next step is to designate an attorney and start the paperwork process (much like the purchase-and-sale agreement used in the U.S.). Real estate agents often will help with an attorney referral. The preliminary offer to purchase may change slightly from company to company but the form is less cumbersome than ones used in the U.S. A 10 percent earnest money deposit is the norm. Your appointed attorney then reviews the property documents and contract.

The seller will provide, via his representative, all pertinent documents, which will include the *escritura publica* or *dominia plena*, (the only two publicly registered, acceptable title documents). Some transactions are initiated via "private" documents, but the transaction time for these will be longer. That's because the seller would first have to apply for *dominia plena* and have it registered prior to selling to you. If this were the case, you might have to commit your funds in escrow for as long as one year while the process plays out.

These pertinent documents will then go to your attorney for review. The attorney will then clear the documents at the "registry," (much like a U.S. county building, where documents are filed and stored) to make sure that there are no lawsuits, tax liens, etc. Your real estate agent acts as the liaison between you, the attorney, the seller and the title insurance company. Your agent will also be responsible for any contingencies that need to be fulfilled before the final closing date. These can include but are not limited to a new survey, road access and water access.

Your real estate agent/company, via your attorney or direct from your attorney, should provide both buyer and seller with English translations of the final paperwork (which will eventually be filed in Spanish) that you or your representative will be signing at the closing. This provides you with a preview of what will be signed and finalized. Buyers can obtain a power of attorney and appoint another person to sign on their behalf. Your agent then provides you with a copy of the closing document with signatures of the buyer and the seller. A few months later, you will get a Spanish Document Title in your name, delivered by your attorney.

A cash deal can be completed in about a week—if all paperwork is in order and an attorney is available—but 30 days is usually standard, especially if financing is needed.

Exploring the power of attorney

Let's say your wife has found a terrific property while on vacation with her college roommates. She is certain it will be the perfect family getaway and her instincts have been right on in the past. However, with jobs and school, there is no way you can visit Honduras for a period long enough to make an offer on the property *and* wait for it to close.

There are ways of solving this dilemma. One is via a power of attorney (POA) that you create, allowing your Honduran attorney, real estate broker or agent to sign on your behalf to accept the property in your name. If the deal is a cash transaction, the POA can be done with as little as a written statement signed and witnessed by another party. If the transaction involves a bank mortgage or seller financing, the document needs to be formalized and registered by a Honduran attorney. For more information regarding how and when to use a power of attorney, consult a reputable real estate agent, attorney or title insurance representative

Types of residency

There are several ways to live abroad. In Honduras, residency often is classified by income flow or investment commitment. Here is a capsule look at the categories.

Retiree (*Pensionado*)

For this type of residency, you would need to show that you have at least $1,500 U.S. per month in income from outside Honduras. This can be a pension-type income (permanent, from a government or financial institution, or a business pension fund or personal funds). That $1,500 U.S. per month then needs to be converted to the equivalent amount of Honduran currency, known as lempiras. You need to allow about six months for processing. Benefits include the importation of personal belongings, including a car, without paying duties, and you are not taxed on your retirement income. Living in Honduras as a U.S. citizen gives you considerable tax benefits, yet be aware that many second-home buyers come to Honduras thinking they can apply for their retirement residency and that the tax-/duty-free shipping is automatic. It is not. You need to apply for a *dispensa* in order for that to happen.

Rentista

This category of residency is available to those who have a monthly income of $2,500 U.S. or more. This income must be from rental properties, investment dividends, interest or other sources that are not related to employment.

Investor

This type of residency requires an investment of $50,000 U.S. or more in Honduras. You need to provide a project description, timeline for investment and proof of having transferred a minimum of $25,000 U.S. into Honduras at the time of your application. It is also necessary to make a cash deposit of $5,000 U.S. in the Central Bank of Honduras to guarantee the investment. The business plan must come together within a three-year time frame. You also need to show how your project would benefit Honduras and its people.

Special presence permits

This last option is a new category that applies to many situations previously covered by regular residency. There are specific requirements, depending on the category of permit. For example, students must provide proof of their studies and economic support. Employees must submit proof of employment, and the employer must also supply documentation for the company. Missionaries and aid workers must provide a letter from the church or institution they are working with, along with proof of economic support.

Remember that laws and requirements can change. If you are considering any type of Honduran residency, you need to communicate with a qualified Honduran attorney.

Safety and security

Political demonstrations sometimes disrupt traffic in the larger Honduran cities, but they are generally announced in advance and are usually peaceful. According to the U.S. Department of State, visitors should avoid areas where demonstrations are taking place, and they should stay informed by following the local news and consulting hotel personnel and tour guides. Up-to-date information on safety and security can also be obtained by calling 888.407.4747 toll-free in the U.S. For callers outside the U.S. and Canada, a regular toll line is available at 202.501.4444. These numbers are available from 8:00 a.m. to 8:00 p.m. Eastern Time, Monday through Friday (except U.S. federal holidays). The Department of State urges American citizens to take responsibility for their own personal security while traveling overseas.

Crime

Crime is common in some areas of Honduras and requires a high degree of caution by U.S. visitors and residents alike. U.S. citizens have been the victims of a wide range of crimes, including assault and property crimes. Criminals and pickpockets have been known to target visitors as they enter and depart airports and hotels, so visitors should consider carrying their passports and valuables in a concealed pouch. Two-man teams on medium-sized motorcycles often target pedestrians for robbery. Honduran police officers generally do not speak

English. The government has established a special tourist police in the resort town of Tela and other popular tourist destinations, including Tegucigalpa, San Pedro Sula, La Ceiba and Roatán, but the number deployed is small and coverage is limited. The San Pedro Sula area has seen occasional armed robberies against tourist vans, minibuses and cars traveling from the airport to area hotels, even sometimes targeting the road to Copan. Copan, the Bay Islands and other tourist destinations have a lower crime rate than other parts of the country, but thefts, break-ins and assaults do occur.

In June 2006, Honduras entered a "Central America-4 (CA-4) Border Control Agreement" with Guatemala, El Salvador and Nicaragua. Under the terms of the agreement, citizens of the four countries may travel freely across land borders from one of the countries to any of the others without completing entry and exit formalities at immigration checkpoints. U.S. citizens and other eligible foreign nationals who legally enter any of the four countries may similarly travel among the four without obtaining additional visas or tourist entry permits for the other three countries. Immigration officials at the first port of entry determine the length of stay, up to a maximum period of 90 days. Foreign tourists who wish to remain in the four-country region beyond the period initially granted for their visit are required to request a one-time extension of stay from local immigration authorities in the country where the traveler is physically present, or travel outside the CA-4 countries and reapply for admission to the region. Foreigners "expelled" from any of the four countries are excluded from the entire "CA-4" region. In isolated cases, the lack of clarity in the implementation details of the CA-4 Border Control Agreement has caused temporary inconvenience to some travelers and has resulted in others being fined more than $100 or detained in custody for 72 hours or longer.

Questions about Honduras

Is the government stable?

Over the last 20 years, the United States has had a significant impact on Honduran economic and governmental reforms. Honduras has increased tourism, allowed more foreign ownership and completed major infrastructure projects. The Honduran government is based upon the United States model, with separation of executive, legislative and judicial branches of government. There are federal elections every four years and officials are limited to one term of office. Voter turnout is among the highest in the hemisphere. Manuel "Mel" Zelaya was elected president by popular vote for a four year term (2006-2010). The government understands the need for absolute stability. Therefore, the laws extend the same protections to foreign investors as to its own citizens. All elected officials serve four-year terms. There are also appointed governors of 18 departments (similar to states). As is true in much of Latin America, Honduras has privatized most businesses and is very interested in attracting foreign investment. An example is that the country's four international airports are now being operated by the same company that operates the San Francisco Airport. An additional $55 million has been earmarked to expand the airports.

What do I need to get to Honduras?

Passport and return ticket are required. A visa is not required for a stay of up to 90 days and holders of U.S. passports are issued a 30-day permit that can be renewed every 30 days for up to a maximum 90-day stay. Departure tax is $30 U.S. yet could change. For additional information, contact the Embassy of Honduras at 3007 Tilden Street N.W., Washington, D.C. 20008, Phone: 202.966.7702, or the nearest Consulate General: California 213.383.9244 and 415.392.0076, Florida 305.447.8927, Illinois 773.342.8281, Louisiana 504.522. 3118, New York 212.269.3611 or Texas 713. 622.7911. Online: *www.hondurasemb.org*

The Honduran Embassy's e-mail address is *embhondu@aol.com*. Interested individuals may visit the Honduran Embassy's website for additional contact information through *www.hondurasemb.org*. For tourist information or suggestions, please contact the Honduras Institute of Tourism at 800.410.9608 (in the United States) or at 800.222.TOUR (8687) (within Honduras only) or visit the website *www.hondurastips. hondurus.com*.

What are the advantages of Honduran residency?

If you have residency status, you can bring in all your household items at one time with a duty-free exemption. You may bring in a new car and boat every five years if you have a retired residency status. To obtain Honduran residency, you should contact the Honduran Consulate in your area, as well as a local attorney who can assist in the process.

What about the education system?

There are several bilingual schools on the island and every town has its own public school through high school. Some students use tutors or correspondence courses that are accredited in the United States and some families send their children to the U.S. or the mainland for their education. College education is usually completed in the U.S. or Honduras.

Can I work in Honduras?

Yes, with the proper work permits. If you have the management skills and investment capital to start a new business, there are many opportunities from which to choose. An attorney can help you acquire a business license and other pertinent documents.

A Look at taxes

Income tax

For nonresidents of Honduras and foreign-owned companies (except those located inside the Free Zones and Industrial Processing Zones), income tax is levied on net income. Taxable income is computed by deducting costs incurred and depreciation expense (capital allowance) from the gross income. Real estate rentals are taxed at 10 percent.

Real estate property tax

(Impuesto sobre bienes inmuebles) Honduras collects annual property taxes based on the *Ley de Municipalidades* (Law of Municipality). The tax rates are levied on the property's declared value and vary depending on the municipality. In the capital Tegucigalpa, the rate is 5 percent for properties located in the Central District. It is from 0.1 to 0.8 percent for properties in the San Pedro Sula, and 0.15 percent for urban properties located in other areas.

Capital gains tax

Capital gains earned by nonresidents from selling real property located in Honduras are taxed at a fixed rate of 10 percent. The taxable gain is the gross selling price less acquisition costs and improvement costs.

There have been sweeping changes in Honduras, especially in the way the country handles the sale of real estate. The spark has been the huge increase in the number of North Americans looking to find a waterfront retreat on the country's plentiful beaches and islands. But changes in Honduras don't even come close in comparison with its neighbor to the south. Nicaragua seems to have come full circle, but some primary players are now wearing different hats. The political alterations, coupled with the emergence of new second-home opportunities on the coast, leads us to a deeper-than-expected dive into an extremely curious region.

CHAPTER FOUR

The New Ortega Nicaragua

*A cautious pause before
a second-home stampede*

Six months before the 1979 Nicaraguan presidential election, the shelves in Managua stores began to empty. People ran out of some fairly basic supplies. Business and foreign investment all but dried up. International organizations closed their doors as the perceived presence of Daniel Ortega's Sandinistas loomed large on the political horizon.

During the Sandinista Revolution of 1979, many private properties were confiscated by the government. Armel Gonzalez, then 17, remembers that his family and friends lost everything. His memories, and those of a generation of Nicaraguans, still are vivid.

cathedral tower, León

HONDURAS

NORTH COAST
Relatively undeveloped semi-arid region

ATLANTIC COAST
Undeveloped Caribbean coastal region. Not currently a second home region.

León

Managua

CENTRAL COAST
Montelimar
La Boquita
El Astrillero
San Juan del Sur

Granada

Lake Nicaragua

Ometepe Island

NICARAGUAN RIVIERA

COSTA RICA

NICARAGUA

"So many of us were broken, lost, homesick," Gonzalez said. "Going through what we did then, there's no way I thought we could ever get to where we are now."

Where Gonzalez and his fellow countrymen are today is the antithesis of 1979. The nation has enjoyed peace and constitutional democracy for more than 16 years and appears to be continuing down the same serene track despite the re-emergence of Ortega, who was re-elected as president in November 2006. Ortega has reconciled with former enemies and former commanders of the right-wing contra army who fought to overthrow him in the 1980s. In fact, the home Ortega had expropriated during his previous term belonged to banker Jaime Morales. For years, Ortega and his comrades used it in strategy meetings during the war against the contras. Morales is now Ortega's vice president. Talk about a turnaround …

So what changed this time? What was so different, especially given that 90 percent of the nation turned out for the 2006 elections? Ten years of civil war are not easily forgotten by many of those who lost everything, including family members.

"Ortega has no wish to be responsible for the loss of the huge momentum that we've established," said Gonzalez, now president of residential property developer Grupo del Sol (*www.grupodelsol.net*). "He understands that it will do him no good to screw it up and he knows the people would not go along with it. He wants to make amends, not a revolution."

Ortega's campaign platform was to continue the economic prosperity through foreign investment and tourism. He has promised to respect private property, one of the reasons the real estate and tourism industries supported his bid for office. His government will not only be checked in Parliament by the opposition, but also several of his key cabinet members will be former contras and current liberals.

"Our businesses and livelihood depend on people like me who were forced into exile for 10 years," Gonzalez said. "Ortega has shown that he understands that. He really has no choice if he wishes to survive politically. He also wants to change his legacy.

"I'm sure some buyers will pull back because of the political changes. But we expect that to change very quickly. In a year, there will still be absolute bargains near the beach. In three years, we will be overrun with foreigners wishing they had bought years ago."

Gonzalez is probably right, especially when it comes to second-home buyers in the U.S. and Canada and their appetite for waterfront communities and intriguing getaways. Many North Americans have heard wonderful stories of Costa Rican getaways with ecotourism, volcanoes, splendid billfin fishing and an obvious place to dream about what's possible in real estate. Fewer second-home seekers have been aware of the undiscovered possibilities of Panama, with its lush landscapes, a modern canal and exotic birds. But mention Nicaragua and the most likely response to surface is: "What's there, anyway?"

But look closely on a map and you will see that Nicaragua's southern border touches one of the most popular regions for second homes in Central America—the province of Guanacaste in Costa Rica, which geographically lies closer to Nicaragua's capital (Managua) than Costa Rica's capital (San Jose). Travel to Nicaragua and wait for the surprises to begin. It is a stunningly beautiful country, with lush tropical forests and miles of sandy beaches. The beachfront area is just now beginning to take off and it is affectionately referred to as "Costa Rica 20 years ago." Major tourism and real estate publications have dubbed Nicaragua's fairly undeveloped coastline "the Nicaraguan Riviera." Major international second-home developments are emerging, with prices that are unheard of in neighboring Costa Rica. New, modern, multi-lane highways connect the country's capital of 1.5 million people to major beachfront locations in less than an hour.

Like most of Central America, there's more to experience in Nicaragua than beaches. There are historical sites to explore, volcanoes to climb, colorful creatures to identify and colonial towns to visit. The capital, Managua, is sandwiched between undeveloped coastline and Lake Nicaragua, one of the largest freshwater lakes in Central America, where islands can be purchased at relatively affordable prices. Nearby lies the colonial city of Granada, where foreigners are restoring old buildings, opening businesses and making second homes in this "non-traditional" city. Many foreigners living in Nicaragua will tell you their favorite quality of the country is its people, known for their warmth and friendliness.

If you cherish adventure and a bit of risk and you truly want to get in on the "ground floor," Nicaragua might be for you. The fact that it is relatively untouched by tourism makes it a fascinating destination for visitors wanting to experience authentic Latin American culture and landscapes—and there are plenty of landscapes. Nicaragua is the largest country in Central America at 129,494 square kilometers, with freshwater lakes and crater lagoons covering 9,240 square kilometers.

For people considering investing and purchasing property in Nicaragua, there are many advantages, including the low cost, of living and labor, sunshine and warm temperatures all year, and the fact that it is an easy and short trip to and from the U.S. A study by INCAE, the Harvard Business School affiliate in Managua, reports that Nicaragua is the safest country, and Granada one of the safest cities, in all of Central America.

Where to buy?
Scanning the attractive areas

Pacific Coast

The Pacific Coast region is separated into three areas:

1. The Riviera and San Juan del Sur,
2. The Central Coast, and
3. The North.

As recently as 1997, there was only one real estate "development" along the Pacific coastline of Nicaragua, and a couple smaller ones were just getting started. Now, in certain areas—especially the Pacific Riviera—you'd be hard pressed to find a stretch of coastline that's not being developed. The Pacific Coast is Nicaragua's hottest property region. Views on this coastline are spectacular, resembling California's Big Sur or Carmel areas. From the drama of crashing waves on boulders and cliffs to calm and secluded beaches, this is arguably Nicaragua's most breathtaking scenery. Yet prices for years to come will remain a fraction of the cost of similar property to the south in Costa Rica.

The Riviera and San Juan del Sur

Thanks to the surfing community, Nicaragua's Riviera has been discovered. Real estate professionals along the Pacific have a saying: "Follow the surfers." Surfers seek out undiscovered territory … places where others have never been. To be the only one riding that perfect wave is a surfer's dream. So when surfers found Costa Rica to be getting a bit crowded, they followed the waves north to Nicaragua. And, in doing so, they fell in love with Nicaragua's real estate. Now, several years later, the appearance of Nicaragua's Pacific coastline has changed drastically. Word was out, the surfers had found paradise. Mainstream developers and real estate investors started moving in, coming north from Costa Rica. And while surfers still frequent the area, the majority of real estate on the coast has nothing to do with surfing anymore. Developments along the Riviera now show more mainstream amenities in their master plans—amenities such as hotels, riding stables, clubhouses, marinas, spas and more.

With a couple of exceptions, most of these developments are in their beginning stages—which makes right now a great time to invest. Off plan and pre construction pricing allows for better capital appreciation in a much shorter time than would otherwise be possible. The caveat here is that not all developments—and not all developers, are the same. With potential for higher gains comes higher risks. Be careful not to believe all the developer promises. If he says that next year there will be a clubhouse and a marina, yet you're standing on raw land, take what he says with a grain of salt and be very cautious. Ask a lot of questions. Alternatively, if there is evidence that something is happening …

Nicaragua's Pacific Riviera stretches from the Costa Rican border north to approximately 30 kilometers south of Managua. It encompasses quaint little fishing villages, such as El Gigante and El Astillero, long stretches of dramatic cliffs, and mountains with sweeping coastal views. Here is where the terrain is most interesting and varied.

San Juan del Sur

San Juan del Sur started life as a sleepy little resort town where some of Managua's wealthy citizens spent weekends in their beach homes. Now the occasional cruise ship docks here and restaurants and bars line the beachfront road. B&Bs, small hotels and luxury resorts are found in the town or nearby. In the heart of town sits the region's most popular resort, *Piedras y Olas*, or Rocks and Waves. With a usual occupancy of about 80 percent, it's difficult to get a room here on last-minute notice. Its reputation for excellent food, great service and beautifully designed accommodations is well deserved.

Just 20 minutes north of town lies Nicaragua's first true luxury ecoresort, Morgan's Rock. Innovative designers combine natural Nicaraguan hardwoods with locally made furnishings to connect guests with nature in a unique and relaxing way. Visitors from around the world come here to enjoy Nicaragua's incredible flora and fauna while being pampered in luxurious surroundings.

The government is building a port for container ships in the San Juan del Sur bay and infrastructure in the area is being upgraded to accommodate a growing population of tourists and residents. On weekends and holidays, San Juan del Sur is active and bustling. Real estate in the town itself is not too attractive; noise, pollution and lack of proper zoning have hurt its development. This is changing, however, as San Juan's current mayor is the first to realize the importance of proper waste disposal systems, infrastructure and zoning to protect the town's future.

Outside San Juan del Sur to the north and the south, developments line the coast. Some encompass beaches ranging from white sand to golden to cinnamon to grey. Be careful in this area (as with all others in Nicaragua), as title issues and empty developer promises can cause problems for buyers. Of course, waterfront property holds value and appreciates well. But don't rule out the view sites where prices are lower and the beach is only a short walk away.

For example, a townhouse development, Villas de Palermo (*www.villasdepalermo.com*), is less than five minutes outside town and offers fully furnished villas with a view of San Juan del Sur bay. And, thanks to Nicaragua's attractive Law 306 (allowing tax-free income and no property tax for buyers for 10 years), these two-story villas provide tax-free income for buyers. Good value for the money and located close to town but without the noise and zoning issues, the development includes a clubhouse with pool, bar, social area, riding stables and a canopy tour on site. Home sites adjacent to these villas are available for those who wish to design and build their own home. A reasonable price, with access to all the above-mentioned amenities and just a short trip to town, makes these sites worth investigating.

Some of Nicaragua's finest developments are a bit farther north in the heart of the Riviera region, from Tola to El Astillero. These developments were the first to form an association to lobby the government for needed infrastructure improvements and were instrumental in pushing the proposed *Costanera*, or Coastal Highway, to approval. Located only an hour from San Juan del Sur and less than an hour from the city of Rivas, this area represents some of the best opportunities for investment in the region. Here, the terrain is beautiful and the beaches are inviting. The area looks much like California's northern coastline, but investing in this region allows for a lifestyle most people could never afford in California.

For example, the benchmark development in this area, Rancho Santana, (*www.ranchosantana.com*), has more than 1,700 acres of hills, forests, and beaches and includes two clubhouses, tennis court, riding stables, an Internet cafe, a couple small shops, a small hotel, restaurant and a bar. Most of the waterfront land here was sold early in the development but there are occasional resales.

The Riviera is also home to the flagship coastal community of Grupo del Sol, a development group quickly becoming known as one of Central America's finest. Situated two hours from Managua, and adjacent to an authentic Nicaraguan fishing village complete with small restaurants and bars, this planned community has begun to take shape in less than two years. No clear cutting or bulldozing of sites is allowed. The homes here are designed to be situated among the trees and visitors regularly see monkeys and flocks of parrots. The largest corporate group in Nicaragua has teamed with American investors to develop a first-class community here, including a master development complete with a signature golf course and condominiums that is in the planning stages.

The Coastal Highway, stretching from the border with Costa Rica to Montelimar, runs right through the San Juan del Sur and Riviera regions. Viewing properties in this area sometimes involves a trip down some bumpy roads during the rainy season, but it's worth the discomfort to invest now and reap the rewards when this highway is complete.

The Central Coast
The Central Coast of Nicaragua is the stretch of Pacific located to the north and south of Managua, within an hour and a half of the city. While the Riviera is the most developed region on the coast, this area is coming on quickly. Pioneer develop-

ers started here in 2002 and a few others followed. Today there are a few developments well under way.

Near El Transito, a small fishing village which provides seafood to Managua and for export to a variety of other countries, development has become extremely popular. One project is a fully master-planned community, complete with clubhouses, pools, social areas, a clinic, golf course, restaurant and planned social activities and events. The development offers several kilometers of building sites on a spectacular coastline, as well as hillside view sites, river frontage and villas that dot the side of a small mountain. Several luxury home owners have formed community service groups and are helping the locals in the town nearby.

Nicaragua's first major vacation resort, Montelimar, is located farther south along the coast yet still only an hour from Managua. Montelimar is an all-inclusive resort developed by Barcelo, a Spanish company, which has been doing business in the Caribbean and Latin America for some time. Since Montelimar's opening, other resorts along Nicaragua's Central coast have sprung up—including boutique-style hotels. The coastline here is not as jagged or spectacular as the Pacific Riviera and the weather is a bit more arid. Much less rain falls in this district and it shows in the vegetation. This region has longer beaches and lies in close proximity to Managua. The majority of Nicaraguans have their beach homes in places like Poneloya, El Transito and Casares. Occasionally you'll find a local willing to sell in this region but be careful and do your due diligence. Shop around and compare prices and amenities. You may find that developers in this region are willing to haggle just a little, as opposed to the ones farther south in the Riviera. Here, building prices may be slightly less expensive than the Riviera, simply due to lower transportation costs from the city.

The North Coast

The northern Pacific Coast of Nicaragua is largely for investors. Large parcels of land are occasionally still available here for relatively inexpensive prices when compared to the Riviera. The north coast terrain is a combination of the Riviera's views and the Central Coast's beaches. Weather is warmer here and, depending on the area, it can be more arid like the Central Coast. Some of Nicaragua's most beautiful tourism spots are in the Corinto region, including the Cosiguiina Volcano Reserve, with its crater lake, wild parrots, scarlet macaws and even a few jaguars. Hiking in the reserve is a memorable experience but getting there from Managua is a four-hour drive, the last hour over pretty rough road.

There is a government plan to upgrade infrastructure due to its desire to augment the existing port in Potosi in the Gulf of Fonseca. Plans are to bring in a ferry from Honduras to cut out three days' journey over the Pan-American Highway. However, like all government projects in Nicaragua, this effort could take years to complete. Larger tracts of land can still be purchased at prices low enough to buy and hold for long-term appreciation.

The North is dotted with small villages and farmland as well as sandy beaches for swimming and warm water in the gulf. The North is what the Central Coast looked like just a few short years ago, with very little outside development or activity. However, as development moves up the coast, this area has all the earmarks of seeing similar projects consistent with the regions farther to the south.

Why not the Caribbean Sea?

Most of Nicaragua's development is taking place along the Pacific Coast. But the country boasts hundreds of kilometers of Caribbean coastline and The Corn Islands' white-sand beaches are comparable to some of the finest destinations in the world. So why not purchase on the Caribbean side of Nicaragua? In a word, title.

The eastern half of Nicaragua is divided into two portions, the RAAN and the RAAS. These are acronyms for Autonomous Regions of the North and South, and they signify that the land there belongs to the indigenous tribes who live there. Think of these regions as the Nicaraguan equivalent of a Native American reservation, where land cannot be sold to foreigners and where even Nicaraguan nationals can buy only under certain restrictive conditions. But there are plenty of people who are willing to sell you the land. And they sound very convincing. A few years ago, one such sly agent made millions selling the Pearl Cays to unsuspecting foreigners. His crimes were so vast that even the Nicaraguan legislature couldn't sort it all out, and he fled the country shortly before arrest warrants were issued. Interestingly, this situation could be changing. There has been discussion in the legislature to release some of this land and it could happen sometime in the not too distant future. But now, even on the popular Corn Islands, taking a chance could result in a lot of wasted effort and money.

Dive resorts on Big and Little Corn Island offer a great place to relax and see some of nature's most breathtaking reefs. The Pearl Cays, while not for sale, can be visited by hiring a boat. The stretch of the Caribbean Sea known as the Miskito Coast offers adventure and eco-travel, including river trips replete with crocodiles and wetland birds.

The purchase process in Nicaragua

Nicaragua is such a new, emerging international second-homes destination that information is not as readily available as in neighboring countries such as Costa Rica and Panama. But reputable real estate companies in Nicaragua can walk you through the process, as they often have accurate information that is difficult to find elsewhere. Many of the real estate players and developers are non-Nicaraguans who have formed partnerships with local real estate companies to sell real estate to foreigners. Frontier Property Group (*www.frontierproperty sales.com*), run by U.S. citizen Gail Geerling and U.K.-based Jocelyn Carnegie, is experienced with several developments on Nicaragua's coastline. Geerling knows that patience is a virtue and, in Nicaragua, it's a necessity. Time is fluid and tomorrow doesn't always mean tomorrow. Just like in Mexico, *manana* may mean tomorrow but it could also mean sometime next week, or next month, or possibly, well … never.

Cultural differences abound and it's part of the fun of living in Nicaragua. But it helps to understand these cultural differences when doing business—especially when purchasing property. One of the most interesting differences is that bothering people is not offensive in Nicaragua. In fact, it's expected. If you are in the process of purchasing property, you (or your representative) will need to follow up multiple times to make sure the process moves along. Leaving your attorney to simply "get on with the purchase" almost always results in disappointment and frustration. Phone calls are best, as are personal visits if you can make them.

The procedure is fairly simple. Except in the indigenous areas, anyone can own property in Nicaragua. There are no restrictions on foreigners owning property. Property can be purchased in the name of the buyer or in the name of a Nicaraguan corporation. Foreign corporations can also be used, but the process becomes more complicated and more documentation is required. It's best to decide how you would like to purchase before entering into a contract.

Once you've agreed on a price for the property, your attorney will prepare a *Promesa de Venta*, or a Promise to Sell. This is a legal document between two parties for the purchase of a property, much like a purchase and sale agreement or earnest money agreement. The *Promesa de Venta* is largely used for homes or raw land, yet can often be skipped if you are purchasing in a planned development. The Promesa de Venta should stipulate a period of due diligence, giving the buyer time to check the title and ensure that it's valid. During this time, the seller must provide to your attorney the title deed (*Escritura Publica*), the *Libertad de Gravamen* (a lien certificate evidencing that the property is free of liens), and the *Certificado Registral* (proving its registry) for the property. Your attorney will then check the documents and give you an opinion of the condition of the title.

It's highly recommended that during this time the buyer obtain a title insurance commitment. By the time all documents required for title insurance are secured and your attorney and the title company rule that the title is insurable, it's usually safe to move forward with confidence. Allow enough time in the *Promesa de Venta* (usually 30 to 45 days) to secure all documents necessary, including the ones needed for title insurance. The title deed is submitted when the purchase is complete.

Next comes a document called the *Testimonio*, which is placed in the public record and notifies any interested party that the property is under contract. This document is like an affidavit, filed by your attorney and testifying that the *Promesa de Venta* was signed. Once all the conditions of the *Promesa de Venta* have been met, it's time to close. Once closed, the property is yours. However, there is one remaining step: Registration of the property under your name.

The same attorney will file another *Testimonio* of the title deed when the transaction is complete. This *Testimonio* is turned into the Nicaraguan equivalent of the U.S. Internal Revenue Service to ensure that the 1 percent transfer tax is paid. Your property can be registered only when this tax is paid. It's an important tax, as the recorded sales price will serve as the basis for your annual property taxes. Once the transfer taxes have been paid, the *Testimonio* is taken to the local municipal office and recorded. This can take several weeks or even months, depending on the region in which you purchase. Registering your property is critical. It will ensure that no one can legally sell that property without your permission.

Follow the two basic rules for doing anything in Nicaragua and your closing procedure can be very simple: 1. Plan ahead. 2. Have a Plan B and Plan C. If you prepare well and plan ahead, your closing can be as simple as signing a document in the comfort of your hotel room just before you leave. Conversely, if you rush out of the country without leaving that simple document signed, your closing becomes much more complicated and time consuming … though it can still be accomplished without a return trip.

Plan ahead

Once you've chosen the property you want to purchase, it's always best to leave a Power of Attorney (POA) before you exit the country. Your agent or consultant can likely recommend several English-speaking attorneys with whom you can leave a POA. You'll need to contact one of these attorneys and arrange well in advance to sign the POA before leaving. These are normally signed in the attorney's office but, for a fee, he can sometimes draft it quickly and bring it to your hotel for signature if necessary. This type of POA is called a *Poder Limitado* or, more commonly, *Poder Especial,* and it must be executed in Spanish. This means that the power you give the attorney is limited to this one purchase transaction and nothing else. The transaction is described within the document in detail; items such as your personal identification information, the specific property details and price are included. When you sign, you are not signing away power to this attorney for anything other than to complete the purchase in your name and register the property for you. This is common practice in Nicaragua and, as opposed to a General Power of Attorney, or *Poder General,* you need not worry that the attorney will be able to sign for you on any other legal document. If you wish, you may designate someone else in Nicaragua to sign the closing documents for you. This can be a friend, your agent or even a different attorney you pay to act on your behalf. It should be someone you trust—don't ask your taxi driver or the nice guy behind the bar.

Choose representation carefully

In addition to following the two basic rules for doing anything in Nicaragua, you'll need to make two very important choices for purchasing property—a good representative and a good attorney.

A good consultant or agent will act as your representative and walk you through the process. This person will be with you every step of the way and will help push to complete all necessary arrangements in time for your closing. To find a good agent, choose a member of the *Camara Nicaraguense de Corredores de Bienes Raices,* which is a real estate association based on the National Association of Realtors code of ethics. The real estate industry is still unregulated and many foreign nationals operate in the country. Proceed with caution.

Attorneys, or *abogados*, function as Notaries as well. In Civil Law countries such as Nicaragua, the idea of a Notary is vastly different than in Common Law countries such as in the U.S. Public Notaries in Nicaragua function as representatives of the government, similar to North America. The difference is that here, the position requires additional education after law school and comes with much more authority, responsibility and liability. A notary must be an attorney, yet not all attorneys are notaries.

It's not as simple as running into your bank and getting a signature and a stamp with Nicaraguan Notaries. They must register each transaction they perform in a book, which serves as a legally binding agreement and can be reviewed by the proper government agency.

Plans B and C

What's the best way to proceed if you can't make up your mind about which property to purchase, or you must return to check funds before committing to a purchase? If possible, it's still best to leave a POA. If the POA is not used because you do not wish to complete the sale, it's simply left unexecuted. You can choose to nullify it later but leaving it is not a problem. However, if you are unable to leave a POA, the easiest solution is to return for the closing. Since this is not always an option, there are several others ... but here is where life gets a little complicated.

Option one

A Power of Attorney can be drafted and executed remotely, with some time and effort. The procedure is as follows:

- Your attorney will draft the POA document in English and send it to you—probably via email.

- You must print the document and sign it in front of a Notary Public in the state where you live.

- Next, you take the POA (signed and notarized) to have the Notary's signature authenticated. This is called an Apostil. Sometimes the entity that handles this is the County Clerk, and sometimes it is an office of the state government—such as the Secretary of State. You may need to phone the government in your state to determine where you can obtain an Apostil.

- You must then have the POA (signed, notarized and apostilled) authenticated at the Nicaraguan Consulate closest to you. You can find the nearest consulate by visiting *www.can cilleria.gob.ni* Once on the site, click the button that says *Consulados de Nicaragua*. There you will find address and contact information for all consulates. (See the notes about Nicaraguan government offices on the next page.)

- Once you receive the document (signed, notarized, apostilled and authenticated by the Nicaraguan Consulate), you'll return it by courier to your attorney's office in Nicaragua. And, while it may sound simple, please remember to use a courier with some form of tracking for packages—such as Fed Ex or DHL. Having gone through this process, the last thing you need is the document to be lost in transit!

- Contact your attorney by phone or email to notify him that the document has been sent and contact him again a week later to ensure that it has arrived. While "overnight delivery" exists in most first-world countries, it usually takes several days for a package to make it to its destination in Nicaragua.

- Having received the POA (signed, notarized, apostilled and authenticated by the Consulate), your attorney will present the document for authentication before the Nicaraguan Ministry of Foreign Affairs in Managua (to ensure that the Consulate's signature is authentic) and complete the transaction on your behalf.

Option one takes time—sometimes as long as several weeks. Plan ahead—and allow plenty of time to get the documents back to your attorney for an on-time closing. When you are ready to close, the seller or your attorney will give you wire transfer instructions. Please remember that everything takes time in Nicaragua. Do not expect to wire the funds the same day as closing—they will not arrive in time and the closing will not happen. Allow at least three working days—not counting Nicaraguan holidays—for the wire to make it through. It is normal for the wire to be sent first and, when it has arrived, for the signing to take place. If this makes you uneasy, wire the funds to your attorney, who can act as an escrow agent. Alternatively, find a U.S. escrow company that will—for a fee—handle the money part of the transaction for you. Do not expect to close with a check—not even a cashier's check. Banks in Nicaragua will hold these checks for up to three weeks and no seller will sign a deed of sale without the funds. If you must pay by check, send it to your attorney or the seller a minimum of three weeks before the scheduled closing date.

A note about Nicaraguan government offices

Dealing with Nicaraguan government offices can be frustrating enough to make you wish for a day at the DMV. Phone ahead to make sure the Consulate is open the day and time you plan to visit. Be sure to ask if they will authenticate your document on that day and at that time. Believe it or not, just because the Consulate is "open" does not mean it is ready to do business. Be prepared and be patient. Clients have arrived during working hours and the person whose signature and seal is needed for the authentication has gone out … or is on vacation … or is resting and will be back after the two-hour lunch.

Each Consulate charges a fee for authenticating documents—usually under $100 USD. They often will not take checks, credit cards, debit cards or any other form of payment besides cash. Try to clarify form of payment and the amount needed before arriving. In other words, be sure to double-check everything before you arrive and plan on spending some time there. If it all goes well and you get everything accomplished quickly, you'll have time to get a rich and delicious Nicaraguan coffee at the nearest coffee house! But don't plan on that coffee …

Alternatively, you can send the document to have it authenticated at the Consulate nearest you. However, please remember that this office will not simply receive the document and authenticate it and send it to you. You will need to track the document and follow up with phone calls every step of the way. You will also need to include a stamped, self-addressed, large manila envelope in your package. Without this, you'll never see your document again.

Helpful tip: In this, the electronic age, we become accustomed to fast and reliable communications and accurate electronic information. When dealing with Nicaraguan Consulates, you'll need to "un-accustom" yourself. They typically do not answer emails. Attempts to communicate with a Consulate in this manner will only prove frustrating. And information on web sites is notoriously incorrect.

Option two

There is one other option for closing and, surprisingly, it's the more straightforward of the two. It is possible to form a corporation using shareholders in Nicaragua, place the property in this corporation and complete the closing by signing over the shares to you. This should be done only in cases where you want to own the property in a Nicaraguan corporation, and if you are comfortable with the people involved.

The shareholders can be persons you designate, or your attorney can choose them for you. The process should be monitored or performed by your attorney. It will cost slightly more—usually around $1,000—for the added setup costs of the corporation. However, when weighing the higher cost against the advantages of saving valuable time and effort, this might be the better option. The *Sociedad Anónima (S.A.)* is the most common corporation used in Nicaragua, for both domestic and foreign investors. There are no restrictions affecting foreign investors and a foreign-owned corporation, in general, is subject to the same laws affecting all local companies. The corporation has capital stock divided into shares and stockholders are liable only to the extent of their contributions. The initials S.A., indicating that it is a corporation, follow the corporate name you select. Your attorney can inform you of all the regulations and be your legal representative to manage the corporation for you. Your legal representative must be a Nicaraguan. The representative does not have to own any portion of the corporation but he is responsible to ensure that you are compliant with reporting laws in Nicaragua. If you use the corporation only to hold property, there are very few requirements.

Always look to title insurance

It's highly recommended that you obtain title insurance when purchasing any property in Nicaragua. Your attorney will need most of the documents listed below to complete a closing. The title insurance company will use the same documents, so it's simple to have copies of these documents sent to the title insurance company at the same time. If you're purchasing in a real estate development, the documents should be simple to obtain. The developer should be able to provide most of them to your attorney and your attorney can obtain any others you need. If you're purchasing outside a development, the process becomes a little trickier but your attorney should be able to obtain all the documents. If you are positive you are using a good attorney and the attorney cannot obtain all the necessary documents, proceed with caution—or not at all. It could indicate that the title is not legitimate or that there are other problems, such as liens or lawsuits against the property.

The following documents are required for closing with title insurance:

1. *Historia Registral*
2. *Libertad de Gravamen*
3. *Solvencia Municipal*
4. *Catastral* survey with appropriate stamps
5. *Antecedentes*
6. Copy of your passport or other ID
7. Power of Attorney (if necessary)
8. Closing statement and receipt for deposit paid

These documents are to assure the attorney that the title history is good, taxes have been paid, the map corresponds with what is indicated on the agreement and there are no liens or legal actions placed upon the property. To obtain title insurance, you'll need to close on the property and produce two additional documents: 9) your title deed, and 10) proof of payment.

Costs of registering your property

Unlike most first-world countries, the title registration process is not automatic in Nicaragua. The day you close is the day you legally own the property and you will be given a copy of the *Escritura Publica,* or public deed. However, to safeguard your investment, the property should be registered under your name at the Registry Office. This can sometimes take several months, depending on which region you choose to make a purchase. Make sure your attorney performs this step for you. Follow up every few weeks to ensure he is on top of the process. Like everything in Nicaragua, certain portions of the closing costs may be negotiable. For example, if you are purchasing a high-ticket property (over $500,000), the attorney may set a flat fee for his services as opposed to a percentage of the transaction.

Typically, you pay the following fees—exclusive of title insurance or incorporation fees:

1.5 percent . . . . Public Deed

1 percent . . . . Transfer Tax

.5 percent . . . . Registration Fees

1 percent . . . . Attorney Fees

$75 . . . . Power of Attorney

$100-$300 . . . . Due Diligence (document research)

Helpful tip: In Nicaragua, few things are "in stone." Time … regulations … work hours … and, in this case, the price paid for property. It is common practice to enter a reduced purchase price on your title deed to avoid a large transfer tax and save on yearly property taxes. In many municipalities, there is no organized assessment system, so this can work. You should know that this practice, although common, is not exactly legal. And it's conceivable that you'd be liable for larger capital gains when you sell your property by reducing the purchase price on the deed. However, do not be surprised if the seller or your attorney asks you, "How much would you like to put on your *Escritura*?"

The eternal dilemma: What should I buy?

The good news is that in Nicaragua, there are endless choices. Unfortunately, that's the bad news too. Some real estate hunters arrive in Nicaragua, see only a fraction of what's available and leave in confusion without ever making the investment. It's important to have an idea of what you're looking for before visiting, because once on the ground the variety and quality of real estate will confuse and dazzle.

When property hunters come to Nicaragua for the first time, they often get "Margarita Madness." After sipping a *margarita* or *nica libre* and watching the brilliant colors of a Pacific Coast sunset, that piece of land with the fantastic view becomes far more attractive. Sit awhile longer and chat with a friendly local or two and Nicaragua seems the perfect paradise. So some visitors sign a purchase agreement on the spot and all is well with the world—until they wake up the next morning and realize that they really didn't come here to take on the responsibility of building a 4,000-square-foot home a couple thousand miles away!

Review your options ahead of time and have an idea of the category of real estate you'd like to purchase before visiting. For example, are you buying for lifestyle or investment? Do you want raw land on which to build or a home you can move into with no fuss? Would you like to rent out your real estate when you're not using it or will you occupy it full time? Or would you rather just buy and hold some land, cashing in later on the potential capital appreciation as prices rise? All of these options—and more—are available in Nicaragua. Answering these questions ahead of time will help narrow your focus and save time, money and a whole lot of confusion.

Flying without a net

Before getting into the categories of property available, it's important to remember one thing: *do not* buy property from a local without a good representative. That nice guy on the barstool next to yours with a piece of property "at a price too good to be true" is telling you the truth: it *is* too good to be true. Property title issues are rampant in Nicaragua. Horror stories abound of visitors who have purchased property only to find out later that the person who sold it to them was not the real owner. Or of the *gringo* who purchased his dream piece of oceanfront, only to find that several others "owned" it as well—and when the happy new owner started building, they came out of the woodwork with a vengeance. Or how about the unsuspecting buyers who bought property which belonged to indigenous tribes or the municipal government—property which is not legally sellable?

As soon as we leave our home countries, the rules and safety nets we're accustomed to no longer apply. If you think that the Nicaraguan government or the court system will do your due diligence for you, you're sadly mistaken. In Nicaragua—as in most of the region—due diligence is the responsibility of the buyer. Don't leave your brains at the border! Do your homework and you'll be absolutely fine. But skip it and it's almost a sure bet you'll have property issues later. These issues are relatively easy to sort through, but not for a foreigner—and certainly not without help. There are established ways and means of checking property you're not sure of but it takes someone knowledgeable to navigate the system. Buying in a real estate development is usually the safest and simplest way to proceed. The developer often does the work for you. But not all developments—and not all developers—are the same.

Raw land for investment

There are still fairly large tracts of land in Nicaragua that you can buy and hold or subdivide. In some areas of the country—especially in the Pacific Riviera—this speculative portion of the market is about maxed out. Developed tourist areas such as Granada and San Juan del Sur are really too far along for buying land simply to hold and flip in a year. Although even in these areas, it is still possible to purchase lots or homes and realize good capital appreciation by holding over a period of time. However, larger tracts of land are available in some areas along the coast, usually located in regions lacking the infrastructure available in more developed areas. The challenge with larger tracts of land is ensuring that title is genuine. Again, this is where due diligence and using a good representative is crucial.

"I was once driving down a road when a group of guys in a truck pulled up and motioned for me to pull over," said Jocelyn Carnegie, who has more than 20 years of international real estate sales and investing experience in emerging markets.

"Turns out they knew I was asking about property and they wanted to tell me about the fantastic beachfront lots they were offering just over the hill. I asked the requisite questions—did they have a title deed for my attorney to review, was the land leased or free hold, were there any squatters, etc. Their answers were satisfactory, so I turned around and drove to the site—only to find a lady living there who insisted the land was hers! Whether the land belonged to her or to the cowboys in the truck didn't matter. The last thing I wanted was to be embroiled in a legal battle to kick someone off a piece of land. And it's the last thing you want too."

Small lots are available for personal use, mostly in areas where others have begun a community. But the really good deals are usually where a large tract of land is involved. The larger the piece, the more likely you'll get a great per-acre price. These large tracts are best purchased with a view to holding them for a few years. Alternatively, splitting the large pieces into smaller ones and selling portions of the property can, over a period of time, pay for the property and leave a nice chunk for you to own free and clear. But the way to make the most money on large tracts of land is to add value by installing infrastructure. Putting in a road, bringing in electrical lines and installing a water system may seem scary. Clearly, this is not an option for anyone who does not want to live in Nicaragua to oversee this work, and it's not an option for anyone without plenty of financial backing. But there are people who can help and qualified engineers and contractors who can do the work.

Back to nature

Nicaragua's climate varies from region to region and is, therefore, perfect for farming. Cash crops such as organic coffee, bananas, pitahayas, mangoes, rice, beans, sorghum and sugar are exported and used locally every day. Nicaraguan beef is some of the finest in the world and cattle are big business in selected areas of the country. Large tracts of farmland can be acquired at reasonable prices in many areas. Of course, as in any other country, the closer you get to the coast and to the cities, the more expensive the real estate. If you're not sure whether you'd like to farm or just have a home, there are a couple of developers offering larger tracts of land which could accommodate a small cash crop or hardwood reforestation (teak, mahogany, cedar or other hardwoods) while at the same time providing the perfect spot for a home with sweeping ocean views, about half a kilometer away from the Pacific's swimming beaches. It's a great way to experiment to see if you'd like farming or reforestation in Nicaragua and hedge the bet with a great piece of oceanview land.

Building your dream home

Most developments along the Pacific Coast offer home sites with ocean frontage or views. Some even offer a few suggested floor plans and might have a building program of some sort. Of course, the simplest route is to purchase a model home, which the developer will construct for you. However, it is possible—with some assistance—to design and build the perfect home yourself using local designers, engineers and contractors. The topography and terrain varies greatly along the coast ... from flat sandy areas to heavily forested mountains. Take a look at several areas and decide which you like best. Then decide how much space you need—a quarter acre? Half acre? More than an acre? Nicaragua's diversity allows for a multitude of options.

Turnkey Properties

Turnkey properties are fully finished units. This category can include condominiums, small bungalows or casitas, or larger homes, and turnkeys can often be purchased at a much better price before construction begins. Turnkey units are far and away the easiest option for property in Nicaragua—no supervising, no contractor hassles, no planning and pushing a builder. The developer builds the unit and hands you the key when it's finished. Often, these units even have furniture packages, which allow you to pay one price for a house full of furniture. For vacation or getaway homes as well as retirement living, turnkey units are great—they're the closest thing to hassle-free investing. And if the developer has a property management program, they're even better. You can place your unit in the rental pool when you're not using it and the income will often offset any normal house maintenance expenses or HOA fees. For additional tips, see Chapter 11.

Nicaragua's property market is just beginning, so property management systems in most areas are a long way from being mature. If you're buying a turnkey unit for investment (as opposed to living in it full time), ask:

- Who is the property manager?
- What plans does he or she have for bringing rentals?
- What are average occupancy rates in this area?
- How often can I expect my unit to be rented?
- What is the average rental price in this region?

You probably won't get definite answers to these questions— property managers don't have crystal balls. But by asking the questions you should be able to get a good handle on whether or not the purchase makes sense. If, for example, you must rent the unit enough to make a mortgage payment, you may choose to purchase in a more populated area such as Granada, The Pacific Riviera or San Juan del Sur. Even the capital city of Managua could work, depending on the area. Alternatively, if you're planning on using your home full time or you don't need the money from rentals, there are a lot more choices available to you in the current market. Less-populated areas in some of Nicaragua's most beautiful settings are a much better option when you'll be living there as opposed to being dependent on rental income.

Hidden gems and advantages

Nicaragua is a country booming with opportunity. It is also one of the most challenging real estate markets because so little information exists on this emerging destination. Like any place, it's best to get "on the ground" and gather information via personal experience and evaluation. Those who have invested in real estate in that country tend to be bullish on its future.

Carnegie was so sold on his first impressions of Nicaragua that he moved there to better understand and take advantage of the second-home market boom. A native of Scotland, Carnegie has lived in eastern and western Europe and has managed international sales for Knight Frank (*www.knightfrank.com*), a London-based, worldwide property brokerage, in addition to commenting and writing on international real estate issues. His present company, Frontier Property Group, targets second-home buyers in a variety of leisurely settings. Carnegie believes the prevailing initial reaction to Nicaragua is linked with images seen more than a decade ago.

"Ask most people what their impression of Nicaragua is and they'll tell you that bandana-clad gangs roam the streets shooting in the air from the backs of beaten-up pickups," Carnegie said. "Or, there are jealous thieves stalking the unwitting traveler on every street corner, AK47-touting drug lords are impossible to avoid and—well, there's some sort of a civil war on, isn't there?"

"We grow up with sweeping preconceptions of far-flung regions of the world," Carnegie said. "Television, newspaper and radio put war and suffering in front of our faces. The images of oppression, dictators and hardship stick in our minds as we grow."

Today, a drastically different environment prevails. Nicaragua is a nation at relative peace. Its government is democratically elected, seemingly committed to a free-market economy and eager to attract foreign investors. A recent study by the Inter-American Institute on Human Rights and a survey of police forces in the Americas revealed that Nicaragua is the safest country in Central America and one of the safest countries in the world. The same study cites that the crime rate in Nicaragua is lower than in Germany, France or the U.S. While Nicaragua is the poorest country in Central America, its people are kind, generous and generally happy. The potholes in the roads and similarly deep communication challenges are balanced with magnificent coastlines, renowned surfing and game fishing, tropical dry forests, rainforests, volcanoes and breathtaking birds. Its fresh food is almost all organic; farmers can't afford sprays. Livestock typically is raised without being pumped with growth hormones.

The BOSIA example:
A sister-island relationship model

The joy and fulfillment of a second home often come from experiences other than sitting with a paperback on a beach or carving up the ski slopes near a family getaway. Sometimes, a second home is purchased following an alluring cultural experience, educational exchange or personal relationship.

A good example has been the Bainbridge-Ometepe Sister Islands Association (BOSIA), founded in 1986 by Kim and Ela Esterberg and some friends on Bainbridge Island, a community of 22,000 just west of Seattle on Puget Sound. The sister island—Ometepe—is a large island in Lake Nicaragua that was formed by two volcanoes. Ometepe, a farming community of 35,000, is a word taken from the Nahuatl language, meaning "two peaks."

In the past 20 years, a few of the hundreds of Bainbridge residents who have visited have returned and purchased property and built second homes on Ometepe, where transportation and communication facilities are limited and most of the island's residents live in basic structures. The two island groups have jointly created schools and water systems and improved health care and education. Bainbridge volunteers import, roast and distribute Ometepe coffee in the Northwest. Lasting friendships have been made among people of all ages on both islands as they continue to work and play together.

David Mitchell, who serves as BOSIA's computer network administrator, recently sold his longtime family home on Bainbridge and built a small home on Ometepe. Mitchell was instrumental in getting wireless Internet to Ometepe and spends about half the year there, usually returning to

Nicaragua in November when the rains dissipate. He is drawn to the island's friendly people yet has seen a definite change in some of the newcomers.

"Other people have come to Ometepe—Europeans, Canadians, Nicaraguans—and built larger homes," Mitchell said. "It's an issue that concerns people there because in many cases the homes take up areas that were once working farms. On the other hand, the construction has brought desperately needed jobs to the island."

Siri Kushner, a Bainbridge Island High School graduate who first visited Ometepe as a student, returned to Ometepe to work and married an Nicaraguan attorney. The couple is uncertain where they will make their full-time home.

"It's hard to watch some of the foreigners developing large parcels of land," Kushner said. "The islanders are really not used to people who live to isolate themselves. There are cultural challenges with the changes and prices are rising. But it's not just Ometepe; young people are seeing prices going up everywhere."

A Personal View:
Luxurious Lifestyle at Bargain Prices

Gail Geerling owns a home on Nicaragua's Pacific Coast that she could never afford in the U.S.

She wakes to the sounds of parrots and howler monkeys, watching the sun rise over brilliant green-hued mountains while waves crash on the rocks below. Her home is built of concrete, to California seismic standards, with tile floors, a state-of-the-art kitchen, clay tile roof,

---

mahogany and cedar crown moldings and trims, and marble and granite countertops. The cost? About one-tenth the price of an equivalent home in California.

"I'm a single woman—blonde, blue-eyed, extremely light skin," Geerling said. "Let's just say that when I came to Nicaragua—a Latin country—I didn't exactly blend. Yet, I've traveled alone across this beautiful country, gotten hopelessly lost more times than I care to count, had flat tires in the middle of the night, given rides to strangers (a course of action I would not recommend for newcomers!), walked alone at 3 a.m. and never once been attacked by anything more dangerous than a mosquito.

"Do I recommend doing all these things on your own? Probably not. I've lived in Central America for almost 10 years and have the experience to go with it. But while I would not walk alone at 3 a.m. in my home town back in Michigan, I feel perfectly comfortable doing it in Granada, Nicaragua.

"And if I had a flat tire along the highway back in the U.S., I would phone someone and sit in my locked car waiting for them—afraid that anyone who stopped to help me might have other motives. Here in Nicaragua, help is likely to be the next passing person. And it's likely to be given with a huge smile and the phrase '*a la orden*,' or 'at your service.'

"The best part? You can buy property here and experience all of Nicaragua's beauty—nature at its best, inexpensive living, access to all the comforts of home, friendly people—and reap a nice reward on your investment as the rest of the world discovers Nicaragua. And property values rise."

A buoyant economy

Nicaragua is growing quickly and opportunities abound. Tourism numbers are fast approaching the million-a-year mark and are growing more rapidly than in any other country in the region. Foreign investment is up over 70 percent from 2002-2005. As a result of years of economic liberalization and the implementation of policies intended to stimulate national and foreign investment, Nicaragua is now one of the most dynamic economies in Central America. In fact, in 2004, Nicaragua experienced the highest GDP growth rate (5.1 percent) of any country in the region, due in large part to a substantial increase in private investment and exports. According to a recent report by International Development Systems Inc. (IDS), Nicaragua was second only to China in terms of growth in garment exports to the United States in 2004. Tourism is now the highest earning sector in the Nicaraguan economy, followed by textiles and apparel, agriculture, forestry and fishing, services and construction.

A further boost to U.S. investors in Nicaragua came with the introduction of OPIC in 2005. The Overseas Private Investment Corporation (*www.opic.gov*) offers political risk insurance, loan guarantees and project financing to U.S. businesses and investors overseas and this provision closes the insurance loop. The U.S. government backs OPIC, so this gives investors a bit more comfort with—and answers most of their questions about—political risk and stability from a U.S. perspective. Perceived risk still acts as a brake to the economy and the real estate market. It's also a contributing factor to this market presenting such a consistent and dependable opportunity. Early investors have seen very good capital appreciation and growing rental return potential. Real estate brokers and market analysts estimate Nicaragua to be comparable to Costa Rica 20 years ago. Many North Americans started buying and investing in real estate in Costa Rica in the late 1980s, with much of the boom spread by word of mouth. Now the coastline is dotted with million-dollar homes, expensive beach resorts and high-end marinas. Property values are approximately five times greater in Costa Rica than on Nicaragua's Pacific Riviera, only 45 minutes to the north. In the past few years, tourism and business have moved from Costa Rica to San Juan del Sur, Granada and the Pacific Coast of Nicaragua. Cruise ships have already started coming to San Juan del Sur. Nicaragua is getting on people's maps and tourism is translating into second-home investments. Real estate values have mirrored the first portion of Costa Rica's curve. Now, 70,000 Americans call Costa Rica their home. They came by the thousands to retire there ... running from California and Florida prices.

Quick Look at Taxes

Income tax

(Impuestro Sobre la Renta) Income earned by non-resident individuals on Nicaraguan-sourced income is

taxed at progressive rates. The taxable income is 70 percent of the gross income, which is deemed to be the net income. For rental income, 70 percent of the gross rent is taxable (therefore, only 30 percent of the gross rent can be deducted). The tax rate becomes 30 percent on amounts greater than $27,955.

Real estate tax

(Impuesto de Bienes Inmuebles or Predial) The property tax is levied at a flat rate of 1 percent. The tax base is 80 percent of the cadastral value of the property (land, buildings and permanent improvements), as assessed by the municipal cadastral office. The tax is paid to the local government (alcaldias municipals).

However, many smaller municipalities do not even collect the tax, due to a lack of knowledge and confusion of land titles. In most cases, paying local taxes in Nicaragua has been described as a voluntary act.

Capital gains tax

Capital gains earned through the sale of real estate are taxed at the ordinary income rates.

Incentives to invest

Nicaragua is the latest country in Central America to introduce generous government-led incentives to entice local and foreign investors, proving that the second-home boom has the government's full backing. The Law 306 Tourism Incentive Program, in place for numerous years already, allows investors to benefit from 10 years of tax-free revenue (including property taxes) from their tourism project investment (see detailed box below). This is a play from Panama's textbook example and success story. In part due to these incentives, inventory will grow over the coming years, but the market seems to be narrowing at the front end. Demand is beginning to outstrip supply. The range of product is also growing, in volume as well as variety. There really is something for everyone here.

Promoting Tourism in Nicaragua

*Information is courtesy of the
United States Embassy web site in Nicaragua*

Summary

Nicaragua is pinning high hopes on tourism as a foreign earner and economic development multiplier. A new tourism incentive law provides several tax benefits to investors and is expected to generate considerable financing in tourism-related projects throughout the country. The Nicaraguan Institute of Tourism (INTUR) is tasked with facilitating and streamlining for investors the process of developing tourism and related projects.

Provisions of new law

After considerable government effort, Nicaragua's National Assembly unanimously approved the Tourism Industry Incentive Law (Law 306) in May 1999. The government successfully eliminated or significantly reduced a number of taxes (import, temporary protection, luxury and value-added taxes) for financiers and investors interested in developing tourism and tourism-related projects in Nicaragua. The country is now beginning to feel the impact of this new law.

Investments outside of Managua qualify for tax subsidies at smaller levels of investment than is the case within the capital. The government also has made it more attractive for investors considering projects in "special districts for tourism planning and development" (e.g., historic areas). There is now a provision for "ad hoc" concessions for 20 years (and a maximum of 59 years) for specific projects on government-owned properties, such as the construction of marinas, piers and airplane runways.

Tourism activities and investment requirements

The Tourism Incentive Laws, which identifies certain minimum investment requirements to receive tax benefits, categorizes the following as tourism-related activities:

- Lodging and hospitality services, including *paradores* (Nicaraguan inns) for traveling tourists. The minimum qualifying investment for a major establishment in Managua is $500,000; the figure is $150,000 outside of Managua. For *paradores*, the minimum investment is $200,000 in Managua and $80,000 outside of the capital. The investment figures for small hotels are $100,000 and $50,000, respectively. An investment of at least $100,000 is required in camping areas to receive tax benefits.

- Investments in "protected areas," public sites of cultural interest and areas designated for historic preservation. Minimum investments for projects in protected areas are $40,000; for historic preservation areas the figure is $100,000. INTUR determines on a case-by-case basis the minimum investment for public cultural sites.

- Air, land, and water transportation, car rentals and the renting of watercrafts for tourists. There is no minimum investment requirement.

- The development of Nicaraguan arts and crafts, the rescue of threatened traditional industries, and the production of native music and folk dance events. There is a $50,000 minimum investment requirement.

- Food, beverage and entertainment services at facilities such as restaurants, recreational centers, nightclubs and casinos, which are clearly related to tourism. *Mesones* (typical food inns) offer traditional and regional cuisine. Minimum investments are $100,000 in Managua and $30,000 outside of the capital to qualify for tax benefits.

- Investments in infrastructure and co-related tourism installations and facilities. The minimum investment is $250,000 in Managua and $100,000 outside of Managua.

- Investments in film production and in events which benefit tourism. There is no minimum investment requirement.

Tourism tax benefits

Under the new law, tax benefits are determined by the type of investment and vary from full exoneration to partial exemptions with regard to import duties, value-added (IGV in Spanish), property and income taxes.

Those involved with (1) hospitality and lodging services; (2) investments in protected areas, public cultural sites and historic preservation areas; and (3) tourism infrastructure and related tourism installations and facilities are fully exempted from paying any import taxes and the value-added tax for design, engineering and construction services. *These same categories are exempted from real estate taxes on property, facilities, and improvements for a period of 10 years* (second homes). Moreover, there are full exemptions from value-added taxes for the local purchase of construction materials and building appliances.

Artisans, traditional industry workshops, and traditional music and folk dance performers should receive full and permanent exemption from income taxes, according to the new tourism incentive law.

Investment registration and process

INTUR is responsible for accepting or rejecting a proposed tourism-related project within 60 days. To facilitate an investor's proposal, INTUR is supposed to consult other government agencies about a project that could impact the environment and local area. The government agencies have 30 days to review a proposal and return their opinions to INTUR. If accepted, the project is registered in the tourism investment registry.

From the implementation date of a tourism-related project, the investor will benefit from the various tax exemptions. Income tax exemptions will not be granted until the project has demonstrated that all of the project conditions, such as a minimum investment, have been met.

Impact of investment

The Nicaraguan government expects tourism, as a result of the new law, to eventually overtake coffee as the country's leading hard currency earner. Tourism Nicaragua's second-largest foreign exchange earner generated approximately $90 million in 1998 (coffee earnings totaled more than $170 million that year).

President Aleman recently said that he wants to convert Nicaragua into the most successful tourism destination in Central America within the next 15 years. Since the enactment of the law through early April 2000, INTUR has approved projects worth an estimated $19 million in tourism-related activities, of which about $4.5 million have actually been executed.

Investment obstacles in Nicaragua

There can be several impediments to doing business in Nicaragua. Although the government is working to establish clear rules applicable to all, the rules of the game are sometimes changed by sudden government decree or political considerations, which can significantly disrupt business planning. The unpredictability of enforcement of contracts and a cumbersome legal system are frequent complaints, and the enforcement of judicial rulings is sometimes uncertain. Requests for bribes do occur.

Property issues are another concern to investors. Resolution of Sandinista-era property claims (including U.S. citizen properties) are slow. Potential investors should consult a local attorney before purchasing property. The current law regarding waterfront properties is unclear and property titles to land on Nicaragua's Caribbean Coast are controversial. There are also high operating costs in terms of electricity, telephone, and transportation (Nicaragua has limited infrastructure).

For Further Information

Copies of the new Tourism Incentive Law and other related information published by INTUR are available by visiting the agency's web site: *www.intur.gov.ni.* To discuss specific tax benefits, INTUR's investment promotion office can answer questions via telephone (505-222-3491) or fax (505-222-6611).

Source: U.S. Department of State

Note that even small investors can take advantage of Law 306, without all the paperwork. Part of this law allows for the sale of units within a 306 project to others, who share in the benefits as long as the unit is placed in a rental pool. For example, if a developer builds 30 villas under Law 306 with the purpose of renting them as a condo-hotel, he can sell the individual units—as long as the buyer signs an agreement to place his/her villa in the rental pool. The buyer can have up to three months' personal use of the unit, then allow the developer to manage the villa for nine months and still qualify for tax incentives under Law 306. So, in essence, the buyer becomes a "partner" with the developer in the Law 306 project. The management group takes a percentage of rentals and owners of the units take the balance as rental income-tax free for 10 years. There is no set standard for management fees, so rental management programs and percentages vary. It's a good idea to speak to the property manager before purchasing, to get information on particular aspects of the rental program such as management fees, how expenses are paid, expected occupancy rates, etc. Often the nine months' rental brings in enough to cover all maintenance expenses for the year and pay off a significant portion of the initial investment.

Investing goals: Risk-to-reward ratio

It's one thing to be able to buy coastal land. It's quite another to be able to find it an affordable and plentiful inventory. The goal of investing in emerging markets is to feel comfortable with your risk-to-reward ratio. Investor confidence is higher than ever and growing. Second-home buyers, tourists and investors are now considering Nicaragua as a destination for business and pleasure due to the low cost but high standard of living as well as the wide variety of opportunities. Nicaragua's growth and optimism is dovetailing with a shrinking world and its real estate market is primed to explode into a growing number of overseas buyers as the world becomes more accessible via the Internet.

Speaking of the Internet, you will want to do your online research before jumping on a plane and visiting our next country, Guatemala.

CHAPTER FIVE

Guatemala:
Huge, Untapped,
Mysterious

... and still in the "diaper" stage of development

Scott Robberson has been around—and now he's staying put. Born in New Mexico, raised in Oklahoma and educated in Washington state, Robberson moved to Guatemala in 1995 to become executive director of the American Chamber of Commerce in Guatemala City. In the interim, he married a Guatemalan woman with whom he is raising two sons, left the chamber job and now is operations manager for Casa Nova Real Estate (*www.casanovarealestate.net*), located in the gorgeous colonial city of Antigua, the country's most popular second-home region for foreign buyers and a 45-minute drive from the capital city.

tikal

Mexico

Flores

Belize

Livingston
Rio Dulce

Lake
Izabal

Honduras

Lake
Atitlan

Guatemala
City

Retalhuleu

Antigua
Guatemala

Monterrico

El
Salvador

Puerto
San José

Pacific beach areas
are undeveloped with
decent surf spots

GUATEMALA

"When I ran the chamber of commerce, everyone asked about safety," Robberson said. "Now, more people are asking about real estate. Once you get a feel for the lifestyle here, it's easy to think about buying a home and staying around. The lifestyle and the region are far preferable to anyplace else that I've lived."

While Guatemala emerged from a 36-year civil war in 1996 and has not experienced the second-home-market activity of some of its Central American family members, more and more transactions are being recorded every year. Reasons for the increase can be traced to more curious, exotic buyers, increased political stability, and the modernization of the real estate laws and land property databases—including the country's title register.

But let's face it ... Guatemala is not typically at the top of the list when buying a second home for recreation, retirement or investment. When somebody says "Central America," most folks' thoughts first drift to Costa Rica, then slip into some warm Belize beach, and then perhaps to the new-found wonders of Panama. Each of those countries conjures up an image of beachfront property, laid-back lifestyle and a certain exoticness that would make your neighbor retiring to a golf course community in Florida jealous.

Introduction and overview

What about Guatemala? It is the largest and most populous of the Central American countries, with a gross domestic product per capita roughly one-half that of Brazil, Argentina and Chile. The agricultural sector accounts for about one-fourth of GDP, two-thirds of exports and half of the labor force. Coffee, sugar and bananas are the main products. The 1996 signing of peace accords, which ended 36 years of civil war, removed a major obstacle to foreign investment. Guatemala ranks right up there on the exotic barometer, but there are a few downsides. First of all, the country lacks beachfront property. Fewer than 300 miles of oceanfront coastline make it one of the most land-locked countries in the region. Guatemala occupies 42,042 square miles, nearly the size of Ohio, but only 200 miles touch the Pacific Ocean. Much of this coastline is dramatic and undeveloped but is comprised of black volcanic sand, making it unattractive for development. The Caribbean coast covers only 70 miles, and much of it lacks actual white-sand beaches. But it is interesting nonetheless (more on that later).

The other downside of Guatemala is the perception of insta-bility. Its history is littered with brutal dictatorships and civil wars. Tensions exist between ethnic Indian groups and the country has one of the highest crime rates in Central America. To make matters worse, Guatemala has been victim to natural disasters, including earthquakes, volcanic eruptions and hurri canes. Most recently it was hit by Mitch in 1998 and Stan in 2005, which killed over 1,500 people and continues to affect the country's economic development.

"Walk down the bad part of any large city at night and tell me what is dangerous," Robberson said. "We are no different. You go out at night in the safe areas of town. Guatemala City's *zona viva* is safe at night, but not after midnight. Antigua is safer than most because the people understand that many tourists come here and crime cannot be tolerated. Are grin-gos more apt to be victimized? Well, if you are retired and carry a video camera, you are probably more at risk. But if you travel in groups, then there is no problem. Are gangs com-mon on the roads? No, but certain areas of the country are safer than others."

A little common sense goes a long way in any country. You wouldn't be reading this book if you weren't in for a little adventure. And, if you are flexible and enjoy calculated risks, you will find Guatemala to be friendly, exotic and geographically varied, with one of the richest cultures in all of Latin America ... thanks to Guatemala's rich Indian ethnicity, which represents up to 40 percent of the country's population (as opposed to being nearly non-existent in Costa Rica and not as pronounced in Panama and Nicaragua). There are traditions, sights and historical exploration opportunities that exist nowhere else in the region. And it is one of Central America's least-expensive countries.

If you are an archeology buff, then you will delight in the exploration of Tikal, where you will find over six square miles filled with thousands of Mayan ruins, under the thick jungle canopy where the sounds of howler monkeys compete with quetzal birds to give a soundtrack that could be taped and sold as musical CDs back in the U.S.A.

If you want cultural immersion, then Guatemala is a terrific option. One of the most popular places to study Spanish is Antigua, with dozens of schools catering to all different levels of instruction. And Antigua itself is one of the best preserved Spanish colonial cities, with many buildings unchanged over hundreds of years. The volcanic mountains in the background provide a stunning backdrop.

Modern cities, including the capital, Guatemala City, feature high-rise buildings, fashionable restaurants, shopping and entertainment districts that boast a cosmopolitan and first-world look and feel. Much of the country lies in temperate elevations, providing a year-round, spring-like atmosphere. And, while oceanfront property is not as prevalent as in other Central American markets, lakefront property is abundant.

Atitlan, located near Antigua, is one of the most picturesque lakes in the world, with dramatic mountainous background and an assortment of second homes mainly for weekend residents of Guatemala City. Lake Izabal sits in an intriguing tropical bowl with numerous islands and twisting rivers. Toss in relatively easy access to the Caribbean and the Lake Izabal area becomes a true hidden jewel of Central America.

U.S.-style second-home communities, which are commonplace in Panama and Costa Rica, are virtually non-existent in Guatemala, so it is a great country for a foreigner to "go native." And the country has some of the easiest access to the United States. Directly to the north is Mexico, so arriving by car is not out of the question. The Pan-American Highway will get you to the Mexican border in a few hours. Numerous direct-flight connections are available to multiple cities in the United States.

Second-home web sites still scarce

Sara Siegel was born and raised in Brooklyn, studied at Ithaca College and moved to Guatemala as a young adult. She earned undergraduate and law degrees in Guatemala City and now acts as an attorney and consultant for real estate investment and development, strategic alliances and government relations. She said Americans tend to buy mostly colonial properties—especially in the large North American community that has emerged in La Antigua Guatemala, or simply "Antigua." Real estate has become very expensive in the popular colonial area where it is increasingly difficult to find land or new construction at affordable prices.

"Although there are web sites for vacation tours and rentals as well as hotel information, there are very few web sites that have reliable information regarding second homes," Siegel said. "There are lovely developments at the beaches but no web sites to promote them or give contact information. At best, most second homes are listed on international web sites that mention Guatemala."

Legalities and ownership

Under Guatemalan law, foreigners can acquire, maintain and dispose of real property with very few restrictions. But foreigners cannot own land directly adjacent to rivers, oceans or international borders—unless that property is purchased by a Guatemalan corporation. Foreign firms developing projects in designated tourism zones are eligible for income tax exemption on revenue from their investments and duty-free importation of any needed goods or materials not made in Central America.

It is relatively easy to form a corporation and buy waterfront property. The entire incorporation process takes three to eight months (depending upon urgency, who you know, etc.) and costs $1,250 to $2,000 depending upon how hard your attorney pushes the process. While the procedure can sometimes be a pain in the neck, the outcome often can make the ordeal well worthwhile.

What You Need to Visit

Passports are required for a stay of up to 90 days. For longer stays, you will need a visa, which requires an application form, a valid passport, one passport-sized

---

photo and the appropriate fee ($25 for tourist visa and $50 for business visa). For travel by minors and general information, contact the Embassy of Guatemala, 2220 R St., NW, Washington, DC 20008-4081 (202.745.4952); or the nearest Consulate: CA (213.365.9251 or 415.788.5651), FL (305.443.4828), IL (312.332.3170), NY (212.686.3837) or TX (713.953.9531). Internet: *www.guatemala-embassy.org*. See Appendix for more details.

Pacific beaches are undiscovered

Steven Moriarty, born in northern Illinois and a graduate of Southern Illinois University at Carbondale, has lived in Guatemala for more than a decade. He has a fair amount of experience dealing with the Guatemalan title process and put it to work when he purchased two parcels for his second-home use.

Several years ago, Moriarty purchased a black-sand, waterfront property on the Pacific Ocean in the tiny town of Iztapa, a dot at the end of the road south of Puerto San Jose, a seaport town southwest of Guatemala City. He paid $9,500 for the parcel, which has approximately 80 feet of waterfront and reaches 290 feet deep and features two almond trees and four coconut trees. In 2006, he purchased the adjacent waterfront lot, slightly larger than his original parcel, for $37,500. He purchased a smaller lot farther inland and drilled a water well to serve both properties.

"As with almost all oceanfront and navigable waterway property in Guatemala, the state owns the property," Moriarty said. "The mechanism to circumvent this is to form a Guatemalan corporation and place the property in the corporation. The foreign national can legally be the legal representative and the shareholder therefore can control the property."

Moriarty said he must register the property with the Office of Control of the Territorial Reserves of State, or OCRET, and sign a 15-year renewable lease. He pays $250 to $300 per year for the lease. Moriarty and other purchasers admit that in some areas, officials will "look the other way" when a non-national (as an individual, not as a corporation) makes an offer on a waterfront property. However, it's advisable that all North Americans attempting to purchase waterfront go through the corporation process. There are exceptions to the corporation requirement if the property was titled prior to a certain date but those properties are not common. Moriarty also created a corporation for a property he purchased from a private party near Sayaxche on the Passion River.

Moriarty's best advice? Always, always hire a reputable attorney.

The five steps:
Buying and registering real estate

First, the seller must obtain a certificate from a Guatemalan property registry verifying that the property is free from liens and financial encumbrances and that the seller is the legal owner. It is this certificate that is later used by the Public Notary (*notario*) for preparing the official property deed (*escritua*). In order to obtain this certificate, the buyer must obtain from the seller the exact information about the property's registry identification numbers and the office where the property is registered.

The next step is to get the cadastral value (*valor catastral*)—that is, the taxable value of the property as determined by the municipal government. If the municipal registry of the property does not have the property value, then the alternative is to request the information from the DICABI (*Dirección de Catastro y Avalúo de Bienes Inmuebles*). The DICABI is a national institution that presides over all of the regional registries throughout the country.

Once the cadastral value has been obtained, the next and most important step for the Notary/lawyer is to prepare and notarize the sale agreement and prepare the public deed. The documents required by the Notary:

- Property Title from the Real Estate Office.

- Actualized certificate of property from General Property Registry (*Registro General de la Propiedad*, or *RGP*)

- Photocopy of the identification of seller and buyer (passport or local identification).

- Certificate from the tax authorities certifying that the Value Added Tax (VAT) has been paid.

- Cadastral value (similar to county assessment) of the property.

The Public Deed is then submitted to the Real Estate Office and recorded in the name of the new owner. The final step is to notify the municipality and/or DICABI of the transaction. This does not affect the validity of the transfer but it is still important as it helps to ensure the proper updating of the cadastral value of the property. Non-compliance with this step carries a fine.

In addition, capital gains earned by nonresidents from selling Guatemalan property are subject to a flat 31 percent withholding tax. The taxable gain is computed by deducting the acquisition costs and improvement costs from the selling price. Any tax paid in a foreign country is deducted from a U.S. taxpayer's domestic liability.

Value Added Tax *(impuesto al valor agregado)*, or VAT, is imposed on the selling of properties in Guatemala and the taxable amount is the selling price. This tax is imposed at the standard rate of 12 percent.

Financing still in the early stages

Financing a real estate purchase for foreigners in Guatemala is relatively new unless you are a resident and can prove your income is generated within the country. The most common alternative to lender financing is seller financing, but more international banks are expected on the scene soon to take advantage of the increasingly popular market.

If you can prove you are a resident—with income—financing doors seem to open quickly. Native Minnesotan Jeffry Paul, an executive for BearCom, a distributor of wireless communications equipment, purchased a primary residence in the Muxbal area of Guatemala City because it was quiet and more secure than other areas, and because new construction was available. He chose a mortgage program from Banco Internacional because he felt the bank offered a competitive rate and was helpful in facilitating the process. He made a down payment of 30 percent and financed the balance on an adjustable-rate mortgage tied to the LIBOR (London Interbank Offered Rate), which began as the British version of the prime lending rate yet now is a readily available index for loans around the world. Paul's interest rate is the LIBOR gauge, plus two percentage points. For example, if the LIBOR was 6.25 percent, Paul's mortgage interest rate would be 8.25 percent.

"The rates were not much higher than you would pay in the U.S. and some of the real estate fees are negotiable," Paul said. "The financing system here is a little strange in that a property has three values: first, the value you pay, which is usually the highest; second, the bank loan value, usually within about 80 percent of the market value, and third, the value for tax purposes, which is significantly less than the other two."

Best bets for a second home: Where to start

You won't find large, multinational developers catering to international second-home buyers in Guatemala. To make matters even more challenging, there is no multiple listing service, central Internet-based national property advertising site, or other means to do a thorough property search remotely. You will simply have to do some serious looking before leaping. Although there are web sites for vacation tours and rentals as well as hotel information, there are few web sites available that have reliable information regarding second homes. Most properties are listed on international sites that offer only a cursory view of Guatemala and little material regarding specific real estate areas and trends. And "buyer beware" is the phrase of the day with real estate professionals. The industry is completely unregulated in Guatemala and no license law is on the horizon. U.S. franchises such as RE/MAX and Century 21 have a presence in the country and provide a decent entering place for your property search.

Antigua, Guatemala Highlands, Lake District

Antigua is by far the most popular destination for foreign property owners. Located less than one hour by four-lane highway from the hustle, bustle, smog and crime of Guatemala City, it may as well be worlds away. Guatemala City is cosmopolitan and modern and has all the trappings and conveniences of a U.S. city, with malls, fast food and every U.S. chain imaginable.

Antigua is colonial, laid back and completely pristine, with no billboards or sprawl and relatively few stoplights. The entire city has been declared a UNESCO world heritage site by the United Nations. The streets are all cobblestones, which lends to strolling and creates an ambience of a slower pace of life. At night, the sky comes alive with stars. Foreigners and villagers peacefully co-exist, and it's a great place for people watching. The central plaza is oozing with character and the city fans out in all directions, with dramatic volcanic mountains as a backdrop. Palaces, convents, monasteries and churches are abundant. One of the most unique hotels in the world is the Casa de Santo Domingo, a convent and monastery lovingly restored into a fancy hotel complete with lit candles and Gregorian chant music playing in the background (and a world-class restaurant to boot). The location is a favorite for weddings.

You could furnish your entire second home in the artisan's market, with its furniture, art work and other goods; prices are jaw dropping if you are a good negotiator. Antigua has dozens of foreign-language schools and students often stay with local families, making the foreign presence an important income generator for many local families. Another benefit of Antigua versus Guatemala City is that the city is relatively crime-free. While pickpockets and petty crime exist, violent crime is rare and foreigners are not a target for crime. Antigua is full of restaurants that cater to tourists and includes everything from high-class outdoor candlelit dining at the Casa de Santo Domingo to ethnic foods, including Thai, Italian and other cuisines. Many foreigners who live in Guatemala have established thriving businesses, from nightclubs to art galleries. Several foreigners also have coffee farms. In buying second homes, foreigners tend to favor restoring old colonial buildings to their original splendor, with updated wireless technology and other conveniences. The owners of several properties have shown a willingness to be flexible on price if they can get their desired terms. Prices in the heavily zoned UNESCO world heritage site have been heading up in recent years.

Perhaps one of the best attributes of Antigua is that while it's *not* Guatemala City, it is definitely close enough to the big city to get all of the urban conveniences, including shopping, healthcare and entertainment. You can also easily access the international airport in less than an hour.

And Lake Atitlan is nearby, which is one of the most beautiful lakes in the world, and is an excellent region to explore second-home opportunities. Sitting at over 5,000 feet, it is framed by three volcanoes and has spring-like temperatures. The lake was formed eons ago when a super volcano collapsed. Nearby villages with exotic names such as Panjachel and Chichicastenango have strong Indian influences and are picturesque (and are also places to pick up bargains on handicrafts).

The Guatemala Caribbean

Who would have ever guessed that Guatemala is part of the Caribbean? With the base city of Puerto Barrios becoming a port of call for cruise ships, more folks are discovering the so-called "Guatemalan Caribbean" and are finding a fascinating area that has limited coastline and white-sand beaches. The city of

Livingston, located on Amatique Bay at the mouth of the Rio Dulce, was founded by escaped slaves. Rivers and marsh land keep Livingston's roads from directly connecting this city to the mainland; there is a sense of isolation and timelessness.

English is widely spoken here and African-inspired folk music adds to its exotic appeal and Garifuna culture. Garifuna (say Ga-RIF-una), or Black Caribs, are a unique cultural and ethnic group. They first appeared in this area over 300 years ago, when escaped and shipwrecked slaves mixed with the native Caribs who had given them refuge. The Garifuna adopted the Carib language but kept their African musical and religious traditions, against the demands of the island's colonial masters.

The real treasure of the Guatemala Caribbean is Lake Izabal, an inland lake connected by the Rio Dulce (sweet river). The Dulce is a navigable river with soaring bluffs along each side and beautiful nature and wildlife. At its upper end lies the town of Frontera, and the river runs about 40 kilometers from the lake before it widens into an area known as Golfete and empties into Amatique Bay at Livingston after flowing through a narrow, spectacular gorge.

Lake Izabal is more than 45 kilometers long and covers about 590 square kilometers. It is surrounded by lush tropical rainforest inhabited by hundreds of bird species, monkeys and many other animals. The waters of the lake are rich in fish. The manatee (fresh-water sea cow) is unique to the lake.. The manatees, in danger of extinction, are the largest mammals in the country and can weigh up to a ton. The lake boasts hot springs as well.

There are several restaurants accessible by boat only and islands with smaller hotels, many owned by foreigners. This truly is a special region that will get more attention in the coming years thanks to cruise ships stopping here more frequently. The centerpiece of Lake Izabal is the Castle of San Felipe, a colonial-era prison now restored to a museum. The region, once very isolated, now is served by modern highways connecting the interior. A modern bridge crossing the lake will bring future development. The Guatemala Caribbean, Lake Izabal and the Rio Dulce are a boater's paradise, with excellent proximity to nearby Belize and the Bay Islands of Honduras.

Medical tips and safeguards

Medical facilities in Guatemala differ from those in the United States. Guatemala City has excellent health facilities but some small towns may have few or no medical facilities. For these reasons, in addition to ensuring you have medical insurance that you can use in Guatemala, consider obtaining insurance or joining a medical assistance program to cover the very high cost of medical evacuation in the event of an accident or serious illness. As part of the coverage, these programs usually offer emergency consultation by telephone. They may refer you to the nearest hospital or call for help on your behalf; they may translate your instructions to a health care worker on the scene. The cost of medical evacuation coverage is minimal for a trip of 30 days. Without this insurance, medical evacuation can cost thousands of dollars.

In some places, particularly at resorts, medical costs can be greater than in the United States. U.S. medical insurance plans seldom cover health costs outside the United States unless supplemental coverage is purchased. Further, U.S. Medicare and Medicaid programs do not provide payment for medical services outside the United States.

Many travel agents and private companies offer insurance plans that will cover health care expenses incurred overseas, including emergency services such as medical evacuations. If your insurance policy does not cover you in Guatemala, it is strongly recommended that you purchase a policy that does. Short-term health insurance policies designed specifically to cover travel are available.

When making decisions regarding health insurance, consider that many foreign doctors and hospitals require payment in cash prior to providing service and that medical air evacuation to the U.S. may cost more than $50,000. Neither the U.S. Embassy in Guatemala City nor the U.S. government will pay to have you medically evacuated to the United States. Uninsured travelers who require medical care overseas often face extreme difficulties. When consulting with your insurer prior to your trip, please ascertain whether payment will be made to the overseas health care provider or whether you will be reimbursed later for expenses that you incur. If you become seriously ill, the Embassy can assist in finding a doctor and notifying your family and friends about your condition.

Guatemalan residence requirements

Ever heard of the laid-back *manana* philosophy? It is always true at government agencies. You should be aware that while the following requirements appear straightforward, applicants for residency often report that unexplained delays in the issuance process makes obtaining a resident visa very difficult. Delays of one, two and even four years are common. During such delays, an applicant's residency status may be uncertain, requiring regular departure from and re-entry into Guatemala in order to re-establish temporary status. If you are applying for residency while living in Guatemala, you should understand that, as foreigners living in another country, you are subject to the Guatemalan legal system.

Guatemalan Immigration Central Office
6a. Avenida 3-11, Zona 4 • Guatemala City
Phone: 2411-2411
Working hours are Monday-Friday from 8:00 a.m. to 4:30 p.m.

Step one: Application for a 90-day residence permit

To apply for the 90-day residence permit at Guatemalan Immigration, the applicant must provide:

- Two recent photographs
- A valid passport
- A letter of sponsorship from a Guatemalan sponsor
- Evidence of the financial resources of both the applicant and sponsor

Present the application and supporting documents at the Guatemalan Immigration central office (see address above). Generally this visa is issued 15 days following application.

Step two: Application for *visa ordinaria*

Before expiration of the 90-day residence permit (step one), an intending resident must apply for a *visa ordinaria,* which permits residence in Guatemala for six months and is renewable thereafter. The applicant must re-submit:

- Another statement of support from the applicant's Guatemalan sponsor
- Evidence of the applicant's financial resources
- A report on the applicant's police record in Guatemala
- A medical report
- A police report from the applicant's prior place of residence in the United States
- A birth certificate authenticated by a Guatemalan Consulate in the U.S.

Pending approval of the *visa ordinaria*, an applicant may work if permission is granted by the Ministry of Labor in Guatemala City. According to Guatemalan immigration authorities, processing of the *visa ordinaria* requires up to two months, during which time only a validated photocopy of the passport is retained by the immigration office.

Step Three: *Visa Ordinaria* Extensions

The *visa ordinaria* may be extended in six-month increments. All the documentation required in steps one and two must be re-submitted again when applying for the extension. At the expiration of the fourth extension (i.e., after two years of residence under the *visa ordinaria*), the applicant may qualify as a legal permanent resident of Guatemala.

Costs (subject to change) are shown in Guatemalan currency, known as the *quetzal,* or "Q":

- 90-day visa, Q100
- *Visa Ordinaria,* Q100
- *Visa Ordinaria* Extension, Q100

The *Oficina de Extranjeros* at the Immigration central office also issues other types of visas to foreigners:

- Student Visa: Valid for one year. Required for primary, high school and university students.
- Courtesy Visa: Valid for one year. Issued to members of the diplomatic community.
- Visas for Foreign Retirees.
- Visas *Temporales*: Issued for 12 months to teachers of foreign students.
- Visas for religious workers: Valid for two years.

The CA-4 Agreement

In June 2006, Guatemala entered a "Central America-4 (CA-4) Border Control Agreement" with El Salvador, Honduras, and Nicaragua. Under the terms of the agreement, citizens of the four countries may travel freely across land borders from one of the countries to any of the others without completing entry and exit formalities at Immigration checkpoints. U.S. citizens and other eligible foreign nationals who legally enter any of the four countries may similarly travel among the four without obtaining additional visas or tourist entry permits for the other three countries. Immigration officials at the first port of entry determine the length of stay, up to a maximum of 90 days. Foreign tourists who wish to remain in the four-country region beyond the period initially granted for their visit are required to request a one-time extension of stay from local Immigration authorities in the country where the traveler is physically present, or travel outside the CA-4 countries and reapply for admission to the region. Foreigners "expelled" from any of the four countries are excluded from the entire "CA-4" region. In isolated cases, the lack of clarity in the implementation details of the CA-4 Border Control Agreement has caused temporary inconvenience to some travelers and has resulted in others being fined more than $100 or detained in custody for 72 hours or longer.

Guatemalan Consulates in the United States

Guatemala has an Embassy in Washington, D.C., and has Consulates in Chicago, Los Angeles, Houston, Miami, New York, San Francisco and some other cities in the U.S.

Americans who need U.S. documents (such as birth, marriage, divorce or death certificates, police certificates/reports, etc.) notarized by a Guatemalan Consulate in the United States should directly contact the Consulate closest to their home in the United States. Once the Guatemalan Consulate has notarized the U.S. document, the Guatemalan Foreign Ministry in Guatemala City must authenticate the signature of the Guatemalan consular officer for the document to be legally valid in Guatemala. See Appendix B.

U.S. court documents must be triple-certified to be valid in Guatemala. The chain of authentication is as follows: the judge signs the document(s); the clerk of the court certifies the judge's signature; and a Guatemalan consulate legalizes (authenticates) the signature of the clerk.

Clearly, Guatemala has not been the first choice in Central America for second home seekers. But boomers are adventuresome and exotic and the country is a prime candidate for both types. Everyone seems to know about Antigua, and are wary of the crime in the major cities. Yet many aging North Americans are calculated risk-takers looking for a bargain, especially if it means living retirement in financial comfort and away from winter's cold. The possibilities in Guatemala are attractive and very few non-nationals have ever investigated its beach areas. And, speaking of beaches, it's time to snorkel over to Belize.

CHAPTER SIX

Time to Believe
in Belize

Cayes, wildlife, ecotourism bringing active buyers

W hat's the big draw of Belize, the country formerly known as British Honduras which lies on the Caribbean coast between Mexico and Guatemala? You can start with the obvious: amenities that are common to all Central American countries—consistently warm weather, clear ocean water, affordable prices, relaxed lifestyle and wonderful local residents. The bonus of Belize, an area slightly smaller than Massachusetts, is that it has shallow, inner coastal waters sheltered by a line of coral reefs and is dotted with islets called "cayes" or "cays" (say "keys") extending almost the entire length of the country. Couple that intriguing coast with the Maya Mountains and the Cockscomb Range in the southern half of the country, the huge forests of the mainland and the ecotourism delights of the Cayo District and you have an inviting destination. Toss in

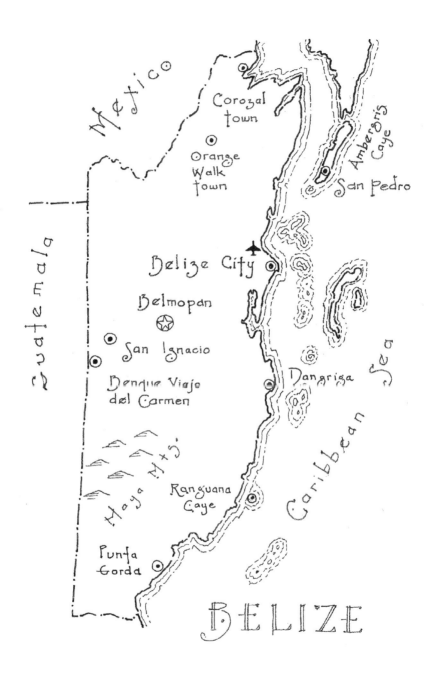

Mexico

Guatemala

Corozal town

Orange Walk town

Ambergris Caye

San Pedro

Belize City

Belmopan

San Ignacio

Benque Viejo del Carmen

Maya Mts.

Ranguana Caye

Dangriga

Caribbean Sea

Punta Gorda

BELIZE

attractive retirement incentives and no capital gains taxes or inheritance taxes and you begin to get a better idea of why second-home buyers are considering the country once labeled "too far south of Cancun" to be a good place to invest. U.S. dollars are readily accepted but the official currency is the Belizean dollar (BZD). Two Belizean dollars equal one U.S. dollar and the ratio has not changed.

Bill Hollingsworth is a trauma surgeon in Columbus, Ohio, a chilly spot for at least six months of the year. He takes a break from the stress and the weather by visiting his second home in Belize. "I chose Belize for the people. Very nice, very friendly," Hollingsworth said. "Also, because English is spoken in Belize. There is no language barrier. The contracts for home buying were simple and easy to understand."

People and Places

While English is the official language of Belize, English Creole is widely spoken and remains a distinctive part of everyday conversations for most Belizeans in the country's six districts. Spanish is spoken by the majority of the people in the Orange Walk and Corozal districts (north of the main district of Belize) and in the Cayo District in the west. In the southern districts, Stann Creek and Toledo, there are people whose first language is Garifuna or Maya. Spanish is also common and is taught in primary and secondary schools in order to further develop bilingualism.

Belmopan, the capital, was built in the center of the country in 1970 following extensive damage caused by Hurricane Hattie in 1961 to the former capital, Belize City. Belmopan, located on higher ground, serves as a hurricane refuge for

Belizeans and has the largest number of hurricane shelters in the country. However, Belize City still remains the hub of commercial activity and has the country's largest airport.

Diane Campbell, a former Realtor in southern California whose husband, Bob, built homes in Malibu, moved to San Pedro Town on Ambergris Caye in 1992. The Campbells continue in similar roles in the country's most popular second-home area, a narrow island that is a short plane ride from Belize City, where they operate Ambergris Caye Properties (*www.ambergriscaye.com/ property.*)

"We felt alive and healthy and happy here more than anyplace we had ever been," Diane said. "All the rest of the stuff—work, immigration—those things made the move possible but they were not the motivating factor. The motivating factor was a passion for this country and what it represents."

The Campbells' primary customers are not unlike the buyers of second homes in other countries. These curious bands of aging baby boomers and early retirees are affluent folks looking for "active retirement" in a healthy and interesting location. Their focus is on outdoor sports, good basic health services and communities they can enjoy and into which they can easily integrate. The single most common dream is a beach house, warm seas, palm trees and an endless summer.

"People often come here with the same set of questions they have in the States," Diane said. "But they have no idea that the first-ever road is now in front of the house or that electricity is now available or that there is an improved airport. What has been increasing property values here is infrastructure improvement rather than speculation. Sure, there are people who say they could have purchased here for pennies years ago, but they probably would not have even considered it because there were absolutely no services back then."

Anyone can sell or buy property in Belize. The cost of real estate—like anywhere else—is obviously driven by location and demand. Property on Ambergris Caye probably is going to be more expensive property than in the retirement communities of Corozal Town (*www.belizenorth.com*), on Chetumal Bay near the Mexican border, or in Placentia, one of the first retirement communities located on a 17-mile peninsula on the country's southern coast (*www.destinationsbelize.com*). Caye Caulker (*www.gocayecaulker.com*), a 30-minute water taxi ride from Belize City, is a longtime fishing village and dive-snorkel haven first popularized by a bunch of hippies in the 1960s. And, if you really want off the beaten beach path, check out the relatively new expat community of Hopkins (*www.hopkins belize.com*), a lazy seaside village about eight miles south of Dangriga on the central coast once described as "the edge between paradise and poverty." Building materials typically are less expensive in the northern portion of the country because they can be imported from Mexico, while homes on the islands and cayes are more expensive to service and typically need additional fortification from the weather. In fact, some areas have no public services and rely on solar and wind power and private septic systems.

Buyer beware

Buying property in Belize is not complicated. Titles are secure, laws are relatively logical and much of what you observe can be drop-dead gorgeous. That said, not only is the country young and developing but everything in sight can seem to be for sale. Some of the properties may no longer be on the market ("for sale" signs can linger in a semi-permanent state) and not all lots will accommodate the second home you would like to build. In addition to the usual zoning rules, many of the country's islands have deed restrictions that run with the land—not unlike the conditions, covenants and restrictions, or CC&Rs, found in many popular view property areas of the States. For the reasons mentioned above and many others, it's always best to use a competent salesperson and an attorney who specializes in Belize real estate and escrow. It's also best to visit, more than once and in different seasons, to gauge the difference between the wet and dry times.

Diane Campbell has encapsulated what many buyers and agents suggest. These tips can really serve all potential purchasers in just about any situation:

First: Plan your visit. There is no sense in "researching" available land from afar if you have not seen at least some areas with your own eyes. The Realtors and other professionals in Belize get an avalanche of requests every day. And it's estimated that only one in 30 of these requests for information results in a person actually visiting. We have searched for years to think of a way to give others the sense of the country from afar—and there simply is no way that works. So just do it. Show up.

Second: Relax and see if you like it. Travel around a little. Listen. You will never learn if you like Belize if you waste time telling other people about your stress level and what it's like in your home country. If you like the stress you came from, then don't even think of moving here. If you like people and nature—if you can sit with another person on a verandah for an hour watching the reef and the birds and can do this comfortably without talking—then you are most likely ready for Belize.

Third: If you think Belize is right for you, start looking for property. Many people make decisions based on price alone and find out in the end that they have missed certain essential items that make the cheap lot cost the most in the end. Observe—and ask questions of the professional who is most likely to be informed on the subject. Where do you look? In the newspaper. In the offices of Realtors. Read listings on real estate web sites. Walk around your favorite area and look for sale signs. Nothing too exotic about it—it's pretty much the same process you would go through at home.

Fourth: If you like it—and you can afford it—buy it. Now. Prices are still very reasonable but are steadily going up. Inventory is going down. Buy what you like, what you can afford and what you will use. Inspect title, boundaries and terrain. Check zoning and the condition of buildings. Use professionals only, including an attorney for title transfer. Find people you can trust and be loyal to them. Build relationships within the community from day one and you will find that buying property in Belize may be the best thing you ever did.

Fees and taxes

While your waterfront property may appear to be an absolute bargain from dreamland, there's a realistic jolt at the closing table that can bring you back to at least semi-consciousness. The General Sales Tax (GST) of 10 percent and Stamp Tax of 5 percent can mean an extra $45,000 for the buyer on a $300,000 property.

The following table provides a brief overview of the expected overall costs of a purchase. Annual property taxes vary depending upon the region.

Stamp duty

5 percent of the purchase price.

Closing costs

Usually done by an attorney but also carried out by some real estate brokers. Typical attorney's fees range between 2 and 4 percent of the purchase price.

Sales tax

10 percent General Sales Tax (GST) on value-added goods.

Annual property taxes

Annual taxes are low by U.S. standards and are based upon the property's assessed value. These taxes are due in April of each year and can be paid at any land department, including the local town council Property taxes typically range from $45 to $300 per year. Property taxes are levied on actual rental income of the property (if it is rented out) or on the assessed rental values, which are likely to be underestimated by the authorities. The tax is levied at 9 percent for occupied properties located in urban areas, but the tax rate varies between 2 and 9 percent in other municipalities.

Capital gains

There is no capital gains tax in Belize.

A word on financing

Most of the properties purchased by North Americans are cash deals, perhaps leveraged by an asset back home. For example, Ohio physician Bill Hollingsworth opted to take out a tax-deductible home equity loan against his primary residence in Columbus to secure the funds to buy his getaway in Belize. While some North American lenders have been mulling a presence in Belize, no lender has made the move. U.S. loan brokers with funding from Europe, Asia and the Middle East are expected to make a run at the blossoming Central American market, and Belizean waterfront and view properties will soon be on their radar screens. Banks in Belize will finance non-residents but the rates and terms have not been appealing. Local banks typically tie their mortgage interest rates to the U.S. prime rate plus about 5 percent. The loan-to-value rate is also tipped in the lender's favor, with a 50 percent down payment required on many loans and a loan term of 10 to 15 years. See Chapter 13 for possible financing alternatives.

Registration and title

There are three different real property title systems in Belize but most of the time the buyer does not have a choice. The system typically is dictated by the location of the property.

Deed of conveyance

This is the oldest form for ownership of property in Belize; Deed of Conveyance is in fact the absolute right to ownership of property. The ownership by means of conveyance may be converted to a Certificate of Title through an application for a first registration. Any subsequent purchaser is issued a Transfer

Certificate of Title. It must always be noted that a Deed of Conveyance is a valid legal title once it has been confirmed that the seller has good title on the property.

A transfer certificate

A Certificate of Title is a physical title to a specific portion of land. While this method is secure, it is the more costly and time-consuming manner to transfer ownership compared to the Deed of Conveyance. The process for Transfer Certificate may drag on for months and may incur high cost in attempts to fast-track the document.

A Land Certificate

A Land Certificate is an absolute title, applying to properties in new or special developments. The government of Belize presently is undergoing a process which calls for the re-registration of all freehold lands under the Registered Lands Act, with the overall goal being a uniform system of nationwide land ownership. This process, though under way, entails much work and re-surveys are yet to be scheduled.

Note that title insurance is not necessary for purchasing property and that closing costs tend to be minimal.

It's always a good idea to consider title insurance. Stewart Title offers the service through Regent Insurance, with the cost being approximately 1 percent of the purchase price of the property.

Coming, staying and working

A passport is required for all visitors to Belize. It should be valid for at least six months beyond the duration of the intended stay in the country. A 30-day visa will be issued on arrival and extensions (up to six months) may be obtained from any Immigration Office for a fee of U.S. $12.50 for every 30 days. Citizens of the United States, Canada, the British Commonwealth, Mexico, Costa Rica and the European Community do not need visas for travel to Belize.

Belize's labor regulations are designed to protect the local job market enable the employment of as many Belizeans as possible. Employment of foreign citizens is possible, however, under certain circumstances. There are two types of work permit applications in Belize:

Application for permission to employ a foreigner

Any foreign citizen who wishes to work in Belize must be a legal resident (having resided in Belize for at least six months) and must be in the country legally, with proper visas and/or permits issued by the Immigration Department. The prospective employer must submit the application for the foreign worker he wishes to hire and proof that this individual is qualified for the job.

Application for temporary self-employment

This category would apply to foreign investors, among others. All applicants must be in the country legally, with proper visas and/or permits issued by the Immigration Department. They are required to produce proof of reasonably sufficient funds for their proposed venture (e.g., local bank statement of account). Applicants must also obtain a reference from the relevant ministry or local organization concerned with the category of work involved. In such situations, the six-month residency requirement is waived and it is assumed that the venture will lead to creation of employment for nationals in the future.

All applications must be presented to the Labor Officers in the respective districts where the person is expected to work. Labor offices generally accept such applications on one particular day of the week.

Retirement and incentives

According to the Belize Tourism Board, anyone 45 years of age or older can qualify for the retirement program. A person who qualifies can also include his or her dependents in the program. Dependents include spouses and children under the age of 18. However, it can include a person up to the age of 23 if he/she isenrolled in a university.

Qualified Retired Persons

To be designated a Qualified Retired Person under the program, an applicant must receive a monthly income of not less than $2,000 U.S. through a pension or annuity that has been generated outside of Belize. There are no exceptions to this rule.

Certification

a. When a company grants a pension, that company has to prove that it has been in operation for at least 20 years by submitting proof of registration.

b. The company that grants the pension shall certify that the pension of no less than U.S. $2,000 per month will be forwarded to a reputable financial institution within Belize. This letter must be signed by the manager, president or a legal representative of the company.

c. Certification by a Certified Public Accountant independent of the company:

- Stating the date the company was established
- Verifying the authenticity of the above-mentioned letter
- Certifying that the obligation signed in favor of the beneficiary is not less than $2,000 U.S. per month.

d. The applicant must present two bank references from the company that is sending the pension.

e. The company granting the pension must present a document outlining its pension plan.

Requirements b-d could be omitted where the company sending the pension is considered to be a Fortune 500 company.

Background check

All applications are subject to a background check to be carried out by the Ministry of National Security.

All persons who have been designated a Qualified Retired Person shall be entitled, on first entering Belize, to import their personal effects and an approved means of transportation free of all import duties and taxes. A Qualified Retired Person shall be exempt from the payment of all taxes and duties on all income or receipts which accrue to him or her from a source outside of Belize, whether that income is generated from work performed or from an investment.

Personal household effects

Qualified Retired Persons have one year from the date that they officially enter the program to import their personal and household effects free of duties and taxes as determined by the Customs Department. Numerous entries are permitted within the one-year period. However, a detailed master list of household and personal effects must be submitted to the Belize

Tourism Board upon approval into the program. After the year has elapsed, goods will be subject to all duties and taxes under the Customs Department.

Transportation

Qualified Retired Persons may import an automobile free of duty and tax. Any boat that is used for personal purposes and for pleasure also will be accepted under this program. A Qualified Retired Person with a valid pilot's license is entitled to import a light aircraft.

Disposal of duty-free Items

If for whatever reason a Qualified Retired Person decides to sell, give away, lease or otherwise dispose of the approved means of transportation or personal effects to any person or entity within Belize, all duties and taxes must be paid by the Qualified Retiree to the proper authorities. Qualified Retired Persons who can show proof that the motor vehicle previously imported into Belize under the program has been disposed of will be granted permission to import another vehicle.

Offenses and penalties

Any person who knowingly makes any false declaration or entry in order to qualify for or renew any exemption or privilege granted under the Retired Persons Incentives Amendment Act commits an offence and shall be liable on summary conviction to a fine not exceeding $1,000.

Fee structure

a. A non-refundable application fee in the sum of U.S. $150, payable to the Belize Tourism Board, must be submitted with the application.

b. A program fee in the sum of U.S. $1,000, payable to the Belize Tourism Board, must be submitted upon acceptance into the program.

c. Upon acceptance into the program, a fee of U.S. $200 must be paid to the Belize Tourism Board for the issuance of the Qualified Retired Person Residency Card.

d. Each dependent is required to pay a program fee of U.S. $750 to enter the program.

How to get there

Like many Central American destinations, Belize is about two hours and 15 minutes by air from Miami and Houston. Direct flights to Belize City's Philip Goldson International Airport are also available from Los Angeles, New York, Atlanta, Dallas, Charlotte, Toronto, Washington, Cancun and Chetumal. Most Central American countries offer direct flights to Belize, including Guatemala, Honduras and Costa Rica. Some tourists find less-expensive fares to Cancun and then take a four-hour bus ride to Belize. Guatemala City also is an international entry point for Belize. The bus ride from Guatemala City is approximately five hours.

From Belize City, connections can be made to Ambergris Caye, Caye Caulker, Caye Chapel, Corozal, Dangriga, Big Creek, Placencia and Punta Gorda, plus various cities in Mexico, Guatemala and Honduras.

Our final Central American country—El Salvador—does not have the snorkeling and diving of the Belize cayes. It does, however, have deserted beaches, outstanding bargains and a terrific airport just minutes from the sand.

CHAPTER SEVEN

The Secret
of El Salvador

Terrific beaches just minutes from the major airport

Five years ago, before the Mexican second-home market began to absolutely explode with aging baby boomers seeking affordable retreats in the sun, an international developer with a superior reputation for quality construction and service was asked why he chose Puerto Vallarta as the prime spot in a very diverse country to build another upscale community. Would not the land be less expensive in a less popular locale? Hadn't Puerto Vallarta already been "found" by the hordes of spring break returnees planning to lock down their place near the sand for future retirement?

"It's all about airlift," the developer said. "The area is going to have a few thousand more flights from the States in the next few years and if people can get there, they are going to buy there."

Guatemala · Honduras

- ⊡ Santa Ana
- ⊡ Sonsonete
- ⊡ Santa Tecla
- ⊛ San Salvador
- ⊡ San Vicente
- ⊡ San Miguel
- ⊡ La Libertad
- ⊡ San Marcelino
- ⊡ La Unión

Pacific Ocean

El Salvador, the smallest country in Central America, has experienced the least amount of ground home activity. It is slightly smaller than the state of Massachusetts and has been called the "Tom Thumb of the Americas."

Volcán
Chaparrastique

EL SALVADOR

If airlift is the key to the second-home door, then El Salvador is the best bargain on the street. It may look like a "fixer upper" because of the country's history with hurricanes, earthquakes, war and poverty but its main airport—now the hub for all of Central America soon will be hosting more than 2.5 million passengers a year—is 20 minutes from the region's Costa del Sol and some of the finest beaches on the West Coast. If there is one single amenity that drives second-home traffic it is waterfront property, and El Salvador has 200 miles of Pacific Ocean coastline that few North Americans have ever seen let alone researched for a real estate purchase.

"The perception has been that El Salvador has been unsafe and devastated by war," said New Orleans native Howard Fluker, who has lived and worked near the capital of San Salvador since 1995 and opened a RE/MAX office in downtown San Salvador in 2007 (*www.worldlandlist.com*). "But I can tell you that I have never been hassled on the street, never been asked for money by a policeman or government official. I can't say that about the rest of the Central American countries that I have visited."

Despite Fluker's experience, crime is common in many areas of the country, especially in San Salvador. Gangs have been known to target Americans who absolutely look like carefree tourists. Be careful of how you present yourself to others on the street and don't spill your life story to cab drivers and hotel clerks. Make sure all of your important documents are tucked away and out of reach of pickpockets. Incidents of assault and robbery have not been as frequent in coastal regions yet always be extremely cautious when traveling at night on rural roads.

El Salvador, from the Spanish term "The Savior," is bordered by Guatemala on the west, by Honduras on the north, by

Nicaragua and the Gulf of Fonseca on the east and by the Pacific Ocean on the south. It is the smallest country in Central America and has the highest density of population in the region. It has the second-largest U.S. Embassy in the world. As mentioned in other chapter the four countries—El Salvador, Guatemala, Honduras and Nicaragua—now have eased entry requirements and visitors no longer have to go through border checks when crossing into neighboring countries. The distance between San Salvador and neighboring capital cities of Guatemala, Honduras and Nicaragua is about the same (four-hour drive). Approximately 70 percent of the regional commerce is concentrated in these four countries.

TACA International Airlines, owned by a Salvadorian family, operates about 65 percent of all the traffic in and out of the El Salvador International Airport (*www.aeropuertoelsalvador.gob.sv*) also known as Comalapa International Airport. TACA, which is expanding its hub in El Salvador, provides nonstop service to San Salvador from Toronto, New York, Washington, Miami, Los Angeles and Chicago and recently purchased a string of regional carriers that will provide additional flights within Central America and the Caribbean. Delta (Atlanta), United, Continental (Houston) and American also provide direct flights to the country's capital city.

La Libertad, an oceanfront community and a popular weekend and second-home spot for many of San Salvador's business leaders, is actually closer to the airport than the capital city. Fluker and others predict that visitors and second-home buyers will soon be heading west from the airport for the warm water and to avoid the big city altogether. View homes in La Libertad are excellent investments, agents say, drawing on both Salvadorian and international vacationers. Playa Costa del Sol, the most expensive beach in the country, is a skinny stretch of Pacific peninsula with gentle waves and attractive houses. There are also coral beaches like Salinitas Beach and plain grey-sand beaches like Costa Azul, Barra de Santiago and Garita Palmera in Ahuachapan.

Compared to U.S. coastal communities, homes in El Salvador are an absolute bargain. For example, Joan Rich Mantecón, a San Francisco Bay-area Realtor who specializes in international second homes (*www.internationaldwellings.com*), listed for sale a five-bedroom, three-bathroom home on the beach at Playa San Diego, south of La Libertad, in May 2007. This fully air-conditioned house had been painted inside and out in 2004, had two swimming pools and a Jacuzzi, a five-room servant-renter quarters, a large gazebo for hammocks, an outdoor BBQ and enough room to park five cars in the backyard. This property is 20 minutes away from the airport and also 20 minutes away from Santa Tecla, where there is a Costco and various malls. There's a seafood restaurant on the beach only steps away and the home's caretakers live across the street. Price? $325,000.

"I first listed a home for a friend in El Salvador that she had received as part of her inheritance," said Mantecón. "Word spread from there and I have been taking more and more listings in El Salvador and Central America. There's no real professional sales organization in many of those areas and many North Americans would rather work with somebody who they know or has some sort of ties to the States."

In addition to the appeal of its variety of beaches (ranging from black sand from volcanoes to a grainy beige), there is the charm and mystery of the historic towering mountain communities steeped in cultural interest of the Mayan civilization. The people are pleasant; same for the year-round climate. While there's an extensive network of pre-Hispanic ruins built between 700 BC and 800 AD along the outlying Indian towns, the great Mayan city of Tazumal lies only 50 miles west of San Salvador. The countryside is alive with exotic birds and native flora.

"El Salvador faces the same reputation that many countries in the sun face," Fluker said. "There's this huge unknown, a sense of fear and lack of services. But didn't people feel the same way about Mexico a few years ago, and I think the same thing was said about Costa Rica at one point. There's a tendency not to want to understand it until you actually get here. Once you see what's available, you begin to get it."

North Americans, other than the thousands of Salvadorians now working in the United States and Canada, have yet to get it. When you compare the second-home energy that baby boomers have brought to Panama and Costa Rica, El Salvador is barely on the map. PROESA, the governmental office in charge of helping foreign investors in El Salvador, began to crank up its "El Salvador Works" (*www.elsalvadorworks.com*) in late 2006, headed by Mauricio Alvarez, investment advisor. The country did not have a Ministry of Tourism until a 2003 survey showed that the country had "the potential and attractiveness" of a tourist destination. In 2004, more than 966,000 visitors arrived in El Salvador, generating approximately $425 million—and the push to bring in more visitors was on.

National network linked to NAR

A foreigner can legally own any land, property or vehicle in El Salvador. Buying land or homes is a relatively simple process—yet it's always best to use an attorney—and all real estate is registered with a government office. The housing industry is strong, with ample product in low-cost housing and upper-income levels. A strategic alliance between the U.S.-based National Association of Realtors and the Salvadorian national real estate board (CSBR) has begun to facilitate the exchange of information and transactions between U.S. and Salvadorian real estate brokers. Developers seem to have focused their attention on the products on either end of the spectrum but have pretty much ignored the broader middle ground. Some town-home developments recently were built in some of the more exclusive residential sections of San Salvador. This has forced developers to price them beyond the means of the average middle-class family. However, a joint effort between the government and private developers has resulted in "housing leasing" legislation. This process involves leasing a home for a period of 15 years, after which title to the home is granted to the tenant. The lease agreement requires much less documentation and proof of income than conventional financing, thus making homes available to a large, important group within the country.

Prime second-home target has been Salvadorians ... in the States

Nearly 2.5 million Salvadorans reside and work outside the country, mostly in the United States. Remittances from Salvadorians working in the United States are an important source of income for many families in El Salvador. In 2005, the Central Bank estimated that remittances totaled $2.8 billion, and bank surveys show that an estimated 22.3 percent of families receive them. Thanks to a strong family structure and connection to their culture, its immigrants keep close ties to their home country and, as a result, they send money back home to relatives. Approximately 92 percent of these funds are

being spent on consumer goods and the government is making an effort to revert some of these funds into more tangible assets, including real estate, according to the National Association of Realtors.

Many overseas Salvadorians buy in their home country but few non-national second-home buyers have been attracted to country. Most foreigners are located in the capital of San Salvador (2 million people, small downtown core) and its surrounding suburbs due to the protection offered by gated villages. While the beach cities have experienced little crime, the country is known for its juvenile street gangs, or *maras*. Given the capital's shortage of available land, developers have been racing to build highrises, especially in the popular Santa Elena zone where the U.S. Embassy is located. Other high-rise projects have been going up in the high-end communities of San Benito, La Colonia Escalon and La Colonia Maquilishuat.

It is the overseas Salvadorians that Todd Gessow, a native New Yorker, and his brother-in-law, Jose Delgado, are attempting to lure to the Jiboa Country Club, a gated community with pool, tennis, basketball and soccer field just five minutes from the beach at San Marcelino. The community is not on the ocean but the developers plan to add a waterfront house for all residents. First-phase lots, many priced between $18,000 and $25,000, sold in a hurry in the 192-lot project. Finished homes are priced from $85,000 to $125,000, with the high end buying a 2,300-square-foot, four-bedroom home. Gessow and Delgado will finance the lots at about 8 percent interest over five to ten years with a 10 percent down payment. They assist owners with bank financing once the owner is ready to build.

"So many Salvadorians live and work in the U.S. and many of them want to come back home to retire," Delgado said.

"While these lots and homes are inexpensive compared to prices in the States, they really are beyond the reach of the average person here. The only ones who can really think about affording something like this are people working outside of the country."

A look at financing

El Salvador boasts a banking system that is a dominant player in the entire Central American region. And American dollars are common. After balancing bucks to the El Salvador colon for years, the dollar was formally adopted as the official currency in January 2001. The latest technology and financial instruments are used by the more than 25 Salvadorian banks that write mortgages. However, most lenders will service only non-nationals who have lived in the country for five years or Americans who have Salvadorian nationality. A few have financed second homes for foreigners with excellent credit and assets. Typically, banks will require a 20 percent down payment on resale homes, 15 percent on new homes and 10 percent on new homes where the bank and developer are actively involved in the project. Loan terms generally run 20 years and interest rates are comparable to those found in the States. Many owners will accept seller financing with a 10 or 15 percent down payment.

Purchasing property in El Salvador

- Foreigners can invest in and buy property in El Salvador. No single person—Salvadorian or foreign—can own more than 245 hectares, or about 605 acres (1 hectare = 2.47 acres). Rural lands cannot be owned by foreigners except for industrial purposes.

- There are no restrictions on foreigners buying urban land. Foreigners should be aware of the need to be cautious about property rights.

- Bank deposits are fairly liberal. Non-nationals can hold dollar accounts and use these accounts when seeking local financing.

- All property is registered in the *Instituto Libertad y Progreso*, a state-owned registry that clearly identifies the owner of the property. The accuracy of this registry, which is currently being computerized, makes property insurance obsolete. This type of registry system is common in Central America and is considered a safe way to guarantee ownership.

- A Notary prepares and notarizes the sale agreement. That person then facilitates the payment of the registration fee (*Derechos de Registro por Venta de Inmuebles*, also known as the Alcabala), which is 0.63 percent of the property price. An additional 3 percent on amounts greater than U.S. $2/,3/1 (250,000 colones) should also be paid as the Transfer of Real Estate Tax (*Impuesto de Transferencia de Bienes Raices*). The deed is then presented to the Registry Office and finally to the Municipality.

The whole process of registering a property can be completed in approximately 50 days.

Transaction Costs		Who Pays?
Real Estate Transfer Tax Over the excess of U.S. $28,571.43 of the total price	3% of purchase price	buyer
Registration Fee	.63% of purchase price	buyer
Notary's Fee	0.15% – 1.00%	buyer
Agent's Fees	5% of purchase price	seller
Costs paid by buyer		3.78% – 4.63%
Costs paid by seller		5.00%
Buy-sell costs This includes all costs of buying and then reselling a property—lawyers' fees, notary's fees, registration fees, taxes, agents' fees, etc.		8.78% – 9.63%

Income tax

Non-residents are charged 25 percent tax on net income, including that derived from leasing or renting second homes.

Capital gains tax

Non-residents are charged 25 percent tax on capital gains earned from selling property in El Salvador. The taxable gain is computed by deducting acquisition costs, improvement costs and transaction costs from the transfer or sale price. Twenty percent is withheld at source as advance payment.

Buying and living

Phil Davies, a telecom engineer, has lived in many of the world's capital cities and decided to stay in El Salvador following his transfer there in 1998. He bought a home in San Salvador in 2006 and he discussed the sale—and life in general—in the Central American country.

What about the purchase?

I bought the house for $190,000 with a down payment of $15,000. I had to pay around $8,000 in taxes and registration fees to the local and national government. I got a 30-year mortgage.

What is the most asked question you receive?

"Is it dangerous?" closely followed by "is it expensive?" Well, it can be dangerous if you go to the wrong places but that applies anywhere in the world. Generally, it is safe. Don't believe the rubbish spouted on some government web pages. El Salvador is a beautiful country. It has its problems, but nothing close to what some of these sites report.

It is quite cheap to live here, but house prices in the city and outskirts are starting to rise a lot. Every price is negotiable and you are expected to try to lower the price of any land, property or vehicle you wish to purchase. Prices are occasionally given in the old, non-existent currency of the El Salvador colone but there is a government-mandated fixed rate of 8.75 colones to the dollar, so the cost is easily translated. Colones don't officially exist anymore but many locals still find it easier to think in colones.

You could live anywhere ... why El Salvador?

I am British by birth but with the very high rate of tax in the UK and the lousy weather that was starting to play havoc with my joints, I decided to look for a warmer and less tax invasive country where I could live in the mid 1990s. I chose El Salvador over all other Latin American countries for a variety of reasons. I like the fact that I can be anywhere in the country in a few hours. It is a hub for all the major airlines. The people are generally great. It has all the advantages of the USA or the UK— great restaurants, clubs, discos, fast food, fantastic malls ...

But it does not have many of the problems. For instance, I can live here, have my salary paid into a bank account here, and as long as it is salary for work outside the country, no tax is paid. I can work here in country and only pay a blanket 20 percent tax on my earnings. So for me, it is very close to perfect.

El Salvador was the one place I felt most at home in. In 1998, when I first arrived, El Salvador was already one of the safest countries in Central America. That trend has continued to the present day. It has a very bad international reputation, mainly due to the war and the human rights atrocities that took place during that war, but you have to look at the country as a criminal that has served his or her time and has no intention of regressing. The people are very friendly and helpful and they remember what the war years were like. They do not want to ever go back to that time.

Is it necessary to learn Spanish?

I should warn you that you will have to speak at least basic Spanish. English is not used a lot in El Salvador but some lawyers, doctors and engineers do speak English very well.

What has been your experience with personal banking?

El Salvador has a very stable currency, the U.S. dollar. The tax situation is very good, with earnings outside of the country not being taxable. This is very common in the whole of Central America. I only paid taxes here when I was working locally some years ago. When I work away, I transfer the money to my local bank account and no questions are asked as to where it came from if the transfer is less than U.S. $5,000. You can do this every day if you wish.

Initially, as a visitor with a 90-day visa or a card granting temporary citizenship, you will only be able to open a bank savings account. But most banks issue a Visa debit card against this type of account and they can be used around the world.

The requirements for a savings account are a passport, an NIT and an address. No other information is normally required. The NIT is the local version of a tax registration number and it can be obtained from the appropriate government office with a passport, even if you only have a 90-day visa. Permanent citizenship is normally granted after five years of legal temporary citizenship and will allow you to apply for mortgages, etc.

At the airport or any border crossing, a 90-day visa is normally issued for Europeans, Americans and Canadians. This can be renewed simply by leaving the country and then coming back in, one hour later if you wish.

How have you found the retail outlets?

San Salvador has four large (by Central American standards) shopping malls. They range from exclusive and expensive to accessible and cheap. There are also building accessories, computer shops, anything you want. Prices are 10 to 30 percent higher than the U.S., as import taxes are applied. Local government taxes are 13 percent. Fuel is much cheaper than in the U.S.

There are many excellent restaurants with just about any type of food you could wish for, and there are also the normal fast-food restaurants like Pizza Hut, KFC, Burger King and Wendys, plus all of the local versions. Prices are, on average, 30 percent lower than in the U.S.

Clearly, El Salvador has not been discovered by second-home buyers around the globe. Its coast, a series of headlands and coves and terrific beach breaks, will first draw the surfers, who will quickly spread the word to their close friends. The consistent world-class waves at El Sunzal and El Zonte, in additio to Punta Roca near the town of La Libertad, will soon have an international clientele who probably will not even venture into the nation's capital. As discussed, one of the best airports in Central America is only 20 minutes away.

"Tourism has finally become a big deal in El Salvador," said Gessow, the New Yorker. "There are now hotels going up on the coast and the government has spent $460 million to improve health care and improve its police force. It is making an effort to be ready when the people start buying second homes. It's not Costa Rica yet but these people are nostalgic about their home country, and the people from the States will figure out what they can buy here for next to nothing."

Now it's time to figure out how to best prepare, and find, your place in the sun. In Part II, we start with a reality check and continue with some property checks.

PART TWO

Preparation, Planning and Renting Strategies

CHAPTER EIGHT

Make Sure Your Dream Meets Up with Reality

*Second home or strictly investment,
your property needs solid fundamentals*

There are certain basics to consider if you are going to make the most of your Central American home investment. It's easy to lose money on an emotional whim. Blue, warm water and picturesque mountains have ways of working wonders on the mind during a long holiday weekend to "just check out the opportunity." Suddenly, your promise of "honey, we won't be writing any checks this trip" turns into torrid excitement and visions of *cervezas* by the pool from November through March. Lots of people can lose money in real estate—even in appreciating Central American locales—so let's try and do the most to protect your hard-earned cash.

Making a profit anywhere—stocks, bonds, commodities, real estate, sales—requires basic understanding and research. Regardless of what you read in the newspaper or see on television, there is no secret sauce that will absolutely guarantee big-time revenue and success. Your return, however, will be gauged differently if you decide it is only for personal use and not necessarily for investment income. How can you put a price on experiences and memories? For now, let's review some basics, explored later in detail, that are often overlooked in an emotional decision.

Central American home ... primarily as a second residence

Picking your place

The three most-used words in real estate—location, location, location—are repeated for a reason. If the property will be solely a personal residence, will its style and layout hold its appreciation over the long term? Then think resale: If you had to sell five years down the road, what would lure the next buyer? Finally, if you had to rent it out, is this the type of property that could definitely catch your eye and possible rental dollars? What appeals to just you may not appeal to the rental pool you will depend upon for consistent income.

Picking your community

Even if the house is perfect, is the neighborhood one that beckons late-afternoon walks and friendly shopping? Do you think most of the people you know would like it, too? Remember, you can always add a bedroom or convert a patio space, but the area is set. Again, play the dual role of renter and retiree. If the parcel will eventually serve as your retirement residence, you need to choose a place where you will be comfortable later in life.

Finding the cash

One of the biggest changes that has occurred in the Central American real estate market over the past five years has been the introduction of financing. And as lenders make more funds available, costs and interest rates will fall. The lower the cost of financing, the greater the cash flow and the higher your return on investment.

Tax is a benefit, but ...

While mortgage interest is deductible on second homes, it's usually not wise to buy a home solely for tax reasons. If your Central American property eventually becomes your primary residence, you can sell it after two years and pocket $500,000 of gain (married couple) or $250,000 (single person). Sale of an investment property would not qualify for such generous tax treatment.

Who's minding the store?

Before you invest in real estate, you must decide how you will handle management. Having tenants, short- or long-term, will require that the property be managed effectively. It's a business, unless you will be the only occupants. This means maintenance and improvement as well as simple rent collection. You will either do it yourself or you will hire others to do it for you. Management is a cost and will diminish your cash flow. Either you will spend your time to do it or you will pay someone else. Choosing the more cost-effective approach will affect the return on your investment.

How much can you handle?

Real estate that will ultimately prove a good investment because of price appreciation might be a challenge every month because of negative cash flow. You are responsible for paying for and maintaining your property regardless of whether or not the property is generating revenue. Before you invest, you need to create and hold a cash reserve to cover those weeks when the house is not rented, when the rent is late or when the toilet needs repair.

Second home viewed through an investor's eyes

Any investment needs to be evaluated for its total rate of return over its holding period relative to alternative investments. The holding period is completely under your control. You might decide to buy a second home as a prelude to retirement—vacation in it now, live in it later. Or your second home could be the stepping-stone investment that appreciates and provides the down payment for a third or fourth vacation rental. The alternatives against which you compare a real estate investment are also subjective. Consider how you would use the money if you didn't buy that second home.

The total return on your investment in real estate is not subjective. Rather, it has several very specific components. If you are evaluating the potential return from a second home, some of these must be estimated. It's usually wiser to be conservative in making these assumptions. The components of total return that affect your profitability are:

Cash flow

Rents provide a stream of income to sustain the expenses of the house and provide profit. In evaluating the investment, you need to adjust your projected rents in two directions. Each year, the rent should be adjusted upward for any increases because of inflation and improvement of market conditions.

The weekly rental income might need to be lowered during slow periods. Talking with other owners or property managers in your market will enable you to get a good feel for what rent levels are and what vacancy rates you can expect.

Potential appreciation

Over your ownership period, the house will change in value—hopefully for the better! With the way Central American properties have been appreciating, there's a good chance the value will increase over time. You have control over when you will sell the property and thus, you can time the market to ensure the best chance of a capital gain. It is rare that investment property *must* be sold, so you can continue to rent it out during slow sales periods and wait for a better time to sell.

Managing, maintaining and renovating

There are expenses attached to owning investment or personal real estate. On the investment side, these need to be offset against cash flow and appreciation in calculating your return on investment. Any expenditure on a rental property to maintain or improve it is an expense that will diminish your near-term return. Also, any outside management expenses reduce cash flow to you. That doesn't mean you should let the property run down or quit your day job to manage it. Two things need to be emphasized here.

First, major changes (repair or remodeling) in the property can be depreciated over an extended period of time. Thus, the amount deducted each year is only a portion of the total expense.

Second, your estimate of repair and renovation expenses is sensitive to your chosen holding period. A roof replacement might be of concern if you are planning to own the home for 30 years but not if your time horizon is five years.

Tax considerations

If your Central American getaway is your primary or secondary residence, the interest you pay to finance the purchase of the house is tax deductible. Because you benefit from this, it represents part of the positive return from your investment. Conversely, rental income is taxable to you and is thus reduced by whatever your marginal tax rate is. Finally, tax schedules will govern the allowable depreciation deductions for major home repairs and renovations. IRS schedules will provide most of the information you need to factor in the tax considerations of real estate investments.

Compare and contrast

You need to adjust your return for the time value of money. In other words, if your rental house yields a return of $10,000 in three years, you need to determine that amount back to today's dollars used elsewhere to see how much it's really worth. Using the return on an alternative investment—perhaps a bank account or certificate of deposit—is usually a good assumption.

All of these considerations can be plugged into a formula that will enable you to get a good estimate of what return you can reasonably expect on your real estate investment. That formula looks rather complicated but merely does what we described above. In fact, most advanced hand calculators have the formula already plugged in. All you need to do is put in your assumptions and you can get an answer that will guide your decision. Check out some of the real estate calculators on the Internet to help you along your way.

Turning the possibilities of a Central American second-home purchase into reality is a straightforward process that requires both thought and work. It should be done jointly by everyone who will participate in the dream house. If you want to include children, close friends and other family members, that's fine. But only if they will have some responsibility—either physical or financial. Planning with people who will eventually lose interest in the property or give up their stake in it will likely leave you stuck with their tastes and thus dissatisfied down the road with what you have.

Take time to picture your place

Whoever participates in the decision making, the best process of picturing your Central American second home involves creating the most detailed picture you can. If, at the end of the process, you can engage all your senses—touch, sight, smell, taste, hearing—in envisioning your dream house, it will seem more real to you and it will motivate you to proceed with confidence. As you develop the vision, remember that the controlling factor is not whether it exists but rather whether you can fully envision it. Creating that kind of vision involves the following steps.

- Begin by setting a time frame. When will you want to reach the goal of your Central American second home? Do you want to wait until retirement to take up residence or will you want to use it, at least part time, well in advance of that? How long do you intend to live there? Answering these questions will not only help you envision the dream location but also set the timetable for the financing process that will enable you to reach the dream.

- Move a little deeper into the process by looking at the things you enjoy now in your leisure time. These will make up the bulk of your activity in the dream location, so the location ought to accommodate them. If you enjoy reading, cultural plays and lectures, then a larger community will be best. Access to golf, fishing, sailing or hiking will dictate a more specific resort community. Don't worry about whether your tastes will change because you will be revisiting the master picture often. You might want to add and subtract activities to account for new interests and limitations. Going through this step will enable you to define the type of location that will best suit your needs.

- Next, focus in on the type of house you want. How much room do you think you need? If you are planning on sharing the home with family and friends, more bedrooms and more living space are needed than if you plan to be there with only your immediate household. How much time do you want to spend dealing with care and maintenance of the property? If you choose a more developed area, would you rather garden or have the time to play golf? Focusing on these decisions will help you choose the type of house as well as the type of ownership that best suits your vision.

- Get more detailed. Think of the configuration of your Central American *casa* and the amenities you want in it. Should it be single level or multilevel? Will you want it "wired" so you have access to the Internet? (This is also important in the interim if you are looking to rent out your investment property.) What type of appliances do you want in the kitchen? Do you want the potential for wheelchair accessibility? In other words, design in your mind the perfect house and then visit it often. The more familiar you become with the house, the more you will want to be in it.

- Revisit the vision. Your tastes might have changed and your family situation might be pointing you in a different direction, both in the near and long term. Go through the process again with your current status. You're doing this to remake the vision but you're also doing it to assess your progress along the road to your dream. As you look at your vision again in light of the changes that have happened to you, also look at your financial position and determine whether your current holdings are on the right track. Is investment in a second home in Central America a better proposition now than it was at your last review? Do you need to be in a different location to take advantage of population shifts and appreciation differences? Answering these questions will provide a valuable "midcourse" correction to your progress.

These are the steps in the visioning process. Creating a vision enables you to have a specific orientation and having that orientation forms your decision making when it comes time to roll the dice. In the next chapter, we explore in more detail how to plug in the financial numbers to make your Central American getaway come true.

It's time to focus on what assets you can tap to make your Central American property a reality. Is there a stock that old Uncle Harry handed to you as a kid that's now in a safe deposit box somewhere? Is there equity in the one rental property you own with your brother? In the next chapter, we ask you to dust off your financial memories and documents to determine what's possible.

CHAPTER NINE

Key to Your Profit Center: Finding the Right Path

Calculating your discretionary income guides property focus

Now that we have an idea of what makes up the big picture, where do you start along the path to your Central American getaway? Learning where to start depends on knowing what you can obligate to your investment. There are two main ways for determining how much you can afford to invest in a second residence, whether it be solely for your use or part-time rental. The first is the asset method. Start by taking stock of your present wealth. Create a balance sheet of your assets and liabilities. Don't forget to include the equity in your primary residence, even though you may be dead-set against borrowing against the roof over your head. Homes are no longer cumbersome and illiquid assets, thanks to the integration of home equity lending with other financial opportunities.

If you have recently gone through a refinance or have children heading off to college, you know all about filling out forms provided by mortgage lenders and university entrance officials. You know the drill—list all of your debts, including credit cards, cars, boats, mortgages and anything else you view as a "minus" on your financial chart. Balance these against all of your assets, including your savings, individual retirement accounts, home value, stocks and bonds and other assets. The net of these two numbers will give you your net worth and be an indication of the amount you have available to transfer into your Central American investment. Record this balance.

Although it sounds simple and gives you a good ballpark number, the actual net number is more complicated. Some of your assets might be unavailable for reinvestment. For example, if your retirement program does not have a loan program attached, those assets are tied up until you reach age 59. Withdrawing retirement savings prematurely subjects the taxpayer to a 10 percent penalty and the withdrawal amount is included in ordinary income for tax purposes. It would take a rather large rate of return to make the alternative investment worth the withdrawal. So to determine exactly what you have available for investment purposes, subtract those restricted retirement savings. What's left is your capacity for acquiring investment real estate.

The resulting numbers here don't have to be great for you to get into the investment real estate game. With as little as $12,000 to $15,000, you can control a modest yet potentially lucrative investment or vacation property in Central America. It may not be your absolute dream home but it can get you in the door somewhere. Once you acquire the property, the actual cash-flow cost to you should be relatively low. Rental income will help offset the monthly costs (including mortgage payment).

The second method to determine your capacity to buy Central American real estate is the income method. This uses cash flow, rather than net worth, as the deciding variable. Once again, it requires offsetting positives and negatives. Calculate all your monthly obligations—mortgage and other loan payments, credit card debt, tuition payments, etc.—and subtract them from your monthly income. We'll call this discretionary net income, and it is the amount that is available to handle the cost of carrying the property. As mentioned, rental income will cover a good part (hopefully all) of the negative cash flow. The ability of your discretionary net income to support an investment property is substantial because of the initial unknowns about the amount of the time the property will be rented. To prove this to yourself, try a little exercise. Look on the Internet or contact a Realtor specializing in Central American property (see Appendix A), and research prices in your targeted area. Now calculate the gross cost of owning that property. This will include the mortgage (pick your own down payment), perhaps a property management fee (10 to 15 percent of the monthly rent) and some amount for replacing house components like plumbing, electricity, roofing, siding and other depreciable items.

When you've calculated this figure, ask Realtors and present owners what you could expect to receive in monthly rent—especially if you are going to rely on rental income to make your plan work. If it's strictly for investment, it's critical to determine how often and for how long you intend to rent it. Decrease this number by 10 percent to account for likely vacancies. Compare the estimated rental income with the gross cost of owning and the balance will either be the net cash flow to you or the amount you need to supply to carry the property. Remember that this is a cash-flow number and ignores the tax benefits of owning investment real estate.

If you are thinking of eventually living in the house full time, consider both your and the renter's preferences. What do renters really want? In a capsule, they typically value convenience to water, transportation and entertainment more than space and landscaping. Choose a property that will appeal to the renter, not to you, if the rental use will absolutely come first in your master plan. Decorate the property to accommodate common tastes, not necessarily yours. Furniture will rub against walls, so use heavy paint that really covers. Appliances will get more wear than usual, so buy those that are reliable.

If you choose a location, you also probably have envisioned your target renter. The next question is what type of property you will look for or build. This is a decision similar to location but focuses more on the configuration of the actual dwelling rather than the neighborhood where it is located. The number and types of bedrooms, the size of the lot and other amenities all will factor into your decision as to the specific property to buy.

Besides looking at the location of the property relative to water, shopping and entertainment, your target renter will be more attracted to a home that suits his or her needs. If you seek families, then a quieter, more spacious property convenient to the pool or beach will be best. Where you are renting to groups of unrelated adults, think about family reunions—multiple bathrooms and larger bedrooms are a must.

With this background, you will be able to choose a property that will be in high demand by potential tenants.

Two suggestions:

- Ask other investors and real estate professionals about the demographics of the rental market. Who will make up the next great wave?

- Talk to resort and vacation community managers about the types of renters who enjoy that community.

Time to drill down on finances

Unless you bring a good business sense and a sharp pencil to your Central American investment, you'll spend many sleepless hours wondering why you ever did this, and feeling worse because your getaway is not exactly around the corner! Before you make your investment in Central America, you need to be honest with yourself. It's time to roll the dice and discover whether this potential financial move will end up benefiting your wealth or whether you would be better off holding the cash in a certificate of deposit. If you can't afford to be in the deal for personal use only, follow these steps:

- Calculate the total cost of the investment. This cost consists of the down payment on the property, the settlement costs of the transaction and the interest foregone because you chose to buy this property rather than invest in something else. The two most common omissions here are to forget the settlement costs and to ignore the opportunities that might have been seized if you had not chosen to invest in real estate. Settlement costs can be more than expected, so get a real figure early in the negotiations. The proper measure of the opportunity cost is the rate of return on some low-risk security like a Treasury Bond.

- Figure an estimate of the monthly cost of owning and maintaining the property. This includes the monthly mortgage payment—including the payment on your home equity line of credit if this is how you are financing the down payment and monthly maintenance, such as utilities and repairs. If you make any major alterations or repairs on the property, you can spread the costs over a number of years. But you should include some monthly charge to your costs of ownership.

- Determine the rent that you can reasonably expect to charge in your market. This can be determined by reference to other properties being rented in the area. The help of a real estate agent will be valuable here. As mentioned, the rent you charge should at least cover the cost of owning and maintaining the house. But you're not going to get this rent every single month. There will be gaps between tenants and some tenants will miss a month or pay late. Because the house will go through periods of vacancy, you need to adjust your rental income estimates to reflect these gaps. Doing so allows you to more accurately project your cash flow. After all, you are not buying the house to lose money.

- Estimate the price at which you will sell the property. This is tricky because real estate markets boom and slump with regularity. You have no way of knowing what the condition of the market will be when you plan to sell. The key here is flexibility—you can usually wait and continue renting the place out until the market rebounds before selling.

- Factor in the tax consequences of your investment. The tax laws favor investment in real estate. Interest paid to finance the purchase of real estate is deductible against income, and major repairs or renovations that enhance the attractiveness of the property to potential renters can be amortized over a number of years and deducted from income as an expense.

All of these positives and negatives will net out to the expected return on your investment in Central America. Remember, your numbers need to be adjusted for the time value of money—a dollar given away today is worth less than a dollar returned tomorrow. Inflation reduces the buying power of money because you forego the use of that money. If you don't adjust for the time value of money, your estimates of the return from your investment will be biased upward. Check with an accounting professional to find the right way to factor in the time value of money.

A tool to help compare properties

There are two keys to finding an investment property that will at least track the market. First, after you choose an investment area using the criteria listed in Chapter eight, find a property for sale whose price is lower than the average price for the entire neighborhood. These properties have the greatest potential for appreciation. In most housing markets, all the units in a given area will eventually move toward the average, so the lower-priced comparable units will be the ones most likely to appreciate the most. Granted, these houses might be under-priced because they need some work, but ultimately they will pay off. Problem developments and condominium buildings/associations can also skew the norm.

Professor Edward Leamer at UCLA developed a creative gauge that can help you evaluate different properties for their appreciation potential. It is a variation on how stocks are evaluated. When analysts look at stocks, they often focus on the price-earnings ratio as a measure of whether the stock is overvalued or undervalued. The higher the number (especially relative to either the market as a whole or to historical averages), the more likely the stock is to decline in price over time. For example, when technology stocks were the place to be in the 1990s, most of them not only had high price-earnings ratios relative to more traditional stocks but also were trading at extraordinarily high price-earnings ratios. Consequently, the "tech wreck" really came as no surprise.

What Leamer proposed was to view real estate in a similar light. In this case, though, the ratio is the price of the investment property to the annual rental it will earn. This calculation will give you a standard by which you can judge the relative potential for appreciation of different properties in different neighborhoods and even in different cities. In other words, it helps you make sound investment decisions by giving you a tool to measure alternative investments against each other. Here's how it works.

- Plan A—Suppose you're looking at a $255,000 property that will rent for $1,500 per month, or $18,000 per year. (We can assume there is no vacancy period but you can figure in whatever you deem to be reasonable.) You are also looking at a $120,000 property that will rent for $850 per month, or $10,200 per year. The price-earning ratio for the first property is approximately 14 (255 divided by 18)while it is approximately 12 (120 divided by 10.2) for the second. The second property appears to be a better candidate for appreciation since it has the lower price-earnings ratio.

- Plan B—For a truly effective comparison of the two properties, you need to make a second calculation. You need to look at the price-earning ratio average for both properties relative to those properties in the same neighborhood. If the ratio for the neighborhood of the first house is 20 while the ratio for the second house is 10, then the first property might be the better buy. It is underpriced relative to its surroundings, while the second property is overpriced.

Although all of this might appear complex, it's really quite simple. After all, you already know the prices being asked for the properties you are evaluating and you should know what rent you can charge once you own them. All that's needed is to find out the averages for prices and rents in the immediate neighborhood and you're done. Any local real estate agent or property manager should be able to help you out with these two numbers. This is a helpful process to go through if you want to choose a property that will propel you to financial success.

The second strategy for finding the most promising investment property is to look for the next hot vacation spot. Some savvy investors simply have followed in the path of large, proven developers who have been extremely successful in other areas. How do you find them? There are several ways to determine the next booming area:

Ask the professionals

As we've stated many times, the people who best understand the housing market are those who are in it every day and who depend on it for their livelihood. If you are interested in where prices will rise the most or where the best rental property buys are in your area, seek out Realtors, developers, builders and city planners. They have a feel for the market and will be able to point you in the direction of the bargains. Try this: Interview a number of the top people in each of these fields and ask them about the future of the community. Try to understand who is now living in the community and who they think will be living in the community in the near future. Find out which neighborhoods they think are the best values and which neighborhoods will be boosted by the development going on in the community. From their answers, you should be able to form a clear picture of where the opportunities for investment are in your area.

Opportunity can come from destruction

What is being torn down in the area that will soon rise anew? Can you buy in this area and perform your own work with the help of local laborers? Often, you can recruit workers from a big contractor's project to work overtime on your project.

Read the local brochure

Not all information is in Spanish. Promotional material, news circulars and community associations have newsletters and bulletins that contain real estate information and potential projects that could affect the value of housing.

Visit the building department

English-speaking officials often are found in local jurisdictions because so many American and Canadian developers are now active in Central America. Ask what major employment, transportation or development projects are on the drawing board. Is the municipality using federal money to place new facilities? When will these come on line and begin to change the location of jobs and residences?

The bottom line is a delicate balance

Harmonizing what you want with what you can afford can be a delicate, sticky balance. It's human nature for our wants to exceed our capabilities, so you will probably never get all you desire. The key to integrating needs and wants is to organize your goal in two different time frames. The first time frame is your best future prediction. Will the place you want to buy now be the same place 20 years from now? Will you seek a different beach or neighborhood? What does your Central American getaway look like down the road? This involves envisioning in great detail the retreat where you will spend your leisure time when you retire from the conventional nine-to-five world. (Is there anybody who *really* still works nine to five?) The more detail you can gather about this place, the greater the chance you will attain your dream or something in the neighborhood.

The second time frame is the present. For many consumers, the first investment/vacation home they purchase will be the one they keep down the road. No stepping-stone moves to see if the grass is greener—or the ocean warmer. If you have not purchased in Central America, the starting point is right here. Ask yourself: Which area—at least at this time—would be best for you? Will the place hold mostly renters in the first five years? What assets would you use to get you there? What can you do now to begin to move toward that goal? If you are currently an investor, in Central America or elsewhere, the solution may be, "how can I leverage/sell property to move closer to my Central American vision of the future?" The answers will be in terms of a particular property, a plan for the property and a strategy to acquire and hold it. You should keep asking yourself that question on a regular basis. Asking will keep you on the path toward your goal.

In Chapter Ten, we suggest some questions to help flush out where you really want to be.

CHAPTER TEN

Critical Choice: Tips on Selecting a Location

Common, specific ideas for family, renters, retirement

The best way to choose a community in which to purchase a Central American getaway is to begin with yourself and your family. You need to know what you want before you can determine where to look. Where do you see yourself ultimately spending the majority of your leisure time? Right now, what would be your best guess even though you cannot be absolutely certain? Work your way through the following process:

How much do we intend to use this home?

You have several options with Central American property: Use it in peak season to maximize personal enjoyment or use it in the off-season to maximize financial gain. If your intent is to use the property only for specific weeks of the year, travel time becomes a significant factor.

What do you do to unwind?

No vacation home will be enjoyable if members of the family cannot do what they find enjoyable. Dad's desire to sit on a remote beach and fish may not suit the adult children's desire for nightlife. Before you make any exploration of Central American home possibilities, come to a clear understanding of what type of atmosphere, amenities and facilities the whole group wants.

Don't bank on a nostalgia trip

If you spent many happy hours on vacation with your family in a particular spot, you might want to return there and buy a home in the same location. This is a legitimate wish but you should consider how important this is to you. Sometimes, you can't go home again. For example, take some areas of Costa Rica—prices have risen, daytime traffic has increased and many of the things you fondly remember have disappeared. More important, your memories are not necessarily shared by those around you. If the vacation home is to provide satisfaction, it must meet the needs of the whole household. Even a seemingly familiar place requires investigation before you seek to relive old memories. Don't let nostalgia for the past come before the more important considerations of the present.

How long will you own this home?

Plan ahead. If you want to hold this place for the long term, think about how the preferences and needs of family members will change over time. Kids grow up and the desire for play space evolves into the need to be with their peers. The young and vigorous will age and slow down. Things that you could once do may now become difficult. Any successful vacation-home choice will reflect a desired holding period. One that stays in the family for generations is of necessity flexible, both in terms of its physical capacity and its access to recreational activities. A vacation home that will be sold in a few years must satisfy the investment criteria defined above.

The next step is to look at some specific communities and some specific properties. There are three important considerations in this process:

Go where you've been

Think about places you've visited, either on vacation or for other reasons, that you think fit your vacation needs. This gives you a leg up because you have a working knowledge of the area, you have some information to use in compiling its merits and demerits, and you can get a good fix on costs (including travel time and expense) in having a vacation home there.

Visit again

This time, look at the whole community through the eyes of someone who will be part of it and not just a short-term visitor. It's important to visit during all the times you intend to be there. The lively winter, beachfront community might turn into a boring, deserted, dead summer town. The seasonal mood should match your needs and you should visit often enough to be able to gauge those moods accurately.

Build a team

Central America is not located just over the next hill. You will be buying a great distance from your principal residence. There are two good ways to identify a real estate agent to use. First, ask

Realtors in your own community or an acquaintance who has purchased in a Central American locale for a referral. This avoids the shot-in-the-dark approach of simply looking up a real estate professional in the phone book. Alternatively, if you don't have a real estate professional that you can ask, use the Internet. If you search on the areas of interest, you will find a number of real estate web sites. You can then e-mail a series of questions that will constitute an interview to screen potential agents:

- How long have you been in business?

- How long have you been doing business in this market? (Obviously, experience is a big plus.)

- Have you had experience with buyers looking at vacation homes from a distance? (Specific familiarity with your type of need is important.)

- Can you give me the names of some of your past customers that I can call? (The agent should be more than willing to share this information with you.)

- Are you a member of a professional organization, like the National Association of Realtors?

- What information will you require from me? (You might also want to ask how often your physical presence will be required.)

- What services do you offer? (You will be dealing at a distance, so an agent who offers all the services needed in the transaction will be more useful to you.)

- What is your usual pricing for an engagement like this? (Price is always the tiebreaker but should never be the prime consideration in a transaction of this magnitude.)

You can, of course, add to this list but it does suggest the basics of what you need to know before proceeding. Going through this process with a number of agents (three is usually the most efficient number) will help you find the best fit for your individual need.

Put yourself in a renter's shoes

Even if you use a terrific real estate professional and even if you think you know everything about the area, there are some very specific factors you need to consider in choosing a location. Each of them can be resolved by answering a series of questions. Next, let's consider the factors, presented in order of importance from the viewpoint of the renter:

Access

The most attractive properties will be those that offer the best access to the things that renters value. For example, renters tend to want to be close to the beach, pool, golf course, recreation center or the famous amenity that brings the local area its reputation. So in evaluating a location for investment, ask (and answer) the following questions. You can score each answer on a scale of 1 to 5 and then compare total scores for each alternative property:

- How close is it to major recreational sites (beach, mountains, golf, etc.)?

- Is the property convenient to major transportation corridors? Consider both roads and public transportation.

- How convenient are shopping, amusements and recreation? Renters often use public space.

- Where is this property located in relation to employment and education centers? If you are seeking a full-time local renter, the closer the better. If you foresee only American beach families, this consideration is not very important.

Safety

In this environment, safety is a high priority for everyone. This is even truer for renters than for owners. In part, this is because owners have more direct control over the security of their properties. Renters will rate alternative properties in part on the safety of the areas these properties are situated. So ask yourself the following questions to rate the neighborhoods where you seek to invest:

- What is the crime rate in your target location as opposed to the area as a whole?

- What security precautions have been taken at the property? As a related consideration, think about what you are willing to spend to increase the safety of the property after you acquire it.

- If the property is a condominium, is the community gated or the entrance tended?

Neighborhood quality

When there is pride in a community, the homes are well kept and inviting. Typically, where the community is strong, house values are high and demand for living in the community is high as well. Most people, renters included, want to live in a vibrant, congenial place. If you are considering an investment property, the quality of the development is a very important factor. It will go far in helping you maintain strong cash flow and high appreciation on the property. The important factors are listed below:

- If you are considering a single-family, detached house, what percentage of the population owns in that neighborhood? Traditionally, high percentages of ownership are associated with better neighborhood quality.

- How strong are the neighborhood organizations? When a community is progressive, the residents will participate.

- Do the adjacent commercial areas in the community attract a large volume of street traffic? Busy areas are more vibrant, exciting and attractive. They also tend to be safer.

A peek at your retirement needs

According to the National Association of Realtors, approximately one-fifth of all second-home owners see the home as a potential retirement residence. If you are considering buying a home in Central America that could turn into a retirement option, there are three considerations you should put on your list as you assess your options:

What is the quality of medical and social services in the area?

As you age, you will come to rely more and more on the helping professions and your own mobility will diminish. Being close to good community hospitals, elder centers and recreational opportunities suitable to age becomes more important as time goes by.

Will the home age with you?

Steps become a barrier as you get older, regular door openings are too narrow, regular countertops are too high for wheelchairs and regular wall studs are often too weak to hold grab bars. Before you decide on a house, inspect its construction carefully not just for now but also for 20 or 30 years from now. We live longer these days and you're likely to spend more time in that house than you think you will.

Can your friends and relatives or medical professionals reach you easily?

The visits might be friendly and enjoyable or they might be necessitated by a crisis, but they will come. Whether you want them to, as a break from the routine of the retirement community, or whether they have to, your friends and relatives will come more frequently if you live near a major airport, train station or bus station. When you select the home, evaluate it for convenience of access.

Many people might not be able to simply become second-home owners and slide down to their Central American *hacienda* at the drop of a hat. For the first few years of ownership, it might be imperative to have renters help you with mortgage payments and maintenance fees. In the next chapter, we explore some methods of locating—and retaining—good renters.

CHAPTER ELEVEN

Strategies to Find (and Keep) Good Renters

Start with relatives and friends, then fill in the blanks

You have a wonderful, romantic, exotic product that consumers want. Your job is to inform the general public of the benefits this product offers them. The basic objective is to match the needs of the renter to the features of your property in such a way that the property stays rented as long as you want it to be. In this chapter, we present marketing ideas that will help you achieve this goal. Just remember, you simply *cannot* attract rental business to your investment property unless that property is in the best condition it can be and shows as well as it can.

The best way to ensure your sanity, and your Central American home's safety, is to first consider renting only to family, friends and neighbors. In a capsule, you *usually* get renters you know and hopefully trust, who will give you less hassle and who are most likely to leave your getaway in the condition they found it. And they quickly become your best—and least expensive—marketing source.

Think about it: How many weeks do you realistically have available? Wouldn't you want to fill your available weeks with somebody you know? Why rent to a stranger who has contacted you off the Internet when the McNultys from the parish church, known for their altar-boy kids, would die to have the two weeks before Labor Day? Second-home owners often underestimate the large pool of potential renters created by the number of neighbors and friends near their primary residence and second home. These two separate and independent areas often can produce more than enough folks to fill your rental calendar. And it's a huge advantage to have personally witnessed how potential renters keep their own homes. You'll rest easier knowing they probably will keep your place in much the same condition that they keep their own home. Conversely, your visit to their home may be the primary reason *not* to rent to them!

Remember, friends know the going rate and usually *expect* to pay—so charge them. If your place clearly is on a resort's 50-yard line and has the best beach, kitchen area and beds, your friends and neighbors will be prepared to pay top dollar for your top spot. (Family sometimes can be a totally different matter but ...) If the getaway is in the middle of nowhere with no obvious amenities (besides serenity) and you have never rented it out, at least consider charging a price low enough to cover your utility and cleaning costs. If you are renting to someone you already know, one of the most important things to do is try to set/review some ground rules before they move in. Discuss any issues (e.g., periodic drinking water, best place to park a rental car, no lifeguard at the pool) that you think could arise while they occupy your place. Preparation always helps prevent some awkward situations down the road.

Marketing in your own backyard

You can reach plenty of potential renters by using local marketing techniques. The power of these is that they can be focused to have the greatest chance of reaching those you wish to attract. When you do advertise locally, be sure to list a phone number or e-mail address that you can use as a message drop, particularly if the rental market is tight. You might be deluged with unnecessary communications if you use your main numbers or addresses.

Consider the following local marketing techniques:

Bulletin boards

These are everywhere and they are very effective. To use them, create an attractive ad for your property. The ad should emphasize the advantages of location as well as the amenities of the property and should contain a color picture. All of this is quite inexpensive. Your cost consists of the time it takes you to compose the ad, the paper it is printed on and the time you need to post it. It helps if you have access to a digital camera, but given the power of the word-processing software that is standard on most personal computers, this is a relatively easy process (and you probably know a 10-year-old who can do it for you in minutes). Common locations:

- *Supermarkets.* Everyone shops for groceries, so the audience here is composed of locals. This is a good place for ads about your vacation home because the family traffic here is strong. Given the volume of ads on supermarket bulletin boards, you might want to take care that your flyer stands out.

- *Coffee shops.* These are today's town squares and they serve the same gathering function. The crowd that loiters here tends to be younger, somewhere between college graduation and first-time home buyer, so the demographics are good for someone offering a place to rent.

- *Local government offices.* You might want to investigate the possibility of using the bulletin board in your local housing office to advertise your rental property.

Merchandising circulars

The Penny Saver-type merchandising newspaper is everywhere. It reaches a geographically targeted audience and generally in read by people who are motivated to find something they need—a car, a boat or a Central American rental. Unlike bulletin board ads, merchandising paper ads will cost you something, with the cost varying with the size of the ad and the length of time the paper carries the ad. Yet given the readership of these merchandising papers—interested in buying and local—this might be a very cost-efficient strategy. Finally, find out if the specialty real estate books that feature homes for sale and rent are open to advertising by individual property owners. These books are used primarily by large property owners and real estate professionals, so it might not happen. But it's worth a try.

Church bulletins

This is an old standby and one glance will tell you about the concentration of real estate advertising in church bulletins.

Marketing your property in the church bulletin gives you an automatic bona fide status with the readers. If you are advertising there, you must be like them, you must be honest and you must be good-hearted. Who wouldn't want you for a landlord? The bottom line here is that local advertising offers the opportunity of reaching high-probability prospects for very little cost. It's well worth thinking about.

Local newspapers

While readership is interested in nearby areas, ads for some Central American properties are popular—especially in colder environs where residents constantly seek sunshine in winter.

The Internet

The Internet is particularly useful for vacation properties where the owner and customer are usually widely separated. It also gives your unit exposure all over the globe. Property owners like Christine Karpinski, an author, teacher and vacation-home owner who wrote the bestselling book *How to Rent Vacation Properties by Owner,* swear by the Internet and say they would not be handling properties by themselves without it. "People new to Internet marketing are always concerned with problem renters," Karpinski says. "In my experience, I've learned that most people spending money for a nice place usually are not going to trash it. There are a lot more good people out there than bad and you can take steps to eliminate the bad ones before they rent."

Internet advertising should be as painless as possible. You can easily create a web site for your property. If you have the computer training (or know someone who does), it is a fairly simple proposition to craft the property page and then place it with any number of popular vacation sites. The "Big Four" vacation rental sites are VRBO (*www.vrbo.com*), Great Rentals (*www.greatrentals.com*), A1Vacations (*www.a1vacations.com*) and CyberRentals (*www.cyberrentals.com*). Each has its own major pluses. For example, CyberRentals will be happy to share all comments about a specific home.

Older snowbirds always seem to pitch in

Karpinski has been a consultant to owners of vacation rental properties for the past five years. Her helpful web site, *www.HowtoRentbyOwner.com*, offers tips for renters as well. Some of her favorite clients are older homeowners who head south for the winter ("snowbirds"). Karpinski said a few of her clients are on set incomes and have set up monthly payment plans. They simply pay a little each month toward their next rental. That way, they can earmark an exact amount each month and don't have to pay one lump sum every year. Typically, the owner would require a reservation deposit, then the balance to be paid in one or two payments. (Most owners require full rent plus a deposit paid prior to the rental period. Payment methods vary but most will take personal checks.)

"I love my snowbirds because many of them are so willing to help when little things go wrong," Karpinski said. "If they see something that needs attention, like a leaky faucet, they just do it. Unlike a family that's renting for a week at prime time, snowbirds are more flexible on their days of arriving and departing."

Satisfied renters will call back and tell their friends

No news here: The key to a successful, moneymaking second home are satisfied renters who want to return because of the special experience they enjoyed at your place. And if they were impressed with their time and accommodation, they are going to tell their friends and acquaintances. Although you often can't be there to place a rose in every room every time a new visitor arrives, make sure you or your representative take the time between cleanings to scoot back to your property and make certain your people are getting the kind of dwelling you want them to enjoy.

The goal is to provide a relaxing environment. Help ensure that goal is reached by investing in great bedding—especially in the largest, or parents', bedroom. Kids are resilient and can curl up in a sleeping bag in the most curious of places. But go out of your way to pamper, and even indirectly coddle, the people most likely to write the check. A great night's sleep brings people back. If they don't receive it, it's often downhill from there. They'll find fault with the inefficient corkscrew, comment on the poor water pressure or complain about getting a splinter while walking on the deck.

At least once or twice a year, put yourself in the renter's shoes. What would you expect to have in a vacation home at the rental price you are charging? When compared to your competition, are your rates fair and in line with the rest of the pack? When it pours rain for three straight days, is there enough to do to keep your renters from harming themselves? While cable television is the scourge of many vacation-bound parents, some owners have found cable has really made a difference for some of their customers. What could be done right away—perhaps deeper cleaning than you are getting from your service—that would make your stay more enjoyable? During the high season, what could you accomplish with $20, one helper (your loving husband?) and four hours dedicated to intense elbow grease? Be sensitive to smell, aware of color.

A couple of times a year, substitute the throw rugs in the kitchen with inexpensive, colorful new ones. Not only do they help give the home a clean and fresh look but such moves also show renters that you care about the condition of your home—and that you expect the same from them.

Top 10 Tips to Keep Renters

Here's a quick honey-do list you can complete with that 20 bucks, one helper and four hours, even in a foreign country. Never underestimate the renter's first up-close look. Remember, these people are on vacation! Make it memorable from the start:

- Buy a welcome mat if you don't have one. This will save you time and effort cleaning interior rugs and it also gives a good impression.

- Clean the front door and make sure the doorknob and lock work and look sharp. It's a pain to wrestle with a difficult lock in the dark.

- If the street numbers are dirty, paint or clean them. If you have a screen door, repair any holes in the screen and wipe the metal frame. Clean all cobwebs from the light fixtures and fingerprints from the entry.

- Don't make any side or backyard area the dumping ground just because most people probably will come and go from the front of the house.

- Make sure your shrubs don't look like grubs.

- Make sure your deck surface is not slippery, sending a visitor for a surprise slide ride.

- Clean all kitchen appliances and don't let the refrigerator resemble a bulletin board. Save the kid photos for home. Replace pans if the scratches resemble golf divots. Make sure drinking glasses shine.

- There should be no mold—anywhere—especially in the bathrooms. If necessary, replace the toilet seat.

- Find an easy, safe place for people to put their keys while they're out of the house.

- Never apologize for the condition of your home. Offer a clean, comfortable home for rent and hope for the best.

Be clear on the terms of the rental

At the time of occupancy, tell the tenant in writing what your responsibilities and theirs are. You will be grateful later on if the tenant does something you forbade or doesn't do something you specified and a disagreement ensues. Unless you are clear at the outset about who will do what, you open yourself up for a lot of headaches.

Use a printed lease, even if you're leasing your waterfront condo to a cousin. This might sound like a burden for you but it will minimize the hassle of disputes that can resolve themselves into a "he said, she said" type of argument. Spell out all the terms that are important to you, such as these:

- How much of a deposit is expected on the property? Usually, the landlord requires the first and last month's rent as well as some amount for damage.

- When and under what conditions will that deposit be returned or kept? Increasingly, the law requires landlords to hold the deposit in escrow and to return it with some form of interest accrual attached.

- When, where and how will the rent be paid? The last day or the first day of the month is traditional but you need to specify whether that day is for postmark or for receipt. You might specify a grace period. But be specific as to how long and clearly state any penalties that will be incurred if the grace period is exceeded.

- Who will be responsible for long-term utility hookups and payment? This can be either you or the tenant. Putting the account in your name ensures continuity of service when a tenant leaves. Because utilities are requiring large payments to reestablish service, continuity is a considerable benefit. Even though you will put some estimate of utility costs in the rent, having the account in your name puts you on the hook for more outlays, whether your tenant pays the rent or not.

- Can the tenant sublet the property? Subletting can reduce the gaps you might experience in tenancy but it will also decrease your control over who is in the property.

- What restrictions will you impose on the use of the property? This will cover things like the number of adults who can live in the house, any pets that are allowed or banned, or any age restrictions on occupancy. It can also cover whether the premises can be used for other than residential purposes.

There are three potential sources for a lease document. First, you can simply draw one up yourself or get a generic form on the Internet or at a stationery store. For most property owners who have a single investment property or whose needs are simple, this is the most cost-effective and efficient way of creating a lease document.

If you have a number of rental properties or if there are some complications attached, you might want to consult an attorney and have him/her draw up the lease for you. In general, it is a good idea to talk with a real estate attorney before you launch into the investment just in case there are local ordinances that will affect your ability to rent your property or your flexibility in its use.

The third source of lease documents is the management company if you own an investment or vacation unit. In many cases, condos are built with the expectation that owners are investors and will seek to lease their property. Generally, the management company will use standard documents that cover all local requirements.

If you have your mind made up to take on all management responsibilities, here are some steps to consider before making that commitment:

- Are you a people person? Do you have the time and patience to field inquiries and calls from potential applicants? Check the costs of hiring a local rental manager who often arrives with solid, reliable leads. Good managers can be worth an entire season's commission by quickly handling an emergency.

- Don't sell in public. More people know about you and your getaway than you realize. Save conversations about your—and your renters'—comings and goings for the friendly confines of your home.

- Friends come first. They're usually good renters. Rent to friends (or friends of friends) you know. They'll usually treat your place with care—and often leave it in better condition than strangers.

- Off-limits space. Don't forget to keep a locked closet or storage area for your supplies and favorite possessions—like a prized surfboard, snorkel or fins you want no one else using. It's also a good idea to load up on cozy comforts like large televisions with DVD and VCR, decent BBQ and all kitchen essentials. You want renters to return and nothing's a bigger turnoff than having only three plates and two forks.

- Bulk is best. Rent by the month or season. It will lessen cleaning and maintenance—and extend the life of your favorite throwrugs.

- Know the territory. While it's unlikely that your group of homes or condos may limit—or prohibit—renters, there may be an age restriction. Research any association guidelines before you rent.

Owning Central American real estate, or any investment real estate, is different from other investments in one very large way—it requires interaction with people. When you own a share of stock and its price falls, you don't need to confront your broker. You just dump the stock. With investment real estate, it's a different ballgame. We get to know the tenants, albeit only electronically sometimes. It's more difficult to simply cut and run because it requires that we confront a real human being. Tough decisions and firm conversations are often necessary in the rental business, and property managers do this for a living. Remember, though, that this service comes at a cost and you will need to factor that into the rent you charge.

Property managers: The *adiós* option

Perhaps you don't want to be in the marketing business. You bought your investment property as a source of income and capital appreciation, and you'd rather do the things you really enjoy. On your scale of pleasure, dealing with renters is not even on the radar. It is possible to hire someone to manage your property, market it, collect rents and arrange for necessary repairs.

Property managers are pretty easy to find. If you've purchased a Central American home in a development, the management of that property will probably come along with the purchase. Either the developer will have an onsite manager, whose job it is to represent the owners in all these matters, or a local real estate firm will have the franchise on marketing and rental management for the development. In many cases, except for specific rentals that you would like to carve out (say, for friends or relatives) and the time you will be using the property, you will be required to use the onsite property management.

For your individual full-time rental unit, you might want to hire your own manager. Realtors will be a good source for developing a list or they may even handle the chores themselves. Be clear on the services that the property manager offers and the cost to you for these services. You should expect that the property manager will send the rents to your specified location (lock box, bank account, etc.) within a certain number of days of the rent due date and ensure the enforcement of any late penalties for unpaid rent. The manager should be available to tenants and responsive to their requests within a (short) specified time period. The manager should also maintain a reference file of reliable tradesmen who can be used to fix anything that goes wrong with the house. Check on references, not only to assure yourself that this property manager is a reliable and effective one but also to see that the property manager has experience in managing your type of property—single-family house, high-rise or garden apartment, condo, high-rent, low-rent, etc.

This might not seem like marketing but it actually is. Using a property manager can ensure that you have as few gaps as possible in the rental period for your house. For this peace of mind, you can expect to pay about 10 percent of the rent for the property management service, though some larger firms demand a 50-50 split of all rental income.

Market managers, restaurant owners and even local Realtors could provide you with a wonderful tip on buying a piece of property that's been part of a local family's estate for decades. As much as they insist that "title insurance probably isn't necessary" do all you can to protect yourself and your investment. In the next chapter, we discuss why taking the extra step to title insurance can be so worthwhile—particularly in a developing region such as Central America.

Title Insurance:
The Strongest Link
to a Peaceful Mind

Make the extra investment—especially in a far-off region

$\mathcal{S}$ince purchasers first began claiming and acquiring ownership of land, there has never been a time when they have
not needed some form of title assurance. The very nature of
land induces a need for title assurance because its characteristics
differ from other forms of property. Land titles are symbolic
because the title is what a purchaser receives when he purchases
real estate (rather than actual delivery of the property.) For this
reason, it is important that a purchaser have the best assurance
possible that his title is valid, unencumbered and free of flaws,

or that the purchaser have an indemnity against loss because of a title defect.

Historically, a purchaser's lack of knowledge of the complexities of land titles has caused him or her to discount the importance of land title assurance. Knowing little or nothing about titles, real estate buyers have consistently relied on the advice of others. They have been led to believe that it is not necessary to look back into a title beyond a couple of previous ownerships; that the public records contain information with respect to every possible title hazard; and that an attorney's opinion gives positive assurance of a safe title. Conditioned as the public has become through traditions and practices, it is inconceivable that a title could be completely lost irrespective of the customary assurances available. Prior to the inception of title insurance, it became obvious in the late 1800s that the U.S. needed a more secure form of title assurance—a form based upon indemnity dollars instead of word-of-mouth reliability. And today, more than 135 years later, foreign purchasers of real estate in Central America face the same dilemma.

The land conveyance process in any country in Central America has become efficient. However, any title defect that can occur in the United States can also occur in any of these countries, with other potential hazards looming on the horizon that are uncommon in U.S. property conveyances. Agrarian claims or expansions, labor liens, property regularization and permitted-use issues can pose significantly detrimental problems to unknowing purchasers of foreign real estate. Moreover, little if no legal recourse is afforded potential purchasers against the Public Notary who closes all real estate transactions in Central America, or against a country's public registry of property concerning title or lien defects, omissions, gaps in ownership or recording errors. A title insurance policy issued on Central American property provides a comfort and security benefit to foreign purchasers and is the only safeguard against title pitfalls resulting in eventual lawsuits and monetary losses regardless of the country.

U.S. title companies bring new coverage and assurance

The real property conveyance process in Central America, like any other civil code system in South America, Mexico, and many other countries in the world, is reliant upon individuals to transfer ownership rights. These highly educated and "handpicked" Public Notaries have the obligation, right and privilege to consummate all real estate transactions within their given territorial jurisdictions. Their acknowledgment and certification procedure provides "judicial certainty" to the authenticity of the process. With this process in place, Central America can be said to have a good land conveyance system. However, one must never lose sight of the fact that it is a system reliant on the performance of various people, not just the Public Notary. Sellers, buyers, agents, surveyors, property recorders and municipal employees all come into the mix. And as we have all learned throughout the annals of time, human beings, though not intending to do so, do make mistakes. Errors are made; individuals are not infallible.

In real estate matters, mistakes can be costly and create significant losses. For that reason alone, reliance upon a monetary indemnification that guarantees remuneration in the event of loss because of a title defect or error is a must. Suing the seller to recover property or money, whether in the United States or in a foreign jurisdiction, is a difficult, expensive, anxious and time-consuming alternative to the viability of title insurance.

Title insurance on real estate located anywhere in Central America is more than just a title insurance policy. It is an in-depth examination concerning title documents and the real estate closing process. In order to issue an Owner's Policy of Title Insurance or a Title Guarantee, as is the case in Costa Rica (*www.stewarttitlelatinamerica.com*) and assume the inher-ent monetary liability that comes with the policy or guarantee issuance, the insuring company must be as certain as possible regarding all of the various elements in the property transfer.

The service and function of the title insurance company is to eliminate risk by examining all of the relevant issues available. When a policy is purchased, a title insurance company's job is to help inform both buyer and seller of the relevant concerns that may be outstanding or in process prior to the consumma-tion of the property conveyance.

This type of investigation coupled with financial indemnifica-tion gives foreign purchasers of real estate comfort and securi-ty. They know that a U.S. company with decades of expertise has examined all of the title matters and ultimately issue a title policy or title guarantee. When compared to the other closing costs associated with real property conveyances in Central America (e.g., transfer taxes, recording and Notary fees), an Owner's Policy of Title Insurance or a Title Guarantee will be one of the least expensive and most important aspects of the sales operation.

What about the *notario publico*?

It is often said that it is the responsibility of the *notarios publicos* to provide title assurance and that they have the same responsibility of title certification as a title insurance company does. That is true. However, it is not often understood that, in the Central American countries, a title policy or title guarantee not only protects against liens, encumbrances and tax issues but also against fraud, misrepresentation, impersonation, secret marriages, incapacity of parties, undisclosed heirs and other hidden risks as provided by the policy. Even the best of *notarios* or attorneys may be unable to discover these title problems. Since title policies or guarantees are fully negotiable contracts of indemnity, a title company can consider and insure a variety of title matters for the benefit of the proposed insured. For example, a title insurance policy has the ability to provide affirmative coverage and endorsements that protect purchasers against risks that may be discovered in the title search process. A *notario publico* cannot offer the same type of assurances. No matter who tells you that title insurance isn't necessary, just remember that it is the only monetary indemnification that you will receive protecting your ownership rights.

Historically, *notarios* have been the main conduit for the real estate closing process in Central and South America, just like Mexico. They provide a "cradle-to-grave" service for the establishment of real property rights in the particular nation. Not unlike other civil code jurisdictions throughout the world, these highly specialized attorneys create judicial certainty in the conveyance of realty and they will not be replaced. In essence, Public Notaries in the Central American countries are the equivalent of the title company (or attorney) we utilize in the United States to close property transactions and establish real property rights. An important caveat to note is that in the country of Belize, the presiding legal jurisdiction is English Common Law and not the Civil Code as is the case in the other Central American countries. In that regard, Belize also uses attorneys to close transactions and provide the certainty in real property conveyances, but they are not *notarios publicos*. They are called solicitors and function in the same manner as a solicitor in England or Canada.

Notarios, however, do not control the development of real estate or what a developer does in its legal entitlement process to insure clear title to the property. Public Notaries are neutral and work for the benefit of the parties in any property conveyance. Development law is normally mandated by the respective country along with compliance at the state, city or municipal level. It is incumbent upon the developer to adhere to procedures and requirements as prescribed by law. It is not the responsibility of the *notario* or the solicitor in Belize to enforce or "police" the development process in any given nation.

Currently, an ancillary turnkey closing service from a title insurance company is available and is being utilized in the Central American countries to help facilitate the real estate closing process. This centralized service can be provided for any type of development, property or project. The heart of the process is that it is coordinated from the local title insurance company acting in a fiduciary capacity as escrow agent and closing coordinator. That company will provide escrow and funding services, closing-package origination to the respective buyers and wire-transfer capabilities to anywhere in Central America—basically applying a U.S. standard of closing assurance on real estate located anywhere in Central America.

Purchasers using this service will have the comfort and security of knowing that their funds are being held in the United States and ultimately will be disbursed by a title company. Those funds will be tied to a fully executed escrow agreement with disbursement instructions as agreed by the parties to the transaction. The company will send a letter of instruction in the closing package, setting out the requirements and procedures, in addition to a settlement statement for the release and payment of the various fees, permits, closing costs and appraisal. Once the package and required information is complete— along with receipt of the needed funds into the escrow account—it is forwarded to the developer for processing, deed preparation and, ultimately, funding to the various entities.

Some documents must be "apostilled" in order for them to be accepted by the *notario publico*—including verification of citizenship, a process that provides certification by the respective buyer's secretary of state. Obviously, these closing matters and required documents can create a paper process that is logistically difficult for most Central American developers, especially when dealing with customers from the United States or Canada.

Investment of any type is a choice. Purchasing real estate in Central America can be one such alternative that provides enjoyment and, hopefully, monetary appreciation and terrific family experiences. A foreign real estate acquisition should be a safe and secure process, and U.S. company affiliates now provide an attractive alternative to the *notarios*. A turnkey closing service provided by a title insurance company is one more creative step in an evolutionary process that provides greater certainty and protection for buyers of real estate in Central America.

PART THREE

The Money Picture

CHAPTER THIRTEEN

Six Solutions to Funding a Second Home in Central America

*Creative options that could provide
the keys to your comfy retreat*

T he "greatest generation" took pride in being debt free. Owning the roof over their heads was a lifelong goal and it took a lot of persuading to get Mom and Dad to even consider the concept of tapping into the equity of a home they already had paid off. Members of this group often were reluctant to spend money on themselves in order to make their lives more comfortable.

Conversely, their children, the bouncing baby boomers, never met a loan they didn't like. They borrow for toys, schools and especially for second homes they see as piggybanks where they can also spend time. The boomers' borrowing philosophy can get extremely creative when conventional financing no longer is in the picture. And financing for Central American properties has been anything but conventional. Today's second-home buyer in Central America often knows what he or she wants—and the possible alternative solutions on how to finance it.

Here are six creative options that might not have entered your big picture when pondering a second-home purchase south of the border. There may even be one that is palatable for Mom and Dad.

Central American real estate IRAs: Great for investors but no personal use

Suppose your best friend from college has pestered you for more than a decade about the financial advantages of investing in real estate in Central America. This person, Lucky Lenny, has struck gold with recreational properties in a variety of locations and has renters clamoring to rent his units every month. Occupancy has been so good that Lucky Lenny could have rented his places during the winter months "three times over," and now he doesn't want to give up the rent money by using the units himself. Larry has evolved from user to user/investor to investor only. Larry appears at the college reunion and he shares with you a lead on the next undiscovered Central American paradise that snowbirds will fall over themselves trying to reach. According to Larry, not only will the place be worth a ton down the road, it also will produce an immediate annual cash flow because of the premiums renters will be more than willing to pay for the winter months.

If you think Central America is an absolute bargain yet you have no money to purchase a property there, do your research and then consider the funds in your Individual Retirement Account. Perhaps you've been seeking an alternative to some lackluster mutual funds that have only been treading water for years. Like foreign stocks, foreign real estate qualifies for an IRA—but you can't use it yourself until you retire. And like Lucky Lenny, you would have to be an investor only. But the move would give you the opportunity of gathering appreciation and equity with the only funds you have available.

In this chapter, we explore how Individual Retirement Accounts—plus some other unfamiliar alternatives—can help you on your way to your goal of an investment home in Central America. These roads could take some extra labor to pave (like finding a trustee or administrator who will establish a real estate IRA) but the effort could provide you with the seed money for a retirement weekend getaway and other financial rewards.

You cannot use IRA money to buy your own residence or any other property in which you live. It has to be investment property. But when you retire, you can direct your IRA to turn it over to you as a distribution at the current market value.

Self-directed real estate IRAs are not only relatively easy, they are also not subject to some of the guidelines that apply to employee-sponsored qualified plans enforced by the Department of Labor. The trustee, as directed by the individual, has complete and total control over the investment. In addition, the trustee, as account holder, has an obligation of investigating each investment to be considered. This personal due diligence is a substitute for the rules that govern some employee-sponsored qualified plans. You can invest self-directed IRA money in a wide range of investments, including stocks, bonds, mutual funds, money market funds, saving certificates, U.S. Treasury securities, promissory notes secured by mortgages or deeds of trust, limited partnerships and ... real estate. This includes single-family homes, timber parcels, terrific getaway condos and office properties.

To prepare for your real estate IRA, designate the amount of your retirement funds that you wish to use in the property deal and open a new IRA account with an independent administrator. The best place to start is an independent community bank—then get set for the possibility of a long afternoon of shopping. Many banks will not service real estate IRAs (some will say "never heard of it") because it must act as owner—pay the taxes, collect servicing fees—which involves paperwork many lenders don't want or need. Community banks, however, often will offer this trust account service for existing customers, especially if the bank can easily see that there's value in the purchase and a great potential for appreciation. And remember, because there are no limits on the number of IRA accounts a taxpayer may have, you will not be restricted to just one purchase.

The guidelines covering real estate IRAs are stringent. If you break one of these rules, you could jeopardize the tax-free status on your account:

- The land or house must be treated like any other investment.
- All rental profits must be returned to the trustee.
- You cannot manage the property. But your trustee can hire a third party—a real estate broker or local manager—to collect rents and maintain or improve the property.
- The house or property (or proceeds from its sale) must remain in the trust until distribution at retirement. If a trustee is instructed to sell the property, funds can be transferred to another account for reinvestment.

"It's a simple case of people selling IRAs not dealing in real estate," says investment advisor Jeff Moormeier, president of Quantum Advisors (*www.quantum-advisors.com*). "What is needed are people who specialize in real estate and deal in it every day, our local Realtors, to understand the self-directed IRA process. It's a huge market that is just starting to emerge."

The challenge with real estate IRAs has been lack of funds to make a meaningful purchase. Historically, real estate IRAs had been purchased with cash and the trust then held the property free and clear. One way to crack a huge financial nut was to get several investors to buy shares in one property. Now some banks are discovering the real estate IRA niche and granting a "non-recourse loan" to the trustee for specific properties. Non-recourse means that if the loan goes into default and the lender needs to foreclose, the property would be the only asset the lender could claim. It's similar to a nonjudicial foreclosure where the property becomes the lender's only focus.

The problem with IRAs involving Central American real estate is a bit more complex. Cash talks—there is no problem finding an administrator to facilitate a Central American property purchase with your IRA funds. However, most U.S. lenders now active in Central America stipulate that their funds secure "second homes," not investment properties. Hence, most consumers wishing to purchase Central American property with their IRAs will probably have to pay cash, unless they have an unusual relationship with a local banker who would be willing to grant a "non-recourse" loan.

(For companies specializing in real estate IRAs, visit My Real Estate IRA—*www.myrealestateira.com*; Sovereign International—*www.worldwideplanning.com*; PENSCO Trust Company—*www.pensco.com*; Sterling Trust Company—*www.sterling-*

trust.com, Lincoln Trust—*www.lincolntrust.com*; Entrust Administration—*www.entrustadmin.com*; Mid Ohio Securities—*www.midoh.com;* or Oarlock Investment Services—*www.oar lock.com.*)

The buddy system

Remember when you went to camp and you had to have a partner for swimming, hiking and clean up? Take that buddy system concept and apply it to purchasing a casita with people you trust and enjoy. Having two or more families, couples or individuals combine their assets and purchase the property as partners makes sense, especially for couples who enjoy being together yet know they will never be able to afford a getaway of their own.

The often overestimated factor in a second-home purchase is time. People who buy a second home and retain a primary residence often do not spend as much time in the second home as they had hoped—especially if it's in another country. And when a block of time surprisingly surfaces, owners often find themselves traveling to a place they have never been or using the time for a family reunion. But with the buddy system, multiple owners can share the time as well as the costs.

Here's how the buddy system works. Let's say the Waterses and the Carrs are diving buddies and have made several trips to the western Caribbean. Nancy Waters has long wanted to return and buy on Roatán, Honduras—an escape from Midwest winters—but she and her husband, Steve, do not have the cash to buy a place outright and can't handle the monthly drag of an extra mortgage payment. But Nancy does have some cash she inherited from her grandmother. One day, during a golf out-ing with David and Pat Carr, Pat discloses that her monthly income has risen significantly due to a job promotion.

Nancy shares that she is longing for a place on Roatán but that even though she has a small inheritance to invest, she and Steve can't swing another monthly mortgage payment. Bingo! A deal is struck whereby the Waterses would make the down payment and the Carrs would make the monthly payments plus pay for all fees for three years. After three years, they agree to the option to refinance or sell the place—a realistic timeframe to reassess the wants and needs of both couples. At that time, the Waterses would get their down payment back with a minimal interest allowance and the two couples would split any appreciation upon sale. If one couple wishes to sell and the other wants to remain, the couple staying has the option to buy out the seller at a price submitted by a mutually approved appraiser. Another possibility is substituting a mutually agreeable new partner for the couple that wants out of the deal.

Seller financing ...
with a plain vanilla home equity starter

Sure, there have been all-cash buyers for gorgeous places in the sun. We've all heard rumors of a dusty Texas oilman, New England attorney or Northwest software executive sauntering out of a Central American taxi and writing a check for a massive hacienda high on a hill overlooking the Pacific. But how many average folks have all cash for a second home in Central America? Maybe years ago they did but not today.

Historically, the most common method of financing property in Central America has been to scrape up a down payment, then pray that a seller or Central American bank would help with the rest. Until recently, U.S. and Canadian banks did not lend money on real estate in Central America and the rates charged by some Central American lenders resembled the sky-high times of the U.S. in mortgage markets of the 1980s. Although Central America remains behind the times in mort-gage banking, remember that not all sellers in Central America—especially in regions close to the coast—are Central American nationals. Sellers are Americans and Canadians who might have to dispose of an investment for reasons beyond their control—loss of spouse, divorce, loss of job. These peo-ple know that conventional bank financing still is in its infant stage and they could very well be open to creative options that they have exercised—or heard about—back home. Never underestimate the possibility of an owner accepting a "seller financing" or "carry-the-paper" proposal, especially if it comes from a person, couple or family the owner enjoys or trusts. And seller financing can benefit both sides. It can provide reli-able income to the seller (especially to a budget-conscious, single senior) while allowing the buyer to bypass the signifi-cant fees and the often higher-than-imagined interest rates brought by conventional financing.

Buyer and seller are free to negotiate terms, including down payment amount and the interest rate on the loan. Often, if the down payment (secured by a home equity loan against the buy-er's primary residence) is minimal, the rate on the loan could be higher than the conventional market, and vice versa. Any type of equally agreeable arrangement can get things rolling. The dealmaker might be a three- or five-year cash-out clause that gives the seller confidence his or her cash is not too far down the road while allowing the buyer time to peruse the new mort-gage offerings by North American lenders, especially Toronto-based Scotiabank (*www.scotiabank.com*), one of the more active lenders in the region. Who knows? You might even get a devel-oper/builder to carry the paper for a few years.

Lease option

It is often difficult to find the right property in a short period of time—especially for an out-of-country buyer. Although you hear about people buying "the first house we saw," potential buyers can also spend months researching house size and style, beach break, water availability, neighborhoods and transportation before finalizing any deal. For those who do not want to be forced to act within a tight timeframe, renting or leasing with an option to buy can be a sensible alternative. As mentioned above, there are more and more Americans now selling homes in Central America that are familiar with financing options other than a flat-out sale. Many real estate agents know of available properties and renting for a year to 18 months is quite common among newcomers from the United States or Canada.

Sometimes, this rental or leased spot can turn into the permanent second home for the renters, which is why a lease with an option to buy is sometimes preferable to a straight lease. A "lease option" allows the renters (potential owners) to buy time to research the area while getting a portion of the monthly rent credited toward the down payment if they decide to pursue the option. The lease agreement includes an option allowing the vacation tenant to buy the property within the lease period. Here's how a typical lease option works.

The owner and tenant agree on a purchase price, often a figure based on today's market value plus an estimate of the average rate of inflation (let's use 3 percent) in the next 12 months. Let's say the agreed-upon amount is $165,000 and represents the home's value 12 months down the road.

The owner charges the tenant a nonrefundable fee for the option to buy. The amount can vary, depending on how eager the seller is to move, the size and quality of the home, etc. Typically, the higher the fee, the better the tenant maintains the property. The one-time fee—let's say it is $1,500—is in addition to the monthly payments and gives the tenant the right to purchase the property for $165,000 at any time within the 12-month lease period.

The monthly rent is typically greater than market rates because no down payment has been made, but a portion of it will apply toward the down payment. The owner and tenant decide what portion will be credited. For example, if the monthly rent is $1,000, $500 of each month's rent could be credited to the down payment. The owner and tenant must be sure to specify both lease and sale terms in the agreement. For example, it's a good idea to set an interest rate ceiling in the agreement or agree that the owner will finance the sale if conventional interest rates are at a certain level. This guards against the tenant being unable to qualify for a loan because interest rates are too high when it's time to exercise the option to buy. Lease option forms are available at some stationery stores that carry professional forms. If you are concerned about the language of the agreement, consult an attorney or escrow officer.

Buy an option

The purchase of an option is the clearest and strongest right that can be granted that gives a potential buyer flexibility in the future. Under this plan, the buyer, or option grantee, is given the right to rent or buy a specified property during a specific period of time. However, the buyer, usually having paid a fee to obtain the option, is under no obligation to perform. To be enforceable, the option should set forth the price, dates and terms on which the option is exercisable.

Right of first refusal

Have you ever stayed in a terrific place that provided you special times and memories and then told the seller: "Let me know if you ever want to sell this place"? You would be surprised how many properties are acquired this way—especially if the renter has gone out of his or her way to take care of the property.

Unlike an option, a right of first refusal does not entitle the holder of the right to force the other party to sell or lease the property. Instead, if and when the seller decides to sell the property, the holder of the right of first refusal can acquire the property for the same price and terms that the seller is willing to accept from a third party. A right of first refusal is not as strong for the potential buyer as the option. That's because it does not set the price for the property in advance and it allows the seller to decide whether and when to sell or lease. A property owner generally will resist granting a right of first refusal because it can negatively impact the marketing of the home. (What outside buyer is going to get excited when he or she knows an inside buyer holds the first right of refusal?) In reality, many owners deal to favorite renters or friends.

Ready to retire?
Reverse your way to Central America

It's true: The primary purpose of a reverse mortgage is to help seniors stay in their homes and live more comfortably in their later years. But let's look beyond the basic box and explore how a reverse can purchase a second home in Central America.

The versatility of reverse mortgages has come a long way since the instrument was first established in 1989. Once perceived only as a last-ditch effort to keep the family home, reverse mortgages are now used to purchase cars, make needed home repairs and improvements, finance education, pay for in-home care, provide supplemental income and buy second homes in other countries. The funds can be used for any purpose.

Here's how the reverse mortgage, which must be attached to a primary U.S. residence, can also be used to acquire a second home south of the border. Let's say June and Ward Cleaver own a home valued at $235,000. Ward is 72 years old and June is 68. They execute a reverse mortgage on their residence based on June's age and an expected interest rate of 7 percent via a HUD Home Equity Conversion Mortgage (HECM), which is one of the more popular reverse options available today. The HECM loan limit, which often follows the increases in the Fannie Mae/Freddie Mac loan limit, varies by geographic area.

The Cleavers net a lump sum of approximately $106,000 on the closing of the reverse mortgage. Shortly thereafter, they purchase a vacation condo in El Salvador, where June loves to snorkel and swim, for $125,000. They use the $106,000 from the reverse mortgage and an additional $19,000 from Ward's retirement funds to own the El Salvador condo free and clear.

After a decade of wonderful vacations and no loan payments, the couple chooses to downsize. They sell their primary residence, pay off the underlying debt from the reverse mortgage and move to the El Salvador condo. Using an average appreciation rate of 4 percent on the primary residence and a 7 percent interest rate on the loan, the balance on the reverse mortgage would have increased to $253,198 from $106,000 while the value of their primary home increased to $347,857 from $235,000. Assuming the home nets that amount upon sale, June and Ward Clever would put $95,659 in their pocket. Also, remember that they have made no mortgage payments for the past 10 years and have no debt on the El Salvador condo.

When did reverse mortgages become an option?

In 1989, HUD tried to help "home-rich, cash-poor" seniors by establishing a program that would enable them to take cash payments out of the home's equity. These reverse mortgages carry a variety of payment options. And repayment of the loan is not required during the homeowner's lifetime unless the property is no longer occupied as a primary residence. The reverse mortgages, however, are still expensive, with fees of 4 percent of the loan amount and more depending upon the program. Financial Freedom Funding (*www.financialfreedom.com*) has a "jumbo" reverse mortgage that is better suited to owners of more expensive homes. The jumbo reverse mortgage is not based on geographic location. In 2007, BNY Mortgage (*www.bnymortgage.com*) rolled out the first fixed-rate reverse mortgage in nearly two decades.

The homeowner cannot be displaced and forced to sell the home to pay off the mortgage, even if the principal balance grows to exceed the value of the property. If the value of the house exceeds what is owed at the time of death, the balance goes to the estate.

The loan is aimed at individuals 62 years or older who own their homes—either debt-free or close to it—and who have a need for additional cash. According to HUD, approximately 70 percent of America's elderly own their own homes and 80 percent of these homeowners do not have mortgage debt. The potential reverse mortgage market continues to be absolutely huge. Reverse mortgage loan amounts to homeowners are based on age, interest rate, type of plan selected, and value of the property. Some second homes qualify for reverse mortgages, but not all lenders offer the second-home option. As of July, 2007 the main players in the reverse mortgage market for second homes were BNY Mortgage and Reverse Mortgage of America (an arm of Bank of America).

All HECM loans are guaranteed by the Federal Housing Administration, the agency established by the National Housing Act of 1934 to stabilize a depressed housing market and provide insurance on loans to homebuyers who otherwise could not find loans. In 1983, the government ceased to control the interest rates on mortgages insured by the FHA and started allowing the rates to "float" with the rest of the market.

National reverse mortgage sources

Reverse Mortgage of America
www.reversemortgageofamerica.com

Financial Freedom Senior Funding
www.financialfreedom.com

BNY Mortgage
www.bnymortgage.com

Wells Fargo Home Mortgage
www.reversemortgages.net

National Center for Home Equity Conversion
www.reverse.org

U.S. Department of Housing and Urban Development
www.hud.gov

National Reverse Mortgage Lenders Association
www.reversemortgage.org

CHAPTER FOURTEEN

Central America Offers an Investment Alternative

*Property outside the United States
provides diversification, potential rewards*

A few short years ago, many of us watched our investment income and net worth diminish significantly because of the woes of the U.S. stock market. Historically, Wall Street has been a pretty good long-term investment vehicle. The "Tech Wreck" that began in the spring of 2000 taught us to be more cautious. It also made us look to investments outside the conventional financial markets. Investing in real property also has been a reliable, consistent investment option. Throughout history, great personal wealth has been attained through real estate ownership. But for most of us, it has been limited to investment in a primary residence. Although Central American real estate also can be a viable investment venue, Americans have had a great deal more trepidation considering properties south of the border because of the highly publicized problems with some governments and acquisitions.

Given today's investment climate, however, Central America provides an alternative, attractive arena for potential investment. It is less expensive than most U.S. destinations and, unlike Hawaii, close enough for some people to actually reach via automobile if absolutely necessary. Real estate in Central America should have a similar appreciation "upside" as does real estate in a U.S. development—coupled with the advantage of use and enjoyment of the property as a second residence. In fact, some Central American projects have significantly higher internal rates of return, with greater near-term value escalation, because of higher demands and less supply considerations given within a respective market or locale. Nonetheless, interested buyers must be savvy and educated because acquiring real estate in all of Central America is not like buying property in the United States.

Never before has there been more information available to the buying public concerning real estate in Central America. Web sites have become more plentiful in many countries, with real estate agents displaying more pertinent information and available property listings. There is greater awareness of property conveyance, tax and legal matters, and greater attention is being placed on safeguarding foreign investment through the use of neutral third-party escrow agreements. In addition, agents are now recommending that buyers obtain a commitment for title insurance, acquire coverage at the time of closing and follow through with the subsequent title insurance policy once the deed is recorded.

It would appear that no one's "crystal ball" has been too clear, nor has anyone predicted big-time run-ups in stock market investments since the dot.com shakeout that began in 2000. While the 2006-2007 stock market performance clearly was positive, it seems more people are content to have cash in certificates of deposit that guarantee a fixed rate of return. However, real estate still represents a strong investment opportunity in many areas of the world. For this reason, if you have an interest in Central American real estate—perhaps you have thought long and hard about the lure of a residence on the beach or a colonial villa in Central America's interior—now just might be the time.

Central America after September 11, 2001

Like the United States, Central America was very quiet in the fourth quarter of 2001. It had already been a difficult year because of U.S. economic woes and recessionary concerns pervading the U.S. economy. Being heavily dependent on trade with its biggest neighbor and business partner to the north, Central America suffered additional financial loss and national anxiety with the turmoil created by the events of September 11.

Americans quit traveling, deciding to stay within the secure confines of U.S. soil. The tourism industry, the lifeblood and a vital part of many Central American gross domestic product, began to suffer. Central America's beautiful and popular beaches, hotels, stores and shops dependent upon U.S. occupancy and money were nearly empty. Real estate companies and their agents wondered, then worried about the state of things to come during the latter part of 2001 and in the future. They asked whether Americans, given all the circumstances and financial uncertainty, would return to Central America. Would the tremendous real estate investment potential that this great region presents to a foreign buying public continue to lure Canadian and American capital?

By early 2002, the prognosis for Central America again became encouraging. Conditions in the United States improved, not only with travel and our willingness to venture outside the U.S. but with the strengthening of the overall economy and outlook. The stock market rebounded to pre-September 11 levels and investor confidence was a little less pensive, less guarded. Investor 401(k) accounts that took a serious whack during September began a gradual rebound during the fourth quarter, signaling a strong rally that U.S. recovery was on its way. With 11 interest-rate cuts by the Federal Reserve during 2001, the U.S. government attempted to jumpstart our sagging economy out of its year-long doldrums.

The residue of 9/11 has made our eyes clearer and our ears keener. We ask more questions and seek more explanations—not just concerning safety and travel but also about major issues and challenges we face every day. The aftermath of 9/11 is one of the reasons potential buyers better understand the issues concerning ownership of land in Central America. They are more willing to learn and to be armed with the right questions. These buyers are simply more savvy and know if their questions cannot be answered by an individual, they will turn to information provided on the Internet. In addition, Central America's real estate developers and agents have increasingly become more aware that purchasers do understand the issues. Buyers are concerned with title matters, use of an escrow agreement, subdivision authorizations, recorded deeds and condominium regimes, capital gains tax implications and property conveyance procedures, to name a few. No longer is the buying public willing to just accept that old adage of "trust me, that's how we do business here in Central America." The margarita syndrome has lost a considerable amount of its swagger and 9/11 contributed to the new focused attitude and approach.

Although taxes can be a huge benefit in the acquisition of real estate, they also can be a burden. In the next chapter, we examine what to expect when considering tax consequences on both sides of the border.

CHAPTER FIFTEEN

Understanding Tax: What to Expect from Uncle Sam

Residency requirements, capital gains exemptions, tax-deferred exchanges

In the United States, American citizens may exclude the capital gain they realize when they sell their principal residence after occupying it for a period of not less than two years during the five years preceding the sale and meeting other specific IRS requirements. There is no federal income tax liability on up to $250,000 gain in U.S. dollars ($500,000 gain for joint filers) on the sale of a primary residence. The same holds true in most Central American countries.

However, if you are a citizen or resident of the U.S., you will be liable for tax on your worldwide income even if you reside outside the U.S. It makes no difference if the country where you are working has no income tax; Uncle Sam still expects you to settle up with him every year. He especially wants to hear from you in the tax year that you sell your second home so that the U.S. benefits from your capital gain, if any. If you are a U.S. resident, you are liable to be taxed on worldwide capital gains at a maximum rate of 15 percent on assets held for more than 12 months and at normal graduated income tax rates on capital gains on assets held for 12 months or fewer.

The U.S. has entered into income tax treaties with many countries, which provide an exemption or reduction in tax rates for particular types of income. A foreign tax credit is granted to U.S. citizens that is equal to the lower of the foreign tax already paid or the U.S. tax payable on the same source of income.

If you are a resident of the U.S., you will also pay state income tax on your worldwide income in the state where you are a resident and to any state in which the income is earned. If the same income is taxed in two states, a tax credit will typically be allowed in one of the states. Some states do not have state income tax.

Underestimated financial options of the Tax Relief Act of 1997

With one stroke of his pen, President Clinton changed the financial status of not only the average American home but also the primary residences of U.S. citizens held abroad. When the Taxpayer Relief Act of 1997 went into law on August 5, 1997, it changed not only the $125,000, one-time home sale exclusion for persons over 55 years of age but also the "rollover replacement rule." In essence, the home began to move from the "shelter" column into the "financial portfolio" column. Under the old law, a taxpayer could defer any gain on the sale of a principal residence by buying or building a home of equal or greater value within 24 months of the sale of the first home. Tax on the gain was not eliminated but merely "rolled over" into the new residence, reducing the tax basis of the new home. If you sold a primary residence and failed to meet the requirements for deferral, you faced a tax on current and previously deferred gain. The old law also contained an once-in-a-lifetime $125,000 exclusion ($62,500 if single, or married and filing a separate return) of gain from the sale of the primary residence.

The intent of the new tax code, which replaces the "rollover" provision and the $125,000 over-55 exclusion, is to allow most homeowners to sell their primary residence without tax. It also dramatically simplifies recordkeeping for many people. Although it's still wise to retain proof of the original cost of the home and significant improvements, tedious collection and retention of invoices and other records to substantiate the cost of home improvements probably won't be necessary. Many taxpayers, including retirees who have already used the one-time over-55 $125,000 exclusion, do not realize they are eligible to sell their primary home again—and do it every two years—under the Taxpayer Relief Act of 1997. The 1997 law repealed all former tax laws on primary residences and significantly changed the role of the home in regard to financial planning. Here are the keys to one of the best ways the average homeowner can now accumulate more wealth for retirement, perhaps buying a smaller home in the States and a primary home in Central America, and an explanation of why the home has become the largest piece in the average taxpayer's financial puzzle.

In order to qualify for the $500,000 capital gains exclusion ($250,000 for single persons), a taxpayer must have owned and used the property as his or her principal residence for two out of five years prior to the date of sale. Second, you must not have used this same exclusion in the two-year period prior to the sale. The only limit on the number of times a taxpayer can claim this exclusion is once in any two-year period. What is often misunderstood is that both the earlier one-time exclusion of up to $125,000 in gain for persons over 55 and the deferral of all or part of a gain by purchasing a qualifying replacement residence are gone. You no longer can utilize parts of either portion and you absolutely do not have to buy a replacement home. Persons who used the $125,000 exclusion can make use of the new exclusion if they meet the two-year residency test. The law enables seniors to "buy down" to less expensive homes without tax penalties. For gains greater than the exemption amounts, a 15 percent capital gains tax usually will apply. Homeowners with potential gains larger than the excludable amounts should keep accurate records in an attempt to reduce their gains by the amount of all eligible improvements.

To qualify for the full exclusion, either married spouse can meet the ownership requirement but both must meet the use requirement. Although exclusion can be used only once in each two-year period, a partial exclusion may be available if the sale results from a change in place of employment or health, or from unforeseen circumstances. If you have owned the house for less than two years, you would receive a proportional amount of the maximum exclusion under special situations. For example, if you owned a home for one year and made a $55,000 profit, the entire $55,000 would be tax free because your total exclusion was chopped in half to $125,000 from $250,000 (and from $500,000 to $250,000 for married couples) because of the one-year time frame. Consumers can turn Central American homes (plus yachts and recreational vehicles) into principal residences simply by meeting the residency requirements. Divorced or separated spouses are not out in the cold. If an "ex" lived in the home for two of the five years before the sale, that person is able to use the exclusion. However, nothing changes on the loss side of the primary home sale ledger—losses on the sale of the primary home still are not deductible in the U.S., Central America or elsewhere. If a nondeductible loss seems unavoidable, it might be a good idea to convert the house to a rental property (where losses are deductible). But you would have to be able to prove the move was not just to avoid taxes. If depreciation were claimed on a property, the maximum long-term capital gains tax liability would be 15 percent to the extent depreciation was claimed.

Two key guidelines: Use and residency requirements

For married taxpayers who file a joint return, only one spouse need meet the two-out-of-five-year ownership requirement but both spouses must meet the two-out-of-five-year use requirement. That is, if the husband has owned and used the house as his principal residence for two of the past five years but his wife did not use the house as her principal residence for the required two years, then the capital gains exclusion is only $250,000.

For those who leave their home because of a disability, a special rule makes it easier to meet the two-year requirement—especially if you were hospitalized or had to spend a significant period in a similar facility. In such cases, if you owned and used the home as a principal residence for at least one of the five years preceding the sale, then you are treated as having used it as your principal residence while you are in a facility that is licensed to care for people in your condition. This rule enables the family to sell the home to raise cash for the expenses without incurring a large tax bite.

The tax-deferred exchange from U.S. to Central American property is not "like kind"

In the United States, a tax-deferred exchange (commonly known as an IRS Section 1031 Exchange) proceeds just as a "sale" for you, your real estate agent and parties associated with the deal. Provided you closely follow the exchange rules, however, the IRS will "sanction" the transaction and allow you to characterize it as an exchange rather than as a sale. Thus, you are permitted to defer paying the capital gains tax. Section 1031 specifically requires that an exchange take place. That means that one property must be exchanged for another property rather than sold for cash. The exchange is what distinguishes a Section 1031 tax-deferred transaction from a sale and purchase. The exchange is created by using an intermediary (or exchange facilitator) and the required exchange documentation. Here are the typical steps:

- You (taxpayer) receive an acceptable offer for your property.
- You assign your seller's rights in the relinquished property purchase and sale contract to the buyer. The buyer gives "your" cash to the intermediary. This is the first leg of the exchange.
- You make an acceptable offer to acquire the replacement property.
- You assign your purchaser's obligations in the contract to the intermediary.

- The intermediary acquires the relinquished property and instructs the seller to deed it directly to you to complete the trade.

In an exchange, you must trade an interest in real estate (sole ownership, joint tenancy, tenancy in common) that you have held for trade, business or investment purposes for another "like-kind" interest in real estate. The like-kind definition is very broad. You can dispose of and acquire any interest in real property other than a primary home or a second residence. For example, you can trade raw land for income property, a rental house for a multiplex or a rental house for a retail property. However, the definition does not include trading a U.S. property for another property outside the country. You cannot trade a home in Tampa for a condo in Panama City—it's not like-kind. However, the IRS does permit a trade of a foreign property for another foreign property on a tax-deferred exchange. For example, if you had a condo in Antigua, Guatemala, and became tired of the colonial look of the area, you could trade it for a cozy place on the beach in Izpata, Guatemala, you could defer the gain by identifying a place of equal or greater value in Izpata within 45 days of the sale of the Antigua condo and then close the deal within 180 days of the sale of the Antigua property. While you would owe no U.S. tax on the deal, you could still face a tax liability in Guatemala because the country would charge capital gains tax, up to 31 percent, on the respective sales.

Considering taxes in different countries

Confusing tax issues can surface when you own property in more than one country. Various taxes related to real estate transactions are calculated differently in Central America and the U.S. The key is to determine in which country you deem your primary residence. Both Central America and the U.S. consider you a tax resident of the country where you keep your principal residence. For example, you may have been living in Central America on a tourist visa the last five years, but for tax purposes you would more than likely be considered a tax resident of Central America. U.S. citizens and residents are required to report and pay tax on income made anywhere in the world, regardless of where they live. In addition, both Central America and the U.S. reserve the right to tax property within their boundaries.

More discussion on second residence ... or rental property

A home and a primary residence have different meanings, benefits and drawbacks to tax persons. For example, do you want the depreciation and maintenance benefits of a rental home or the mortgage-interest deduction of a second residence? A personal residence cannot be depreciated. An individual can have several homes yet only one primary residence. A home refers to where a person is physically living, as long as his or her stay is more than a temporary one. Primary residence involves both physical presence in a place and intention to make that place one's home. Residence without "the intention to remain indefinitely" generally will not constitute primary residence. An individual's motive for changing primary residences—even for tax reasons—does not raise red tax flags. However, consumers must show at least some sort of intent to establish a primary residence.

If you are considering making your Central American home your permanent residence, now or in the future, you should begin planning for a change in primary residence. If you have been using your Central American home as a rental, consider converting it to personal use for a period of at least two years. That way, if you have to sell unexpectedly, you can keep up to $500,000 in gains tax free. However, use caution and keep a paper trail. Some people who retain homes and remain active in business or community affairs in their original states are finding that state tax officials are challenging their change of personal residence. The states say that these folks are still residents for income or estate tax purposes because they have not abandoned their original personal residences. However, when intent conflicts with facts and circumstances, determining which residence is actually an individual's primary residence can be confusing. The determination is usually based on the individual's objective and facts such as:

- Payment of local taxes
- Time spent in state of residency
- Continuous car registration and driver's license
- Furnishing and appointing primary residence more extensively

You will also want to consider the potential of U.S. state income tax consequences of a change of residence. If you have bonuses coming, stocks options or other deferred compensation (as is the case, for example, with many corporate executives), plan carefully how you receive these funds relative to your move to avoid excessive state income taxes. Many states have become more aggressive in enforcing their sales and use tax laws. They have gone to great lengths—examining U.S. Customs reports, auditing tax gallery sales, personal checkbooks and credit card statements, and sharing that information with other states. Some states have enacted strict filing responsibilities and record retention statutes with respect to individuals who flip-flop principal residences.

A home does not have to actually be used to qualify as a residence. If there is no rental or personal use of a residence for an entire year, it can be designated as a "qualified residence" and mortgage interest can be fully deducted. If it is rented a majority of the year and used just two weekends by the owner, no interest can be deducted under the personal-residence rule. The U.S. rule is that personal days must exceed the greater of 14 days or 10 percent of rental days. The personal-use requirement must be met before a property can be designated a qualified residence. If the home is rented more than 140 days, there will have to be 15 days of personal use before the interest can be deducted fully under the residence rule. Since the 1986 Tax Reform Act left mortgage interest on first and second homes intact, accountants and tax advisers have asked clients to weigh renting versus personal use very carefully. The deductibility of rental expenses and mortgage interest enters a gray area when you alter the cut-and-dried 14-day or 10 percent guideline. If you have the ability to rent winter and summer, you can also get in more personal-use days under the 10 percent rule. A Central American resort might have the potential for 250 rental days a year, allowing the owner to use it for 25 days without forfeiting its rental status.

Another way to pick up a day or two on the beach without eating into your 14-day or 10 percent limit is to clean the house yourself between renters, perhaps monthly snowbirds from the Midwest. Days spent maintaining the house do not count toward your personal use limit. You can even deduct travel costs to get to the house and expenses such as paint and cleaning supplies. The house also must be rented at fair-market value. If you rent to relatives at discount rates, the IRS may rule that the house is not a business and disallow many of your deductions.

It's a good idea to consider a second home—for rental or personal use—simply because houses will continue to appreciate in many areas of Central America for some time. The boom is likely to continue especially in the most popular areas. If you want that getaway all to yourself but find you can't afford the mortgage payments after you buy it, go ahead and rent it. You can juggle rental and personal use status from year to year. The getaway that was once viewed only as a luxury is now not a bad place to stick your savings. And in a few years, you may even be able to retire into what has become the best investment you ever made.

Use may matter to your lender

The personal residence or rental question also will surface when dealing with a lender. In Chapter Thirteen, we offered some creative ways you may not have considered to help you get in the door of a second home. However, the conventional method typically entails making a down payment (from savings, liquidating other assets) or taking out a home equity loan on your primary residence for the "down." The remaining balance then can be financed over a term similar to the loan on your primary home—30 years, 15 years or a variety of adjustable rate mortgage periods. If the home is a second residence, the rates probably will be more favorable than if the home is a rental unit, commonly referred to as a "nonowner occupied" dwelling. In fact, some lenders will not finance investment properties in Central America, only second homes or primary residences. If you plan to rent out your home, a lender willing to make an investor loan will want to see proof that you're actually going to generate a cash flow that will help pay the monthly mortgage plus taxes and insurance. In many cases, the lender will ask for a cash flow statement for a property showing its rental history. And don't count on your bank to take all of a home's estimated rental income into consideration. Even for a property with a long rental history, most lenders will only consider 75 to 80 percent of the total take. If possible, make purchase offers contingent upon your loan being approved—some lenders will not extend funds in condominium developments where there are renters other than owner occupants. Also, make sure you know all insurance costs for your new property.

A second home in Central America can also be a long-term tax shelter for future retirement. For example, if you are 45 years old and plan to slow down at 60, you can buy a rental home disguised as vacation home, furnish it, enjoy some personal use time and have renters pay for it. When you have carved every bit of tax depreciation advantage out of it, you can move in and convert it to a full-time private residence while still renting it out a couple of weeks a year. And because most mortgages "front-loan" interest, you will have used up most of your tax deductions from the mortgage in the 15 years you were working and renting the home. In the later years of the mortgage, when interest deductions are relatively low, you probably will be less concerned because your income will have fallen off. Although future tax proposals undoubtedly will change the current tax landscape, second homes in any environment should be spared the big axe when compared to other proposed restrictions on real estate investments. You can sell your primary residence, pocket the gain and retire to your second home in Central America. If you no longer like the Central American getaway you purchased years ago, make sure you have lived in it two years as your primary residence, sell it, pocket the gain and move on down the beach to another home (though you could owe some capital gains tax in your Central American country).

Congress really helped the potential for second homes

Unknowingly, when members of Congress approved the Taxpayer Relief Act of 1997, they completely overhauled and multiplied the possibilities for second-home purchase, use and sale. Ironically, the reason why taxpayers are able to reap the advantages of having two homes in the first place can be directly traced to our members of the U.S. House of Representatives and Senate. Why are we able to deduct the mortgage interest on two homes rather than just one? It's because congressional members "needed" two homes—one in their home state and another in the nation's capital. (Some accountants even refer to the curious guideline as the "Congressmen's Rule.") When you couple the ability to own two (or more) personal residences simultaneously, then toss in the capacity to convert a rental property into a personal residence, you will be overwhelmed to discover the windfall profits brought by simple combinations of appreciation and tax savings. But never forget—you can always move in to your rental and you can sell your primary residence every two years and pay no U.S. tax.

More than one home— in the United States or Central America

As most taxpayers know by now, the 1997 tax legislation added a generous exclusion for sales of primary residences. If you own one or more residences, there are some tax-saving strategies to be considered, chess moves to be made—all legal and proper—but preparation and timing are always important. The basic gain exclusion qualification rule is simple: You must have owned and used the home as your main residence for at least two years out of the five-year period ending on the date of sale. To repeat: If you are married, the full $500,000 capital gains break ($250,000 for singles) is available as long as one or both of you satisfies the residency and ownership guidelines.

Now, if you *do* decide to become adventuresome and buy a spot in a remote Central America jungle, will you ever be able to sell it? In our Conclusion, we explore that while the baby boomer group is immense, it should not underestimate the appetite for different experiences of the next generation of second home buyers.

Pondering the Exit: If You Buy, Will You Be Able to Sell?

The number of prospective buyers will continue to be strong

As amazing as the housing market was in the United States between 2000 and 2005, the second-home market in Central America was even more prolific for U.S. and Canadian buyers seeking appreciation for their vacation or retirement residences. In some Central American markets, it has not been uncommon for foreign purchasers to realize at least a 30 percent increase in home values over a two-year period. It really isn't hard to understand. Owning a residence has long been the way Americans create personal net worth. Houses have historically accounted for the largest and single most important acquisition one makes. If our disposability of income reaches a threshold where we can make prudent investments, real estate has long been a lucrative avenue.

If you roll the dice and buy in Central America, who will be *your* likely buyer? With the number of people looking to real estate to acquire wealth and leisure time, the resale prospects for a well-situated home in Central America appear to be extremely bright. And for at least the next 20 years, the numbers are overwhelming. According to the U.S. Bureau of the Census and the National Center for Health Statistics, the number of Americans aged 45 to 64 increased 34 percent from 1990 to 2000 and now sits at approximately 71 million. Every day, the 50-plus population is growing by 10,000 people, and this trend is expected to continue for the next 20 years. Right now, an American turns 50 every seven seconds.

Why is this important to the outlook for Central American real estate? This is the largest, healthiest and wealthiest group ever appearing on the U.S. growth landscape and it is just beginning to grasp the concept of buying abroad. Much like their parents—members of the "greatest generation"—targeted Florida, the boomers will target Central America because of the different experience, the attraction to perceived risk and the thrill of the exotic. In many cases, it's simply the lure of the beach and a step outside the predictable second-home box. Remember the popular advertising line "this is not your father's Oldsmobile"? Central America, except for some long-time retirees who saw the light early, "is not your father's second-home spot." That was Florida, now too expensive and a touch too common for the boomers' tastes. Some may say they will buy in Florida or Arizona but you can never rely on what this group collectively says it will do.

"Baby boomers are famous for believing one thing and then behaving totally different from what they think they do," says Eric Snider, who has a doctorate in social psychology and serves as Shea Homes' marketing director for Trilogy, the homebuilding company's upscale, active adult communities. "They are after exclusivity, amenities and personal experiences. Boomers are all about personal experiences."

In a 2004 economic study prepared by the Urban Institute for AARP, authors Barbara Butrica and Cori Uccello contend that boomers will amass more wealth in real terms at retirement than will the two previous generations. Median household wealth at age 67 will grow from $448,000 among 2004 retirees to $600,000 among boomers. Income at retirement is consistent with trends in wealth at retirement, the study shows. Projected household income at age 67 will increase from $44,000 among current retirees to $65,000 among boomers.

As we mentioned in Chapter Thirteen, baby boomers never met a loan they didn't like. The bottom line is that they will continue to drive the second-home stampede to Central America because they like to be creative with financing and they love having the status—and the actual experience—of a second home. Owning a property in a place as mysterious as Central America will further push their fun and romance buttons.

And they will introduce Central America to their children. If you think the baby boomer group was immense and steered the housing market plus every element of the retail industry, get ready for a throng that contains many of their consumer-crazy children—the proud members of Generation Y. These youngsters, born in 1979 or later, will have 74 million members (an estimated 3 million more than the boomers) and make up 34 percent of the population by 2015. They will prefer homes that will be useful rather than prestigious and they will be willing to trade size for lifestyle and convenience factors. Doesn't that sound like a small bungalow close to the beach or a casita with a view of the mountains?

Members of Generation Y have been under the radar and haven't even shown up yet with their checkbooks. Will they also be buying memories of great family times under the Central American sun? Absolutely. And the numbers will be overwhelming.

PART FOUR

Helpful Sources

Realtors Specializing in Central America

Agents in Canada

Terry Moranis
Prudential Sadie Moranis Realty
35 Lesmill Road
Toronto, ON M3B 2T3
Phone: 416.449.2020 **Fax:** 416.449.1975
Email: *terrymoranis@sadiemoranis.com*
URL: *www.sadiemoranis.com*

Ursula Morel
RE/MAX Sea to Sky Real Estate Whistler
4333 Skiers Approach
Whistler, BC V0N 1B4
Phone: 604.935.3635 **Fax:** 604.932.1140
Email: *ursula@ursulamorel.com*
URL: *www.ursulamorel.com*

George Pelyhe
Groupe Sutton Immobilia, Inc.
785 Mont-Royal E.
Montreal, PQ H2J 1W8

Phone: 514.529.1010 **Fax:** 514.597.1032
Email: *geopel@montreal-real-estate.com*
URL: *www.montreal-real-estate.com*

Agents in Costa Rica

James Aoki
Rico Realty Corporation
200 Mts. al Sur Cinco esquina de San Luis
de Tilaran
Tilaran, Guanacaste 18-5710
Phone: 506.695.8562 **Fax:** 506.695.5663
Email: *ricorealty@hotmail.com*
URL: *www.ricorealty.com*

Eddy Barquero
Metro Cuadrado Bienes Raices CR S.A.
Tibas 50 Este Rincon Poblano
San Jose, Tibas 1200 PAVAS
Phone: 506.297.7575 **Fax:** 506.241.2019
Email: *info@metrocuadrado.info*
URL: *www.metrocuadrado.info*

Thomas Battaglia
Century 21 Coastal Estates
Playa Tamarindo
Santa Cruz, Guanacaste
Phone: 506.653.0300   Fax: 506.653.0600
Email: tom@coastalestates.org
URL: www.c21costarica.com

Olivia Benavides
Century 21 Marina Trading Post
Front of Principal Entrance
Hotel Playa Flamingo
Santa Cruz, Guanacaste 166-5130
Phone: 506.654.4004   Fax: 506.654.4401
Email: olivia@century21costarica.net
URL: www.century21costarica.net

Rene Bradley Aoki
Rico Realty Corporation
200 Mts. al Sur Cinco esquinas
de San Luis de Tilaran
Tilaran, Guanacaste 18-5710
Phone: 506.695.8562   Fax: 506.695.5663
Email: ricorealty@hotmail.com
URL: www.ricorealty.com

Hernan Carazo
Ocean Realty Costa Rica
P.O. Box 98-1007
San Jose, Guanacaste
Phone: 506.290.6529   Fax: 506.291.2824
Email: Hernan@costaricaoceanrealty.com
URL: www.costaricaoceanrealty.com

Ernestina Carman
Coldwell Banker
Frente a la Fabrica de hielo
Playa del Coco, Guanacaste
Phone: 506.670.0805   Fax: 506.670.0403
Email: tina@coldwellbankercr.com
URL: www.coldwellbankercr.com

Robert Davey
Century 21 Marina Trading Post
Flamingo, next to Marie's Restaurant
Flamingo 166-5150
Phone: 506.654.4004   Fax: 506.654.4401
Email: bob@century21costarica.net
URL: www.century21costarica.net

Tony Dimaggio
ABC Realty
Playa Tamarindo

Santa Cruz, Guanacaste
Phone: 506.653.0402   Fax: 506.653.0793
Email: abctam@racsa.co.cr
URL: www.abccostarica.com

James Drews
Coldwell Banker Dominical Realty, S.A.
Playa Dominical, Peninsula de Osa
Dominical, Puntarenas
Phone: 506.787.0223   Fax: 506.787.0220
Email: james@cbcostarica.com
URL: www.cbdominical.com

Cynthia Duran Rodriguez
Hacienda Pinillo
5 km. South of Tamarindo—
Villareal intersection
Santa Cruz, Guanacaste 66
Phone: 506.680.3000   Fax: 506.680.3165
Email: cduran@haciendapinillo.com
URL: www.haciendapinillo.com

Greg First
Century 21 Marina Trading Post
P.O. Box 166-5150
Flamingo Beach, Guanacaste
Phone: 506.654.4004   Fax: 506.654.4401
Email: greg@century21costarica.net
URL: www.century21costarica.net

Jeffrey Fisher
Century 21 Coastal Estates
Main Street
Tamarindo, Guanacaste
Phone: 506.653.0300   Fax: 506.653.0600
Email: greatplaces@hotmail.com
URL: www.costaricarealestate.com

Michael Fonseca
Century 21
Main Street
Tamarindo, Guanacaste
Phone: 506.366.8349   Fax: 506.653.0600
Email: mike@micari.net

Luis Garro
RE/MAX Connection
Jaco Beach, Pastor Diaz Av.
Jaco, Puntarenas 130 4023
Phone: 506.643.3510   Fax: 506.643.4005
Email: connect@racsa.co.cr
URL: www.costaricaconnections.com

Thomas Ghormley Hessell
Century 21 Jaco Beach Realty
Apartado Postal 25, Playa Jaco
Garabito, Puntarenas 4023
Phone: 506.643.3356 **Fax:** 506.643.2959
Email: *tom@c21jaco.com*
URL: *www.c21jaco.com*

Linda Gray
Coldwell Banker Coast to Coast Properties
Main Street, P.O. Box 98
Playas del Coco, Guanacaste 5019
Phone: 506.670.0805 **Fax:** 506.670.0403
Email: *linda@coldwellbankercr.com*
URL: *www.coldwellbankercr.com*

Jimmie Gray
Coldwell Banker Coast to Coast Properties
Main Street, P.O. Box 98
Playas del Coco, Guanacaste 5019
Phone: 506.670.0805 **Fax:** 506.670.0403
Email: *jim@coldwellbankercr.com*
URL: *www.coldwellbankercr.com*

Sheila Hawke
Coldwell Banker Coast to Coast Properties
Playas del Coco
Playas del Coco, Guanacaste 5019
Phone: 506.672.0227 **Fax:** 506.672.0227
Email: *sheilahawke@yahoo.com*

Harvey Hofmann
Coldwell Banker Coast to Coast Properties
Main Street, P.O. Box 98
Playas del Coco, Guanacaste 5019
Phone: 506.670.0805 **Fax:** 506.670.0403
Email: *harvey@coldwellbankercr.com*
URL: *www.coldwellbankercr.com*

David Hollander
Coldwell Banker Dominical Realty S.A.
Playa Dominical, Peninsula de Osa
Dominical, Puntarenas
Phone: 506.787.0223 **Fax:** 506.787.0220
Email: *daveed@cbcostarica.com*
URL: *www.cbdominical.com*

John Logan
Century 21 Marina Trade
Playa Flamingo
Santa Cruz, Guanacaste
Phone: 506.654.4004 **Fax:** 506.654.4004
Email: *loganjl2002@aol.com*
URL: *www.century21costarica.net*

Jim Main
Ocean Pacific Realty
#16, Sunrise Commercial Center
Playa Tamarindo
Tamarindo, Guanacaste
Phone: 506.653.1300 **Fax:** 506.653.1302
Email: *jim@oceanpacific-realty.com*
URL: *www.oceanpacific-realty.com*

Lou Maresca
Century 21 Coastal Estates
Playa Tamarindo
Santa Cruz, Guanacaste
Phone: 506.653.0300 **Fax:** 506.653.0600
Email: *lou@coastalestates.org*
URL: *www.c21costarica.com*

Shawn Maricle
Century 21 Coastal Estates
Playa Tamarindo
Santa Cruz, Guanacaste
Phone: 506.653.0300 **Fax:** 506.653.0600
Email: *shawn@coastalestates.org*
URL: *www.c21tamarindo.com*

Federico Marin
Marschu International Realty
Apartado 2963
San Jose 1000
Phone: 506.384.2216 **Fax:** 506.222.5523
Email: *fams04@yahoo.com*
URL: *www.marschu.com*

William Marks
Coldwell Banker
50 Km. N. Hotel Sol
Playas del Coco, Guanacaste
Phone: 506.392.3734
Email: *billy@coldwellbankercr.com*
URL: *www.coldwellbankercr.com*

Chip McGraw
Coldwell Banker Nosara Realty
Toll free: 866.372.4447
Cell: 506.8390.4908
URL: *www.cbnosara.com*

Sean McGraw
Coldwell Banker Dominical Realty S.A.
Playa Dominical, Peninsula de Osa
Dominical, Puntarenas
Phone: 506.787.0223 **Fax:** 506.787.0220
Email: *sean@cbcostarica.com*
URL: *www.cbdominical.com*

Connie Moreno
Century 21 Coastal Estates
Playa Tamarindo
Santa Cruz, Guanacaste
Phone: 506.563.0300 Fax: 506.563.0600
Email: *connie@coastalestates.org*
URL: *www.c21tamarindo.com*

Faith Mullins
CRDC Real Estate S.A.
Villas Celina
Playa Hermosa, Guanacaste
Phone: 506.672.0011 Fax: 506.672.0011
Email: *windstar@racsa.co.cr*
URL: *www.crdcrealestate.com*

Javier Munich
Coldwell Banker
Playas del Coco
Playas del Coco, Guanacaste
Phone: 506.670.0805 Fax: 506.670.0403
Email: *javier@coldwellbankercr.com*
URL: *www.coldwellbankercr.com*

Viale Nicholas
Century 21 Coastal Estates
Main Road – Next to Hotel Diria
Tamarindo, Guanacaste 005
Phone: 506.653.0300 Fax: 506.653.0600
Email: *nviale11@aol.com*
URL: *www.costarica1realestate.com*

Gustavo Odio
Axxis Realty International
Uvita Puntarenas 200 Mts.
antes Gas Station
Uvita, Puntarenas 682300
Phone: 506.743.8206 Fax: 506.743.8205
Email: *go@axxisrealty.com*
URL: *www.axxisrealty.com*

Gerald Ogilvie
Coldwell Banker Coast to Coast Realty
Playas del Coco, Guanacaste
Phone: 506.670.0805 Fax: 506.670.0403
Email: *gerald@coldwellbankercr.com*
URL: *www.coldwellbankercr.com*

Alvaro Ortiz
Century 21 Marina Trading Post
P.O. Box 166-5150
Flamingo Beach, Guanacaste
Phone: 506.386.6825 Fax: 506.654.4401

Email: *alortiz@racsa.co.cr*
URL: *www.century21costarica.net*

Angela Passman
Guardian Angels CR
APDO 106-4006
San Antonio de Belen, Heredia
Phone: 506.832.2450
Email: *angela@guardianangelscr.com*
URL: *www.guardianangelscr.com*

Emilia Piza Escalante
Contactos BR
P.O. Box 125-2120
San Francisco, Goicoechea
Phone: 506.240.1704 Fax: 506.240.6673
Email: *bienesraices@emiliapiza.com*
URL: *www.emiliapiza.com*

Mark Price
Century 21 Coastal Estate
Tamarindo
Santa Cruz, Guanacaste
Phone: 506.653.0300 Fax: 506.653.0600
Email: *marks@coastalestates.org*
URL: *www.c21costarica.com*

Angela Rossy
Tierra y Sol Real Estate
Parque Valle Del Sol, Suite 228
Pozos, Santa Ana
Phone: 506.203.0028 Fax: 506.203.0032
Email: *info@tierraysolrealestate.com*
URL: *www.tierraysolrealestate.com*

Natalia Sancho
Costa Rica Global Association of Real Estate
Playa Tamarindo
Santa Cruz, Guanacaste
Phone: 506.653.1320 Fax: 506.653.1321
Email: *nataliacrgar@yahoo.com*
URL: *www.gar.or.cr*

Jaime Seminario
Easy Real Estate, S.A.
West Palm Estates #137, Playa Grande
Playa Grande, Guanacaste
Phone: 506.653.1426 Fax: 506.653.1426
Email: *jaimeseminario@yahoo.com*
URL: *www.easyrealestate123.com*

Chris Simmons
RE/MAX Ocean Surf Realty, Tamarindo

Sunrise Centre
Tamarindo
Phone: 506.653.0073 **Fax:** 506.653.0074
Email: *csimmons@racsa.co.cr*
URL: *www.remax-oceansurf-cr.com*

Margaret Sohn
Great Estates of Costa Rica
P.O. Box 98-1007
San Jose
Phone: 506.290.6529 **Fax:** 506.291.2824
Email: *margaret@greatcre.com*
URL: *www.greatcre.com*

Roxana Soto
Tico Network
200 Sur Colegio Vocacional
La Ceiba, Alajuela
Phone: 506.841.1475
Email: *roxana_cr@yahoo.com.mx*

Ronald Umcina
Coldwell Banker Coast to Coast Properties
Playas del Coco
Playas del Coco, Guanacaste
Phone: 506.670.0805 **Fax:** 506.670.0403
Email: *rumania@coldwellbankercr.com*
URL: *www.coldwellbankercr.com*

Luis Urrutia
Casa Canada Group
Ave. 2, Calle 38 y 40
San Jose
Phone: 506.386.7946 **Fax:** 506.222.8233
Email: *lurrutia@casacanada.org*
URL: *www.123costaricarealestate.com*

Roma Vargas-Gutierrez
Casa Bruno Real Estate
550 m. Este del Cruce Guadalupe-Moravia,
Ave. Central
Guadalupe, San Jose 2100
Phone: 506.280.5217 **Fax:** 506.280.5120
Email: *info@casabrunorealestate.com*
URL: *www.casabrunorealestate.com*

Paola Vendemiati
Century 21 Coastal Estates
Playa Tamarindo
Santa Cruz, Guanacaste
Phone: 506.653.0248 **Fax:** 506.653.0600
Email: *paola@coastalestates.org*
URL: *www.c21costarica.com*

Frank Viale
Century 21 Coastal Estate
Playa Tamarindo
Santa Cruz, Guanacaste
Phone: 506.653.0300 **Fax:** 506.653.0600
Email: *frank@coastalestates.com*
URL: *www.c21costarica.com*

Pennye Wheeler
Century 21 Marina Trading Post
Flamingo Beach
Guanacaste
Phone: 506.654.4004 **Fax:** 506.654.4401
Email: *pennye@century21costarica.net*

Pamela Wright
St. Patricks Paradise S.A.
Playas Del Coco
500 m. North of Villa Del Sol Hotel
Playas Del Coco, Guanacaste
Phone: 506.670.0796
Email: *2pamelamarie@gmail.com*
URL: *www.coldwellbanker.com*

Ashley Young
Century 21 Marina Trade
Playa Flamingo
Santa Cruz, Guanacaste
Phone: 506.654.4004 **Fax:** 506.654.4004
Email: *ashleyyoung@mydogolf.com*

Andres Zamora
RE/MAX Ocean Surf Realty, Central Valley
2 Blocks North and 50 mts.
La Sabana, San Jose
Phone: 506.231.7878 **Fax:** 506.235.6669
Email: *andresz@racsa.co.cr*
URL: *www.andresz.com*

Agents in El Salvador
Marida Alfaro
Concepto Y Desarrollo S.A. De C.V.
Av. Antiguo Cuscatlan E 6-8
Col. La Sultana
Antiguo Cuscatlan
Phone: 503.2243.5698 **Fax:** 503.2243.5685
Email: *malfaro@concepto-sv.com*
URL: *www.concepto-sv.com*

Patricia Gonzalez de Barriere
Exelaris Inversiones
Final 93 Avenida Norte

Residencial Monaco Senda A #19
Colonia Escalon
San Salvador
Phone: 503.2275.5800
Email: *patriciadebarriere@yahoo.com.mx*

Mery Guevara Marquez
Guevara Marquez S.A. de C.V.
Calle y Colonia Roma #G-1
San Salvador
Phone: 503.2245.0324

Eva Montenegro de Vega
Eva Felisa M. de Vega
91 Ave. Norte y 3 C.P. Pasaje #6 & #2
San Salvador
Phone: 503.2263.0841 **Fax:** 503.2263.0841

Marco Tulio Salazar Amaya
Rapiventas Salazar Bienes Raices
5 Ave. Nte. y 17 C. Pte.
Centro Comercial Las Roas No. 3
San Salvador
Phone: 503.2221.2484 **Fax:** 503.2271.1392
Email: *markojr@navegante.com.sv*

Joe Velasquez Quintanilla
Ai Casa S.A. de C.V.
Calle Los Sislimiles 3130 Col. Miramonte
San Salvador
Phone: 503.2211.2272 **Fax:** 503.2260.0955
Email: *josemiguel@aicasa.com*
URL: *www.aicasa.com*

Agents in Guatemala

Victor Arreaza Martinez
Administracion Servicios y Projectos-
ASYPRO
4 Calle y 17 Avenida esquina,
16-48 Zona 3, Plaza Trino, Segundo Nivel
Oficina No. 8
Quetzaltenango
Phone: 502.5810.9971 **Fax:** 502.7767.0562
Email: *victorarreaza@asypro.com*
URL: *www.asypro.com*

Luis Arriola Samayoa
Precision Inmobiliaria
31 Ave. "A" 5-58 Zona 11, Residencial V
Guatemala 01011
Phone: 502.5202.5082 **Fax:** 502.2434.6243
Email: *luisarriola@amigo.net.gt*

Armand Boissy
Atitlan Solutions
Calle Santander, Comercial San Rafael
Local #6
Panajachel 07010
Phone: 502.5493.6161 **Fax:** 502.7762.0959
Email: *armand@intelnet.net.gt*
URL: *www.realestateatitlan.com*

Edward Carrette
RE/MAX Grupo Inmobiliario
Torre La Pradera, Of. No. 1007
Blvd. Los Proceres Z10
Guatemala City 10
Phone: 502.2385.4333 **Fax:** 502.2385.3226
Email: *edcarrette@remax.net*
URL: *www.realestateguatemala.com*

Edwin Estrada
Soluciones Bienes Raices
Carretera El Salvador, Km. 14.3 Puerta
Parada Plaza
Sonibel Locales 2A
Phone: 502.6637.1252 **Fax:** 502.6637.1252
Email: *solucionesbienes@intelnet.net.gt*
URL: *www.solucionesbienes.cjb.net*

Jeff Ghiringhelli
RE/MAX Grupo Inmobiliario
Torre La Pradera, Of. No. 1007
Blvd. Los Proceres Z-10
Guatemala City 10
Phone: 800.694.8072 **Fax:** 800.507.6529
Email: *jghiringhelli@austin.rr.com*
URL: *www.realestateguatemala.com*

Ana Gonzalez de Ruano
Century 21
17 Calle "A" 12-03 Zona 11, Mansca 1
Guatemala
Phone: 502.5715.0640 **Fax:** 502.2474.4276
Email: *anamariaruano@yahoo.com*

Edward Pearse
ETAP, S.A.
198 Plazuela Del Conquistador
Antigua Guatemala, Sacatepequez 03001
Phone: 502.7832.1029 **Fax:** 502.7832.8831
Email: *edpearse@gatewaytoantigua.com*
URL: *www.gatewaytoantigua.com*

Maria Luisa Perezalonso
CORSESA
Boulevard Vista Hermosa 22-65, Z-15

Guatemala
Phone: 502.2429.1212 **Fax:** 502.2429.1213
Email: *marialuisaperezalonso@hotmail.com*

Margarita Sagastume Morales
Propiedades Exclusivas/Grupo Propiex
5a. Av. 15-45, Zona 10, Edif. Centro
Empresarial
Torre 2, of 408
Guatemala 01010
Phone: 502.2333.7155 **Fax:** 502.6634.1250
Email: *propiex@terra.com.gt*
URL: *www.propiex.com*

Sara Lois Siegel
Representaciones Monterrey S.A.
Ave. Reforma 10-00 Zona 9
Penthouse Edif. Condominio Reforma
Guatemala City 01009
Phone: 502.2334.5233 **Fax:** 502.2331.5214
Email: *slsiegel@intelnet.net.gt*
URL: *www.centralamericaninvest.com*

Agents in Honduras

Michael Cox
Roatan Brokers
Box 131
Coxen's Hole, Roatan
Phone: 504.403.8200
Email: *mcox2000@pacbell.net*
URL: *www.roatanbrokers.com*

Gustavo Ralph Heinemann Nathusius
Heinemann Bienes Raices
Blvd Moraza, Edificio Bemac No. 2036
Local A 2
Tegucigalpa
Phone: 504.239.0799 **Fax:** 504.235.6263
Email: *heinemann_br@cablecolor.hn*

Roberto Houghton
Terrenos y Constructions S. de R.L. Tecon
S. de R.L.
Col. La Esperanza, Final Blvd Morazan
No. 4802
Tegucigalpa
Phone: 504.236.7495 **Fax:** 504.221.2156
Email: mtecon@hondutel.hn

Lawrence Schlesser
Roatan Real Estate
Main Street Mall, A5
Roatan, Bay Islands

Phone: 504.445.1612 **Fax:** 504.445.1767
Email: *larrys@roatan-realestate.com*
URL: *www.roatan-realestate.com*

Jurgen Timpel-Werther
Inversiones Multiples De Copan
Santa Rosa de Copan
Colonia Loma, Linda
Phone: 504.662.1204 **Fax:** 504.662.0521
Email: *info@copaninvest.com*
URL: *www.copaninvest.com*

Phil Weir
Roatan Life Real Estate
Anthony's Key Resort, Sandy Bay
Roatan, Bay Islands
Phone: 504.445.1965 **Fax:** 504.445.1965
Email: *philweir@roatanlife.com*
URL: *www.roatanlife.com*

Agents in Italy

Enrico Giuli
Enrico Giuli International Real Estate
Via Dante 10
Cerreto d'Esi (AN), ITALY 60043
Phone: 39.0732.678975 **Fax:** 39.0732.670406
Email: *info@enricogiuli.com*
URL: *www.enricogiuli.com*

Agents in Jamaica

Lorraine Levy-Finlason
Valerie Levy & Associates, Ltd.
134 Constant Spring Road, Suite 23
Kingston, Jamaica 8
Phone: 876.931.4471 **Fax:** 876.931.4445
Email: *lorraine@vlarealtors.com*
URL: *www.vlarealtors.com*

Agents in Mexico

Felipe Alvarez-Icaza Longoria
Grupo Define, S.A. de C.V.
Miguel Laurent No. 17, Piso 5
Desp. 502-503
Col. Del Valle Cd.
Mexico, D.F. 03100
Phone: 52.55.5559.1459
Fax: 52.55.5559.7518
Email: *fai@gdi-bienesraices.com*
URL: *www.gdi-bienesraices.com*

Enrique Angulo Marquez
Consultoria Y Gestoria Inmobiliaria
Colima Esq. Insurgentes No. 3800
Fracc. Suarez
La Paz, B.C.S. 23060
Phone: 52.612.125.1470
Fax: 52.612.125.1470
Email: *eangulo@prodigy.net.mx*

Pedro Arellano Arroyo
Arellano Corporation Group
Paseo Jacarandas 21-A
Fracc. Chula Vista
Chapala, Jalisco 45900
Phone: 52.376.766.3055
Fax: 52.376.766.3675
Email: *pedroarellano@laguna.com.mx*
URL: *www.pedroarellano.com*

Mario Aviles Barroso
Opcion Avil., S.A. de C.V.
Blvd. Manuel Avila Camacho 1994-502
San Lucas Tepetlacalco
Tlalnepantla, Edo. de Mexico, C.P. 54055
Phone: 52.55.5361.6061
Fax: 52.55.5398.7072
Email: *avil2000@hotmail.com*

Jaime Barrios Knight
Jaime Barrios Y Asociados, S.C.
Rio Amazonas No. 85 Desp. 202
Col. Cuauhtemoc
Mexico 06500
Phone: 52.55.5533.4533
Email: *jbarrios@prodigy.net.mx*

Federico Barton Guajardo
J.Q. Bienes Raices
Av. Del Prado No. 1 Fracc. Club Deportivo
Acapulco, Guerrero 39690
Phone: 52.744.484.4440
Fax: 52.744.484.4158
Email: *acapulco@jqrealestate.com.mx*
URL: *www.jqrealestate.com.mx*

Rene Billard Bayle
Cabo San Lucas Properties
Boulevard L. Cardenas
Colonia Centro
Cabo San Lucas, B.C.S. 23410
Phone: 52.624.143.3262

Fax: 52.624.143.3262
Email: *cslprops@cabonet.net.mx*
URL: *www.mexonline.com/cslprop1.htm*

Enrique Blazquez Guerrero
Grupo GB Construcciones & Inmobiliaria
S.A. De C.V.
Boulevard Adolfo Lopez Mateos #201
Lc.110
Santa Cruz Acatlan
Naucalpan 53150
Phone: 52.55.5363.4048
Fax: 52.55.5363.4029
Email: *grupogb@prodigy.net.mx*
URL: *www.grupogb.com*

Leon Borenstein Braun
Radisson Resort Acapulco
Av. Monterrey No. 15-1-B
Fracc. Lomas De Costa Azul
Acapulco, Gro 39850
Phone: 52.744.463.4259
Fax: 52.744.483.7591

Robert Brown
Baja Properties
89 Laguna Vista, Col. Campo Del Golf
San Jose Del Cabo, B.C.S. 23400
Phone: 52.624.142.1910
Fax: 52.624.142.0987
Email: *escaped5555@hotmail.com*
URL: *www.escapeproperties.com*

Enrique Cantu Garza Gallardo
CIMA Inmobiliaria
Belisario Dominguez 809
Planta Alta, Colonia Reforma
Oaxaca 68050
Phone: 52.951.502.5072
Fax: 52.951.503.0504
Email: *ventas@cimainmobiliaria.com*
URL: *www.cimainmobiliaria.com*

Duane Christie
Century 21 Mexico
2345 Paseo De La Reforma
Mexico, D.F. 11930
Phone: 52.55.5251.6700
Fax: 52.55.5251.6710
Email: *irfcsb@aol.com*
URL: *www.century21mexico.com*

Gloria Cruz Vazquez
Tierra Cruz Bienes Raices
Guerrero 3320
Nuevo Laredo, Tamaulipas 88270
Phone: 52.867.714.7985
Email: *gloriatierracruz@hotmail.com*

Manuel De La Torre
Alianza Realty, S.C.
Insurgentes Queretanos #88-1
Col. San Francisquito
Queretaro 76040
Phone: 52.442.213.8811
Fax: 52.442.223.6219
Email: *alianzarealty@televicable.net.mx*

Debra Dobson
Prudential California Realty
Cabo Gold Division
Matamors Int. Posada el Marlin
Cabo San Lucas, B.C.S. 23410
Phone: 52.624.104.3226
Fax: 52.624.143.6432
Email: *debra@prucabogold.com*
URL: *www.prucabogold.com*

Ted Downward
Century 21 Paradise Properties
Km. 4.5 Carretera Peninsula CSL AL SJC
Cabo San Lucas, B.C. S. 23450
Phone: 52.624.143.1101
Fax: 52.624.143.1008
Email: *paradise1@paradiseproperty.com*
URL: *www.paradiseproperty.com*

Victor Ivan Ebergenyi
Costa Realty S.A. de C.V.
Kukulcan Plaza, Loc. 408-A Zona Hotelera
Cancun 77500
Phone: 52.998.885.1551
Fax: 52.998.885.1551
Email: *iebereganyi@costarealty.com.mx*
URL: *www.cancunrealty.com*

Marco Ehrenberg
Ehrenberg & Associates/Pisces Real Estate
Madero Esq. Blvd. Marina, #1
P.O. Box 137
Los Cabos, B.C.S. 23410
Phone: 52.624.1431588
Fax: 52.624.1436612
Email: *marco@piscesrealestate.com*
URL: *www.piscesrealestate.com*

Alejandro Erhard Lozano
RE/MAX Py V
Carretera Nacional Km. 268
Colonia El Encino
Monterey, N.L. 64986
Phone: 181.8317.8283
Fax: 181.8317.8286
Email: *aerhard@remax-pyv.com*
URL: *www.remax-pyv.com*

Joan Feinstein
Coldwell Banker Riveras
145 Camino De La Plaza
Cabo San Lucas, B.C.S. 23410
Phone: 52.624.143.0202
Fax: 52.624.143.1348
Email: *feinstein.joanie@cbriveras.com*
URL: *www.pedregal.com*

Roberto Flores Fernandez
Promociones Mercadeo y Servicios
S.A. De C.V.
Circuito Jardin No. 7
Fracc. Alamos 3rd Seccion
Queretaro 76160
Phone: 52.442.212.8077
Fax: 52.442.212.6224
Email: *promessa@infosel.net.mx*
URL: *www.promessa.com.mx*

Maria Antonia Flores Morales
Grupo Inmobiliaria Vincent S.A. de C.V.
Abasolo #20-1, Col. Miguel Hidalgo
Tlalnepantla 54060
Phone: 52.55.5365.6046
Fax: 52.55.5365.5995
Email: *vincentt@avantel.net*

Wayne Franklin
Tropicasa Realty
Pulpito 145-A, Col. Emiliano Zapata
Puerto Vallarta, Jalisco 48380
Phone: 52.322.222.6505
Fax: 52.322.222.2555
Email: *franklin@tropicasa.com*
URL: *www.tropicasa.com*

Maria Del Carmen Galindo Rodriguez
Zuksa Bienes Raices
Blvd. Lomas Campestre No. 1167
Fracc. Lomas de Agua Caliente
Tijuana, B.C.S. 22440

Phone: 664.621.1113 Fax: 664.621.1113
Email: *zuksa@telnor.net*
URL: *www.zuksa.com.mx*

Aldo Jose Garces Flores
Pancho's Villas Real Estate
Lazaro Cardenas 295
Col. E. Zapata, Puerto Vallarta
Jalisco, C.P. 48380
Phone: 52.322.223.0569
Fax: 52.322.223.0570
Email: *aldo@panchosvillas.com*
URL: *www.panchosvillas.com*

Maria De Jesus Garcia Juarez
Data Habitat Bienes Raices
Bugambilia 303, Local 13
Bahias De Huatulco, Oaxaca 70989
Phone: 52.958.587.0218
Fax: 52.958.587.0875
Email: *datahabitat@yahoo.com.mx*
URL: *www.datahabitat.com.mx*

Maria Barbara Gaxoet Bravo
C21 Roriz y Cia
Cda. de Libra 781-1
Fracc. Jardines de Satelite
Naucalpan, Edo. de Mexico, C.P. 53119
Phone: 52.55.5343.4293
Fax: 52.55.5343.8131
Email: *bgaxoet@prodigy.net.mx*

Paul Geisler
Dream Homes of Cabo S.A. de C.V.
B-1, Blvd. Mijares Es. Manuel Doblado
San Jose Del Cabo, B.C.S. 23401
Phone: 800.403.6597
Fax: 52.624.142.6343
Email: *pgeisler@prodigy.net.mx*
URL: *www.dreamhomesofcabo.com*

James Gladgo
Century 21 Paradise Properties
Km. 4.5 Carretera Peninsula CSL AL SJC
Cabo San Lucas, B.C.S. 23450
Phone: 52.624.143.1110
Fax: 52.624.143.1008
Email: *jim@paradiseproperty.com*
URL: *www.century21baja.com*

Vicente Gonzalez
Century 21 Maya Real
Calle 19 No. 111 Altos Monte Cristo
Merida, Yucatan 97133
Phone: 52.999.948.0900
Fax: 52.333.948.0900
Email: *vgonzalez@mayareal.com*
URL: *www.mayareal.com*

Michael Green
Tropicasa Realty
Pulpito 145-A at Olas Altas
Puerto Vallarta, Jalisco 48380
Phone: 52.322.222.6505
Fax: 52.322.222.2555
Email: *michael@tropicasa.com*
URL: *www.tropicasa.com*

Enrique Alfonso Guadiana Machado
Promotora Azteca
Av. Profa. Carmen Rivera 51-B
Col. Insurgentes Oeste
Mexicali, Baja California 21280
Phone: 52.686.566.2133
Fax: 52.686.566.1382
Email: *eguadiana@inmobiliariamexicali.com*
URL: *www.inmobiliariamexicali.com*

Teresa Gutierrez Valles
Caribbean Realty
Centro Comercial Marina Local 4 "A"
Edificio D
Puerto Aventuras, Quintana Roo 77750
Phone: 52.984.873.5098
Fax: 52.984.873.5158
Email: *rental@cancun.com.mx*
URL: *www.puertoaventurasrentals.com*

Manuel Hernandez Ontiveros
Hernandez Realty Group, S.A. de C.V.
Carr-Chapala-Ajijic #36-38
Ajijic (Chapala) Jalisco 45920
Phone: 52.376.766.2103
Fax: 52.376.766.2104
Email: *hrealtygroup@prodigy.net.mx*
URL: *www.hernandezrg.com*

Isaac Holoschutz
Zenix
Fco. Petrarca 223-1001
Col. Chapultepec Morales
Mexico, D.F. 11560

Phone: 52.55.255.4545
Fax: 52.55.255.3344
Email: *isaac@data.net.mx*
URL: *www.zenix.com.mx*

Beverly Hunt
Laguna Real Estate
#24 Carretera Ajijic-Chapala
Ajijic, Jalisco 45920
Phone: 52.376.766.1174
Fax: 52.376.766.1186
Email: *lagunarealty@prodigy.net.mx*
URL: *www.lagunamex.com*

Reyna Veronica Juarez Leon
Century 21 Terranova
Paseo Tabasco 411, Centro
Villahermosa, Tabasco 86000
Phone: 993.312.0628
Email: *verojuarez2002@hotmail.com*

Julie Kershner
Prudential California Realty/
Cabo Gold Division
27 Blvd. Mijares
Posada El Marlin
San Jose del Cabo, BCS 23400
Phone: 520.204.5450
Fax: 52.624.105.2668
Email: *julie@juliekershner.com*
URL: *www.juliekershner.com*

Tere Kimball
Prudential California Realty/
Vallarta Division
Blvd. Francisco Medina Ascencio Km. 3.5
Zona Hotelera
Puerto Vallarta, Jalisco 48300
Phone: 52.322.294.1612
Fax: 52.322.293.3987
Email: *tere.kimball@prurealtypv.com*

Adolfo Kunz Bolanos
Kunz Y Asociados S.A.
Paseo De La Reforma 403-1001
Colonia Cuauhtemoc
Mexico, D.F. 06500
Phone: 52.55.5553.5575
Fax: 52.55.5207.6427
Email: *kasa@kunz.com.mx*
URL: *www.kunz.com.mx*

Rogelio Ledesma Torres
Promociones Mercadeo y Servicios
S.A. de C.V.
Circuito Jardin #7, Alamos 3 Seccion
Queretaro 76160
Phone: 52.442.212.8077
Fax: 52.442.212.6224
Email: *rledesma@promesa.com.mx*
URL: *www.promesa.com.mx*

Reyna Leon-Aguilera
Century 21 Terranova S.A. de C.V.
Paseo Tabasco #411
Villa Hermosa, Tabasco
Phone: 52.933.312.0628
Fax: 52.933.311.0526
Email: *c21terranova@prodigy.net.mx*

Jose de Jesus Lopez Soto
Habitat Desarrollos, S.A. de C.V.
Venustiano Carranza 122-5
Aguascalientes 20000
Phone: 52.449.915.2257
Fax: 52.449.915.7877
Email: *jjlopezsoto@aol.com*

Adrian Loustaunau Pellat
Loustaunau & Asociados
Zacatecas #47 L-1
Esquina Conception I.. De Soria
Hermosillo, Sonora 83000
Phone: 52.662.215.2224
Fax: 52.662.215.2224
Email: *adrian@loustaunauyasociados.com*
URL: *www.loustaunauyasociados.com*

Donna Machovec
Tropicasa Realty
Pulpito 145-A at Olas Altas
Puerto Vallarta, Jalisco 48380
Phone: 52.322.222.6505
Fax: 52.322.222.2555
Email: *donna@tropicasa.com*
URL: *www.tropicasa.com*

Lynda MacMahon
Manager, International Realty
A Division of The Hernandez Realty Group
Colon #2 A
Ajijic, Jalisco 45920
Phone: 52.376.766.5122
Fax: 52.376.766.4909

Email: *lynda@mexicodreamhome.com*
URL: *www.mexicodreamhome.com*

Luis Madariaga
Real Solutions S.C.
Paseo de la Reforma #115-1003
Paseo de las Lomas
Mexico, D.F. 01330
Phone: 52.55.5442.9999
Fax: 52.55.5442.9999
Email: *gante@prodigy.net.mx*

Luis Horacio Madariaga Audiffred
Century 21 Wallsten
Ave. Constituyentes 345, Piso 6
Mexico 11830
Phone: 52.55.5276.0200
Fax: 52.55.5272.3600
Email: *luis_madariaga@terra.com.mx*

Irma Patricia Martinez Nieblas
Bahia Kino Bienes Real Estate
Ave. Mar de Cortez y
Calle Topolobampo 3201
Bahia Kino, Sonora 83348
Phone: 662.242.0037 Fax: 662.242.0055
Email: *kinobayrealestate@prodigy.net.mx*
URL: *www.kinobayrealestate.com.mx*

Linda Miller
Property Solutions Real Estate Sales
Plaza Nautica Condominiums
Cabo San Lucas, B.C.S. 23451
Phone: 52.624.143.1688
Fax: 52.624.143.1788
Email: *cabolinda@cabotel.com.mx*
URL: *www.propertysol.com*

Kyoshi Monge Kotake
Long Realty Bienes Raices
S. de R.L. de C.V.
Blvd. Colosio No. 437-A, Villa Satelite
Hermosillo, Sonora 83280
Phone: 52.662.217.3234
Fax: 52.662.217.3234
Email: *yoshi@longrealty.com*
URL: *www.longrealty.com*

Luis Moreno Valencia
Century 21 Cupatitzio
Roma 1852, Int. 5, esq. Paseo Gral.
Lazaro Cardenas
Col. Jardines del Cupatitzio

Uruapan, Michoacan 60080
Phone: 52.452.523.0321
Fax: 52.452.523.0321
Email: *cnt21upn@prodigy.net.mx*

Linda Neil
The Settlement Company
Salvatierra No.120
La Paz, B.C.S. 23000
Phone: 52.612.123.5056
Fax: 52.612.123.5242
Email: *linda.neil@settlement-co.com*
URL: *www.settlement-co.com*

Flemming Nielsen
Snell Real Estate
Punta Ballena Resort
San Jose Del Cabo, B.C.S. 23400
Phone: 52.624.145.8226
Fax: 52.624.145.8227
Email: *flemming@snellrealestate.com*
URL: *www.snellrealestate.com*

Mark Nieman
Inmobiliaria Suenos del Sol, S.A. de C.V.
Rosario Morales #201, Esq. Zaragoza
Plaza San Marcos L-5, Col. Maranhon
Cabo San Lucas, B.C.S. 23410
Phone: 52.624.143.2797
Fax: 52.624.143.2797
Email: *cabosol@cabonet.net.mx*

Jaime Niembro Montemayor
Ajijic Real Estate, S.C.
Calle Morelos #4
Ajijic, Jalisco 45920
Phone: 52.376.766.2077
Fax: 52.376.766.2331
Email: *jaime@ajijic.com*
URL: *www.ajijic.com*

Hector Obregon Serrano
Century 21 Obregon & Obregon
Paseo del Moral No. 431
Col. Jardines del Moral
Leon, Guanajuato 37160
Phone: 52.477.773.3477
Fax: 52.477.773.3478
Email: *hmobregon@aol.com*
URL: *www.century21obregon.com*

Luis Ornelas Reyes
International Realty Group
Blvd. Kukulcan Km. 7

Plaza La Hacienda, Local 34/Zona Hotelera
Cancun, Quintana Roo 77500
Phone: 52.998.883.0028
Fax: 52.998.883.0029
Email: *luisornelas@internationalrealtygroup.com*
URL: *www.internationalrealtygroup.com*

Bryan Pacholski
Snell Real Estate
Palmilla Resort Sales
Carretera Transpeninsular Km. 27.5
San Jose Del Cabo, B.C.S. 23400
Phone: 52.624.144.5200
Fax: 52.624.144.5201
Email: *bryan@snellrealestate.com*
URL: *www.snellrealestate.com*

Cesar Paredes
Global Commercial &
Investment Real Estate, Corporation
De Mexico, S.A. De C.V. TCN Worldwide
Rio Tiber 224-A, Col. Del Valle
Garza, Garcia, NL 66220
Phone: 52.818.400.0660
Fax: 52.818.115.6770
Email: *cparedes@att.net.mx*
URL: *www.globalcom-inv.com*

Stanley Patenaude
P.O. Box 368
Cabo San Lucas, B.C.S. 23450
Phone: 52.624.143.0852
Fax: 52.624.143.0852
Email: *stanley@cabotel.com.mx*

Rodolfo Pena Rosas
Grupo Pecasa – Bienes Raices
20 De Noviembre 1329
Nuevo Laredo, Tamaulipas 88000
Phone: 52.867.713.6600
Fax: 52.867.712.7511
Email: *grupopecasa62@msn.com*

Isaac Podbilewicz Tenenbaum
Libra Administraciones y Promociones
S.A. de C.V.
Hacienda de Cristo #4 Echegaray
Naucalpan 53330
Phone: 52.555.360.3455
Fax: 52.555.363.2239
Email: *isaac@librabienesraices.com*

Lelia Riggs
Hernandez Realty Group

Carr. Chapala Ajijic #36-38
Ajijic, Jalisco 45920
Phone: 52.376.766.2103
Fax: 52.376.766.2104
Email: *lriggs@prodigy.net.mx*
URL: *www.hernandezrg.com*

Salvador Rodriguez Lopez
Rodriguez Llerenas y Asociados, S.C.
Homero No. 1933, 5 Piso Col.
Los Morales, Mexico 11510
Phone: 52.555.557.9867
Fax: 52.555.557.9813
Email: *rodriguezlleren@infosel.net.mx*

Raul Martin Salamanca Riba
Sayro Bienes Raices, S.A. de C.V.
Otatal 15
Col. Carrizal
Santiago de Queretaro 76030
Phone: 442.215.0102 **Fax:** 442.215.0102
Email: *sayrobr@prodigy.net.mx*
URL: *www.sayro.com.mx*

Michael Schaible
Baja Properties
Plaza Coral Baja
San Jose Del Cabo, B.C.S. 23400
Phone: 52.624.142.0988
Fax: 52.624.142.0987
Email: *broker@bajaproperties.com*
URL: *www.bajaproperties.com*

Judi Shaw
RE/MAX Playa del Carmen
Ave. 10 con Calle 16, Scotiabank Plaza
Playa del Carmen, Q.Roo 77710
Phone: 604.628.7247 **Fax:** 408.547.9767
Email: *judi@resorts-real-estate.com*
URL: *www.resorts-real-estate.com*

Fay Sloane
El Grupo Bienes Raices
Heroe De Nacozari #121
Bucerias, Nayarit 63732
Phone: 52.329.298.1212
Fax: 52.329.298.1213
Email: *fbsloane@move2mexico.com*
URL: *www.move2mexico.com*

Tad Snell
Snell Real Estate
Palmilla Resort Sales

Carretera Transpeninsular Km. 27.5
San Jose Del Cabo, B.C.S. 23400
Phone: 52.624.151.5201
Fax: 52.624.145.8213
Email: *tad@snellrealestate.com*
URL: *www.snellrealestate.com*

Chris Snell
Snell Real Estate
Villas Del Mar Sales,
Carretera Transpeninsular Km 27.5
San Jose Del Cabo, B.C.S. 23400
Phone: 52.624.142.4873
Fax: 52.624.142.4874
Email: *snell@snellrealestate.com*
URL: *www.snellrealestate.com*

Wendy Straumann-Knapp
W.F.R. Cape S de RL de CV
Carretera Transpeninsular Km. 19.5
San Jose Del Cabo, B.C.S.
Phone: 52.624.144.0288
Fax: 52.624.144.0172
Email: *wendy@rionda-knapp.com*
URL: *www.rionda-knapp.com*

Tim Vanni
Chilson & Associates International Real
Estate Co.
285 Camino de La Plaza, Space 2
Cabo San Lucas, B.C.S. 23410
Phone: 52.624.143.1778
Fax: 52.624.143.1779
Email: *tim@chilsoninternational.com*
URL: *www.chilsoninternational.com*

Jay West
Cabo Realty
Local #3
Calle De La Marina y
Camino Viejo San Jose
Cabo San Lucas, B.C.S. 23410
Phone: 206.347.3325 Fax: 619.819.5500
Email: *west@caborealty.com*
URL: *www.caborealty.com*

M. Thomas Yablonsky
Exotic Realty S.A. de C.V.
Las Palmas 1, Local 2, Marina Vallarta
Puerto Vallarta, Jalisco 48354
Phone: 52.322.221.2377
Fax: 52.322.221.0079

Email: *exoticrealty@hotmail.com*
URL: *www.remaxexoticrealty.com*

Agents in the Netherlands

Alexander Roos
Van Eijsden, Ter Borgh & Roos B.V.
Sloterkade 84
Amsterdam, Netherlands 1058 HJ
Phone: 31.2061.78858
Fax: 31.2061.76598
Email: *roos@ebr.nl*
URL: *www.ebr.nl*

Agents in Nicaragua

Maya Arguello
Global Real Estate
Rotonola Ruben Dario
1C Sur 20 varas abajo
Managua
Phone: 505.270.2413 Fax: 505.278.2108
Email: *globalre@turbonett.com.ni*
URL: *www.globalrealestate-ni.com*

Jocelyn Camaja
Frontier Properties S.A
UK: +44 (0) 207 1 93 83 43
European cell: +33 (0) 6 70 05 19 89
Nicaragua cell: +505 897 – 1107
Email: *jac@frontierpropertysales.com*
URL: *www.frontierpropertysales.com*

Gail Geerling
Arenas Bay Town
Edificio MovilPhone
Managua, Nicaragua
Phone 1: 505.278.6888
Phone 2: 505.270.3002
Fax: 505.278.8256
Email: *gailgeerling@yahoo.com*

Yelba Carvajal Jiron
Enterprise Real Estate
Colonial Los Robles #154
Managua
Phone: 505.270.2612 Fax: 505.278.6643
Email: *presidencia@enterpriserealestate.com*
URL: *www.enterpriserealestate.com*

Vamia Delgado Obregon
Financiera E Inversiones S.A. Division
Bienes y Raices

Hotel Crowne Plaza, 1C. Este
1/2 C. Norte
Managua
Phone: 505.254.5375 **Fax:** 505.254.5376
Email: *fisavamia@hotmail.com*

Aurora Gurdian de Lacayo
Aurora Bienes Raices
La Estancia de Sto. Domingo #28
Managua
Phone: 505.276.2506 **Fax:** 505.276.2508
Email: *auroralacayo@yahoo.com*
URL: *www.aurorabienesraices.com*

Maria Lacayo Fonseca
Real Estate Center (REC)
Colonial Los Robles III Etada No. 13
Managua
Phone: 505.278.3810 **Fax:** 505.278.3811
Email: *info@realestatenica.com*
URL: *www.realestatenica.com*

Julio Lacayo Gurdian
Aurora Beachfront Realty
Texaco 300 Feet towards the Water
San Juan del Sur, Rivas
Phone: 505.884.7141 **Fax:** 505.276.2508
Email: *jclacayo@gmail.com*
URL: *www.aurorabeachfront.com*

Nestor Perez Ubilla
Financiero E Inversiones S.A. Division
Bienes y Raices
Hotel Crowne Plaza, 1C. Este, 1/2 C. Norte
Managua
Phone: 505.254.5375 **Fax:** 505.254.5376
Email: *gofisa@cablenet.com.ni*

Abraham Ruiz
Blandon Bienes Raices
Colonial Los Robles 7 Etapa, #214
Managua
Phone: 505.278.5306 **Fax:** 505.277.0297
Email: *blandonbienesraices501@hotmail.com*

Rosario Siero de Tefel
Territorio Bienes Raices, S.A.
Villa Fontana Norte, atras de la Casa #30
Managua
Phone: 505.270.5728 **Fax:** 505.278.3024
Email: *etefel@turbonett.com.ni*
URL: *www.territoriorealestate.com.ni*

Manuel Sotelo Bolanos
Sotelo y Novoa Bienes Raices
Pali Altamira 2 1/2 Cuadra Abajo #437
Managua
Phone: 505.277.3401 **Fax:** 505.278.2790
Email: *info@soleoynovoa.com*
URL: *www.soteloynovoa.com*

Alvaro Sacasa
Portonica Real Estate
Phone: 505.265.8435
Cell: 505.841.0917
Email: *alvarosacasa@portonica.com*
URL: *www.portonica.com*

Rosario Tefel
Territorio Bienes Raices
Villa Fontana Norte Casa #30 detras
Managua
Phone: 505.270.5728 **Fax:** 505.278.3024
Email: *etp@cablenet.com.ni*
URL: *www.territoriorealestate.com*

Agents in Panama

Jose Boyd
Boyd's Realty
San Francisco, Calle 74
Ave. 3B Sur, No. 90
Panama City
Phone: 507.270.4753 **Fax:** 507.270.4752
Email: *boydreal@investinpanama.net*
URL: *www.investinpanama.net*

Felix Carles
Bienes Raices y Seguros Carles, S.A.
P.O. Box 2728
Panama
Phone: 507.226.1120 **Fax:** 507.226.6871
Email: *fcarles@carlesrealtors.com*

Ivan Carlucci
Inversiones Natasha S.A.
Panama
Phone: 507.300.1111 **Fax:** 507.223.3993
Email: *icarlucci@inversionesnatasha.com*
URL: *www.inversionesnatasha.com*

Jose Angel Delvalle
SUCASA
Via Espana #50 Edf. Sucasa
Panama

Phone: 507.302.5433 Fax: 507.263.1260
Email: *jadu@unesa.com*
URL: *www.gruposucasa.com*

Frank Morrice Arias
Century 21 Semusa Realty
Plaza Semusa, 74th Street, San Francisco
Panama, Paitilla 55-0883
Phone: 507.270.6050 Fax: 507.270.6051
Email: *fmorricea@semusarealty.com*
URL: *www.semusarealty.com*

Agents in Puerto Rico

Omayra Borges Gomez
Reality Realty
Ave. Troche, V-12
Caguas, PR 00725
Phone: 787.745.8777 Fax: 787.745.4593
Email: *borgeso@realityrealtypr.com*
URL: *www.realityrealtypr.com*

Ivan Zavala Steidel
Reality Realty
P.O. Box 7529
Avenida Troche V-12
Caguas, PR 00725
Phone: 787.745.8777 Fax: 787.745.4593
Email: *realty@caribe.net*
URL: *www.realityrealtypr.com*

Maria Oquendo
Maria Judith Oquendo
P.O. Box 9065262
San Juan, PR 00906
Phone: 787.449.1393 Fax: 787.282.7011
Email: *mjoa@coqui.net*
URL: *www.mjoyasociados.com*

Miguel Aran
Miguel Aran Real Estate
Ave. Ponce de Leon 1605
Cond. San Martin, Suite 106
Santurce, PR 00908
Phone: 787.724.1559 Fax: 787.724.1558
Email: *realtor@coqui.net*

Juan Charles
Juan Charles & Associates
1606 Ponce de Leon Avenue, Suite 700
Bogoricin Building
Santurce, PR 00908
Phone: 787.977.0403 Fax: 787.724.6780

Email: *charless@caribe.net*
URL: *www.juancharles.com*

Rodolfo Del Toro
Rodolfo Del Toro & Associates
Paseo San Juan C-10
Catedral Street
San Juan, PR 00926
Phone: 787.748.0427 Fax: 787.761.9165
Email: *rdeltorocips@prtc.net*

Gianna Mendez Zamora
Home Team
PMB 417 Avenida De Diego 89, Suite 105
San Juan, PR 00927
Phone: 787.790.5186 Fax: 787.790.5186
Email: *giameza@coqui.net*
URL: *www.hometeampr.com*

Pedro Gonzalez-Gorgas
RELOxpress
P.O. Box 363501
San Juan, PR 00936-3501
Phone: 787.717.6543 Fax: 787.701.8045
Email: *pgonzalez@reloxpress.com*
URL: *www.reloxpress.com*

Ligia Hernandez
RELOxpress
P.O. Box 363501
San Juan, PR 00936-3501
Phone: 787.781.8020 Fax: 787.781.8090
Email: *lhernandez@reloxpress.com*
URL: *www.reloxpress.com*

Adalgisa Gambedotti
TIRI Real Estate
Camino Alejandro #9
Guaynabo, PR 00969
Phone: 787.789.0000 Fax: 787.789.8000
Email: *tiri@coqui.net*
URL: *www.tiri.com*

Carmen Malaga
Piramide Real Estate Brokers
Urb. Corrientes, CO-25 Quebrada Grande
Trujillo Alto, PR 00976
Phone: 787.283.7573 Fax: 787.292.0092
Email: *carmen@piramide.com*
URL: *www.piramide.com*

Janice Ramos
Angelus Real Estate

Montecillo Court, Apt. 3408
Trujillo Alto, PR 00976
Phone: 787.435.7437 **Fax:** 787.293.2469
Email: *angelus@prw.net*
URL: *www.angelusrealestate.com*

Rolando Acosta
Universal Real Estate
Calle 519 Bloque 184, #30, Villa Carolina
Carolina, PR 00985
Phone: 787.647.0179 **Fax:** 787.276.2451
Email: *rolandoacosta@centennialpr.net*
URL: *www.universalrealestate.com*

Aida Caraballo
Aida M. Caraballo Real Estate
P.O. Box 9384
Carolina, PR 00988
Phone: 787.317.1355 **Fax:** 787.762.8010
Email: *aidamcaraballorealty54@yahoo.com*

Agents in the United Kingdom

Humphrey Harrison
Harrison & Cartier, Ltd.

39 Flower Lane
London NW7 2JN
Phone: 44.208.959.6588
Fax: 44.208.959.7994
Email: *humphrey@harrisonandcartier.com*
URL: *www.harrisonandcartier.com*

Bill Jackson
Bill Jackson International Ltd.
45 Bridge Street
Hereford, Herefordshire HR4 9DG
Phone: 44.143.234.4779
Fax: 44.143.235.2229
Email: *billjackson@billjacksoninternational.com*
URL: *www.billjacksoninternational.com*

Michelle Wilmot
Jackson International Ltd.
45 Bridge Street
Hereford, Herefordshire HR4 9DG
Phone: 44.143.234.4779
Fax: 44.143.235.2229
Email: *billjackson@billjacksoninternational.com*
URL: *www.billjacksoninternational.com*

Central America Agents in the United States

Alabama

Jerry Keehn
RE/MAX by the Bay
23800 US Hwy. 98
Fairhope, AL 36532
Phone: 251.928.7474 **Fax:** 251.928.7438
Email: *hlbolton@bellsouth.net*
URL: *www.jerrykeehn.com*

Arizona

Alice Martin
Arizona Association of REALTORS®
255 E. Osborn, Suite 200
Phoenix, AZ 85012-2358
Phone: 602.248.7787 **Fax:** 602.351.2474
Email: *alicemartin@aaronline.com*
URL: *www.aaronline.com*

William Powers
Realty Executives International, Inc.
2398 East Camelback Road, Suite 900
Phoenix, AZ 85016
Phone: 800.252.3366 **Fax:** 602.224.5542
Email: *billpowers@realtyexecutives.com*

Donna Lewis
Lake Pleasant Regional Association
of REALTORS®, Inc.
10451 Palmeras Drive, Suite 203 North
Sun City, AZ 85373-2013
Phone: 623.974.0555 **Fax:** 623.974.3789
Email: *dalewis8@aol.com*
URL: *www.lprar.com*

Claire Jean Prager
Coldwell Banker Residential Brokerage
2890 E. Skyline Drive, Suite 250
Tucson, AZ 85718

Phone: 800.973.7827 Fax: 520.529.1880
Email: *claire@claireprager.com*
URL: *www.claireprager.com*

Camille Rivas-Rutherford
Coldwell Banker Residential Brokerage
2890 E. Skyline Drive, Suite 250
Tucson, AZ 85718
Phone: 520.250.5192 Fax: 520.577.5417
Email: *camillrivruth@aol.com*
URL: *www.camillerivasrutherford.com*

Roy Grimm
Buyer Brokers Realty of Sedona
1370 W. Hwy 89A
The Old Market Place, Suite 1
Sedona, AZ 86336
Phone: 800.282.2959 Fax: 928.282.2858
Email: *Roy@RoyGrimm.com*
URL: *www.SedonaRealEstate.com*

Diane Jackson
The Jacksons International Real Estate
20 Rockridge Drive
Sedona, AZ 86336-4774
Phone: 928.821.2237 Fax: 928.203.4677
Email: *diane@arizonabuyers.com*
URL: *www.arizonabuyers.com*

Luminous J
Service First Realty, LLC
2085 Contractors Road, Suite 1
Sedona, AZ 86339
Phone: 928.274.2265 Fax: 928.204.1662
Email: *luminousone@esedona.net*
URL: *www.sedonalandandhomes.com*

Arkansas

Harold Bagwell
Coldwell Banker Ozark Real
Estate Company Branch
2303 Old Country Road
P.O. Box 451
Pocahontas, AR 72455
Phone: 870.892.7653 Fax: 870.892.7651
Email: *harold.bagwell@coldwellbanker.com*
URL: *www.coldwellbanker.com/ozark*

California

Carlos Saborio
RE/MAX Beverly Hills
9454 Wilshire Blvd, Suite 150
Beverly Hills, CA 90212

Phone: 310.205.0905 Fax: 310.205.0070
Email: *carlossaborio@yahoo.com*
URL: *www.carlossaborio.net*

Steve Goddard
RE/MAX Beach Cities Realty
400 S. Sepulveda Blvd, Ste 100
Manhattan Beach, CA 90266
Phone: 800.861.3333 Fax: 310.376.6522
Email: *steve@stevegoddard.com*
URL: *www.stevegoddard.com*

Yolanda Velasco
The Real Estate Group
P.O. Box 175
Manhattan Beach, CA 90266
Phone: 310.376.4573 Fax: 310.376.7231
Email: *yvelasco777@yahoo.com*

Jason Buck
Coldwell Banker
68 Malaga Cove Plaza
Palos Verdes Estates, CA 90274
Phone: 310.265.4268 Fax: 310.373.2340
Email: *jasonbuck@datafrrame.net*
URL: *www.jasonbuck.com*

Leon Katz
Commercial Brokers, Inc.
3510 Torrance Blvd, Suite 220
Torrance, CA 90503
Phone: 310.678.6510 Fax: 310.868.2515
Email: *leon@cbire.com*
URL: *www.cbire.com*

Gloria Godet
Century 21 Exclusive REALTORS®
22829 Hawthorne Blvd.
Torrance, CA 90505-3615
Phone: 310.373.5252 Fax: 310.791.1921
Email: *realtyrus@att.net*
URL: *www.getlahomes.com*

Susan Barlin
Barlin & Associates Realty
860 E. Carson Street #113
Carson, CA 90745
Phone: 310.507.8888 Fax: 310.507.8887
Email: *barlins@prodigy.net*
URL: *www.barlinrealty.net*

Trinidad Lim
RE/MAX Capital Center
1242 San Fernando Road

San Fernando, CA 91340
Phone: 818.838.0635 Fax: 818.838.0686
Email: *trinidadlim@trinidadlim.com*
URL: *www.trinidadlim.com*

Jim Summers
Coldwell Banker – Greater Valleys
10324 Balboa Boulevard
Granada Hills, CA 91344
Phone: 818.360.3430 Fax: 818.366.7484
Email: *jimsummers@realtor.com*
URL: *www.jimsummers.com*

Rose Falocco
RE/MAX Estates
706 Lindero Canyon Blvd, Suite 746
Agoura Hills, CA 91377
Phone: 805.402.3395 Fax: 805.579.9350
Email: *rose@rose4realestate.com*
URL: *www.rose4realestate.com*

Nadia Haddada
Coldwell Banker Residential
930 Prospect Street
La Jolla, CA 92037
Phone: 858.232.7867 Fax: 858.459.1375
Email: *nadia_haddada@yahoo.com*
URL: *www.condohomesrealestate.com*

Griselda Mendoza Cadman
Interglobal Independence
4140 Oceanside Blvd, Suite 159-407
Oceanside, CA 92056
Phone: 760.940.0423 Fax: 760.414.1910
Email: *griselda@interglobalhomes.com*
URL: *www.interglobalhomes.com*

Robert Warburton
The Warburton Co. International Network
Emerald Plaza Center
402 West Broadway, Suite 400
San Diego, CA 92101
Phone: 530.265.4973 Fax: 619.595.3150
Email: *warburton@warburtoncompany.com*
URL: *www.warburtoncompany.com*

Ralph Haverkate
Tarbell REALTORS®
74-245 Highway 111, Suite 100
Palm Desert, CA 92260
Phone: 760.902.0512 Fax: 775.855.2323
Email: *ralph@rhaverkate.com*
URL: *www.rhaverkate.com*

Gregory Golden
Prudential California Realty
71949 Highway 111
Rancho Mirage, CA 92270
Phone: 760.275.3612 Fax: 435.417.2800
Email: *greg@GregoryGolden.com*
URL: *www.GregoryGolden.com*

Nurcys Grimes
Coldwell Banker Residential Real Estate
6833 Quail Hill Parkway
Irvine, CA 92603
Phone: 949.552.2000 Fax: 949.559.7173
Email: *ngrimes@coldwellbanker.com*
URL: *www.ngrimes.cbsocal.com*

Kostantinos Theodorou
KT Home Loans, Inc.
26501 Rancho Pkwy So., Suite 102
Lake Forest, CA 92630
Phone: 949.215.2879 Fax: 949.215.2869
Email: *Kosta@KTHomeLoans.net*
URL: *www.MortgageLoanGuy.com*

Terry Theodorou
Buy a Home in America, Inc.
26501 Rancho Pkwy So., Suite 102
Lake Forest, CA 92630
Phone: 949.215.2879 Fax: 949.215.2869
Email: *terry@buyahomeinamerica.com*
URL: *www.buyahomeinamerica.com*

Theodore Deuel
Deuel International Group, Inc.
24022 Calle De La Plata, Suite 400
Laguna Hills, CA 92653
Phone: 949.707.4999 Fax: 949.859.0617
Email: *tdeuel@deuelinternational.com*
URL: *www.deuelinternational.com*

Danielle Carlson
World Star Realty
1717-B West Orangewood Ave.
Orange, CA 92868
Phone: 714.978.9100 Fax: 714.978.9300
Email: *danielle@cdcre.com*
URL: www.cdcfinehomes.com

Lana Le Chabrier
Thor Trust
610 Anacapa Street
Santa Barbara, CA 93103
Phone: 805.966.5446 Fax: 805.966.3517
Email: *vesier@yahoo.com*

Linda Dorris
Coldwell Banker
Gay Dales, Inc., REALTORS®
444 S. Main Street
Salinas, CA 93901
Phone: 831.424.0771 Fax: 831.424.1750
Email: *ldorris@coldwellbanker.com*
URL: *www.lindadorris.com*

Barbara Cooke
Pacific Rim Realty
4341 Rosina Court
Concord, CA 94518
Phone: 925.408.9488 Fax: 866.207.1930
Email: *brokerbarbara@gmail.com*
URL: *www.brokerbarbara.com*

Joan Mantecon
Coldwell Banker
36 Tiburon Boulevard
Mill Valley, CA 94941
Phone: 415.380.3995 Fax: 415.388.5084
Email: *joan@internationaldwellings.com*
URL: *www.internationaldwellings.com*

Gerardo Padilla
G.P. Real Estate, Inc.
50 Airport Parkway
San Jose, CA 95110
Phone: 408.437.7731 Fax: 408.528.7725
Email: *padillag@pacbell.net*

Juan Penalva
Coldwell Banker C & C Properties
5800 Fagan Drive
Redding, CA 96001
Phone: 530.244.1777 Fax: 530.221.5231
Email: *edp2000@charter.net*
URL: *www.barilocherealestate.com*

Colorado

Manfred Chemek
Manhelm International
12403 E. Amherst Circle
Aurora, CO 80014
Phone: 720.748.4040 Fax: 720.748.6530
Email: *mchemek@manhelm.com*
URL: *www.manhelm.com*

Omar Rocwa
Urban Echo Realty
3000 S. Jamaica Ct., Suite 250

Aurora, CO 80014
Phone: 303.570.5310 Fax: 303.755.0261
Email: *omar@urbanechorealty.com*
URL: *www.urbanechorealty.com*

Kay Corken
Marx Real Estate Corp.
20269 E. Smoky Hill Road, Suite B61
Centennial, CO 80015
Phone: 303.761.4006 Fax: 303.761.7334
Email: *kcorken920@aol.com*
URL: *www.kaycorken.com*

Leah Begalle
Prestige Real Estate Group
520 Zang Street, Suite 200
Broomfield, CO 80021
Phone: 303.268.0570 Fax: 303.280.1333
Email: *lbegalle@prestigerealtygroup.com*
URL: www.*thecathyandleahteam.com*

Nancy Mikoda
Prestige Real Estate Group
520 Zang Street, Suite 200
Broomfield, CO 80021
Phone: 888.887.7617 Fax: 303.280.1333
Email: *nancymikoda@qwest.net*
URL: www.*nancymikoda.com*

Jason Pavlovic
Prestige Real Estate Group
520 Zang Street, Suite 200
Broomfield, CO 80021
Phone: 303.268.0577 Fax: 303.280.1333
Email: *jpavlovic@prestigerealtygroup.com*
URL: *www.prestigerealtygroup.com*

Rise Staufer
RE/MAX Alliance
225 South Boulder Road
Louisville, CO 80027
Phone: 303.664.6519 Fax: 303.926.4055
Email: *rise@stauferteam.com*
URL: *www.stauferteam.com*

Richard Staufer
RE/MAX Alliance
225 South Boulder Road
Louisville, CO 80027
Phone: 303.550.1292 Fax: 303.926.4055
Email: *rick@stauferteam.com*
URL: *www.stauferteam.com*

Heidi Burose
Perry & Company
8000 E. Belleview Avenue, Suite B-20
Greenwood Village, CO 80111
Phone: 303.399.7777 **Fax:** 720.489.1823
Email: *heidi@heidiburose.com*
URL: *www.heidiburose.com*

Peggy Worthington
Prestige Real Estate Group, LLC
9200 E. Panorama Circle, Suite 140
Englewood, CO 80112
Phone: 303.799.9898 Fax: 303.721.8515
Email: *peggyworthington@msn.com*
URL: www.*peggyworthington.com*

Jennifer Elpers-Wells
Keller Williams Realty
10646 W. Walker Place
Littleton, CO 80127
Phone: 303.668.1208 **Fax:** 720.489.3908
Email: *jelperswells@yahoo.com*

Genie Bodson
Prestige Real Estate Group, LLC
1745 Shea Center Drive, Suite 100
Littleton, CO 80129
Phone: 303.346.4060 **Fax:** 303.268.0300
Email: *gbodson@prestigerealtygroup.com*
URL: *www.magic-genie.net*

Ingrid Glancy
RE/MAX Classic
345 Milwaukee Street
Denver, CO 80206
Phone: 800.571.5789 **Fax:** 303.320.4169
Email: *ingridg@denverhome.net*
URL: *www.denverhome.net*

Lance Chayet
Hanover Realty/Hanover Commercial
13095 West Cedar Drive, Suite 102
Lakewood, CO 80228
Phone: 303.399.9000 **Fax:** 303.763.5470
Email: *hanoverrealty@aol.com*
URL: *www.hanovercolorado.com*

Ilse Hemmer
Keller Williams Preferred Realty
1333 W. 120th Avenue, Suite 216
Westminster, CO 80234
Phone: 303.601.3930 **Fax:** 303.452.9620
Email: *ilsehemmer@kw.com*
URL: *www.ilsehemmer.com*

Joe Martinez
RE/MAX Northwest, Inc.
12000 Pecos Street, Suite 160
Denver, CO 80234
Phone: 303.255.4334 **Fax:** 303.255.4396
Email: *joe@denverhomesells.com*
URL: *www.denverhomesells.com*

Raymond Mallard
United Property Brokers, Inc.
3515 S. Tamarac Drive, Suite 100
Denver, CO 80237
Phone: 303.671.9311 **Fax:** 303.694.2520
Email: *upbi@aol.com*
URL: *www.unitedpropertybrokers.com*

Nancy Stocker
Mock Realty Company
825 S. Broadway
Boulder, CO 80305
Phone: 303.497.0627 **Fax:** 303.499.8425
Email: *nancystocker@mockrealty.com*
URL: *www.mockrealty.com*

Laura Kerl
Metro Brokers – Laura Kerl Real Estate
100 N. Main Street
Mail: 65 Fairview Blvd.
Breckenridge, CO 80424
Phone: 970.406.1212 **Fax:** 970.547.1878
Email: *laurakerl@topproducer.com*
URL: *www.laurakerl.com*

Pamela Boyd
Pamela Boyd Real Estate
P.O. Box 320
Dillon, CO 80435
Phone: 970.389.7450 **Fax:** 970.513.0588
Email: *captpamela@yahoo.com*
URL: *www.pamelaboydrealestate.com*

Ruth Krinke
Steamboat Real Estate, Inc.
P.O. Box 775247
635 Yampa Street
Steamboat Springs, CO 80477-5247
Phone: 970.879.5000 **Fax:** 970.879.5591
Email: *ruthk@amigo.net*
URL: *www.steamboatrealestate.com/ruth
krinke.shtml*

Dena Schlutz
Estate Professionals

9767 North 89th Street
Longmont, CO 80503
Phone: 303.588.7532 **Fax:** 303.772.2928
Email: *dschlutz@qwest.net*

Hilda Schlutz-Barrientos
RE/MAX of Longmont
2350 17th Avenue
Longmont, CO 80503
Phone: 303.588.7578 **Fax:** 303.774.7080
Email: *hildaschlutz@remax.net*

Jorgette Krsulic
Jorgette & Boris, REALTORS®
965 Pico Point
Colorado Springs, CO 80906
Phone: 719.227.7200 **Fax:** 719.227.7202
Email: *jorgette@realtor.com*
URL: *www.coloradocasa.com*

Liliane Rowe
ERA Shields Real Estate
5475 Tech Center Drive, Suite 300
Colorado Springs, CO 80919
Phone: 719.535.7349 **Fax:** 719.548.9357
Email: *lrowe@enashields.com*
URL: *www.rowepropertiesintl.com*

Dan Roda
RE/MAX Properties, Inc.
1740 Chapel Hills Drive
Colorado Springs, CO 80920
Phone: 719.388.2446 **Fax:** 719.466.7696
Email: *droda1547@msn.com*
URL: *www.danroda.com*

Elizabeth Donn
Americasitas Real Estate
P.O. Box 7793
Colorado Springs, CO 80933
Phone: 719.632.3666 **Fax:** 719.636.3666
Email: *elizabethdonn@msn.com*

Robbie Pepper
Jim Smith Realty
P.O. Box 3850
Pagosa Springs, CO 81147
Phone: 970.264.3200 **Fax:** 970.264.3220
Email: *robbie@frontier.net*
URL: *www.pagosarealty.com*

Lee Holfeltz
Coldwell Banker Massey Real Estate

Consultants
29919 U.S. Hwy 160
South Fork, CO 81154
Phone: 719.873.5131 **Fax:** 719.873.5380
Email: *lhol@amigo.net*
URL: *www.cash4cashflows/leeholfeltz*

Toni Wyrick
Wyrick Real Estate Resources, Inc.
718 E. Main Street, Suite A
Montrose, CO 81401
Phone: 970.252.0065 **Fax:** 970.252.0065
Email: *toniwyrick@msn.com*
URL: *www.toniwyrick.com*

Raymond Bowers
Peaks Real Estate/
Sotheby's International Realty
615 W. Pacific
P.O. Box 1653
Telluride, CO 81435
Phone: 970.728.0708 **Fax:** 970.728.0710
Email: *ray@captainrayrealtor.com*
URL: *www.totaltelluriderealestate.com*

Suzanne Dugan
Suzanne J. Dugan, Broker
P.O. Box 3768
Vail, CO 81658
Phone: 800.595.8955 **Fax:** 970.476.2564
Email: *dugan@sdugan.com*
URL: *www.sdugan.com*

Connecticut

Robin Gregory
Diversified Investments International
1129 Manchester Road
Glastonbury, CT 06033
Phone: 860.633.6348 **Fax:** 860.633.6348
Email: *robingregory@cox.net*

Stella Montana
Prudential CT Realty
1583 Post Road
Fairfield, CT 06824
Phone: 203.255.2800 **Fax:** 203.255.1149
Email: *stelmontana@hotmail.com*

Doris Smart
William Raveis International
2525 Post Road
Southport, CT 06890

APPENDIX A

Phone: 203.341.7261 Fax: 203.319.1042
Email: *smartd@raveis.com*
URL: *www.raveis.com*

Geoffrey Smart
William Raveis International
2525 Post Road
Southport, CT 06890
Phone: 203.341.7261 Fax: 203.319.1042
Email: *smartg@raveis.com*
URL: *www.raveis.com*

District of Columbia

Angela Eliopoulos
Long & Foster/Global Owner Properties
1680 Wisconsin Avenue, NW
Washington, DC 20007
Phone: 202.944.8400 Fax: 202.944.8424
Email: *angela@globalowner.com*
URL: *www.globalowner.com*

Harriet Pressler
RE/MAX Allegiance
1720 Wisconsin Avenue N.W.
Washington, DC 20007
Phone: 202.333.5757 Fax: 202.333.5854
Email: *harrietpressler@mris.com*
URL: *www.harrietpressler.realtor.com*

Patricia Bonds
Weichert REALTORS®
1930 18th Street, N.W.
Washington, DC 20009
Phone: 202.326.1010 Fax: 202.544.4063
Email: *patriciabonds@aol.com*
URL: *www.patriciabonds.realtor.com*

Florida

J. Enrique Iguina
Summer Beach Realty
5456 First Coast Highway
Amelia Island, FL 32034
Phone: 904.753.3333 Fax: 904.261.8411
Email: *eiguina@aol.com*
URL: *www.realestateofamelia.com*

Marie Farrell
RE/MAX Coastal Real Estate
50 A1A North, Suite 108
Ponte Vedra Beach, FL 32082

Phone: 904.742.8534 Fax: 904.685.2188
Email: *marie@mariefarrell.com*
URL: *www.mariefarrell.com*

John Haynes
Pelican Real Estate & Development Co., Inc.
15900 Front Beach Road
Panama City, FL 32413
Phone: 850.230.4514 Fax: 850.230.3763
Email: *rashaynes@yahoo.com*
URL: *www.johnmhaynes.com*

Jean-Paul Groshaeny
Crye-Leike Coastal Realty
4447 Commons Drive East, Suite 110
Destin, FL 32541
Phone: 850.654.7700 Fax: 850.654.7742
Email: *jeanpaul.groshaeny@crye-leike.com*
URL: *www.coastalrealtyfla.com*

John Sylvia
RE/MAX Town and Country Realty
1315 Tuskawilla Road, Suite 101
Winter Springs, FL 32708
Phone: 407.366.1934 Fax: 407.366.7265
Email: *jsylvia@att.net*

Molsey Edwards
Edwards International Realty &
Financing, Inc.
250 International Parkway, Suite 114
Heathrow, FL 32746
Phone: 407.771.4188 Fax: 407.771.4308
Email: *molsey@edwardsintl.com*
URL: *www.edwardsintl.com*

Willie Risner
The Property Place
3436 S. Hopkins Avenue
Titusville, FL 32780
Phone: 321.269.3777 Fax: 321.269.2322
Email: *risnerera@gnc.net*

Paul Lastra
Coldwell Banker Residential Real Estate, Inc.
7600 Dr. Phillips Boulevard, Suite 146
Orlando, FL 32819
Phone: 407.352.6800 Fax: 407.351.8468
Email: *team21@sale-pending.com*
URL: *www.sale-pending.com*

Rosita Armada
Century 21 Real Estate Professionals
1412 Shelter Rock Road

Orlando, FL 32835
Phone: 407.484.8590 Fax: 407.295.4573
Email: *rositare@aol.com*
URL: *www.rositaarmada.com*

Mike Acevedo
Keller Williams Homestead Realty
4124 Town Center Boulevard
Orlando, FL 32837
Phone: 407.313.5205 Fax: 407.313.5205
Email: *orlandoboundrealtor@yahoo.com*
URL: *www.mikeacehomebuyerssellers.com*

Alexander Van Grondelle
Keller Williams Realty
3980 Town Center Boulevard
Orlando, FL 32837
Phone: 407.529.7253 Fax: 321.221.2919
Email: *alex@hotpropertystore.com*
URL: *www.secondhomesales.com*

Michiyo Hoshino
Enjoy Realty, Inc.
P.O. Box 531015
Orlando, FL 32853
Phone: 407.947.2031 Fax: 407.264.6513
Email: *luckymi777@hotmail.com*

Belton Jennings
Orlando Regional REALTOR® Association
P.O. Box 609400
Orlando, FL 32860-9400
Phone: 407.513.7260 Fax: 407.691.7922
Email: *ceo@orlrealtor.com*
URL: *www.orlrealtor.com*

Carolynn Mouat
A1A Internet Realty, Inc.
609 Shorewood Drive, Suite D201
Cape Canaveral, FL 32920
Phone: 321.960.1515 Fax: 321.784.0645
Email: *move_2_florida@yahoo.com*
URL: *www.floridabuyeragent.com*

Sonja Beuzelin
Paradise Properties of Brevard, Inc.
1640 Hwy. A1A
Satellite Beach, FL 32937
Phone: 321.795.6261 Fax: 321.727.1664
Email: *sbeuzelin@cfl.rr.com*
URL: *www.sonjainternational.com*

Salvador Aleguas
Sal Aleguas REALTOR®
695B S. Courtenay Parkway

Merritt Island, FL 32952
Phone: 321.452.3212 Fax: 321.452.7561
Email: *salaleguas1@cfl.rr.com*
URL: *www.relocate-america.com/sal*

Alfonso Chacon
Coldwell Banker
15100 N.W. 67th Avenue, Suite 110
Miami Lakes, FL 33014
Phone: 305.821.4700 Fax: 305.821.2277
Email: *alfonsochacon@msn.com*
URL: *www.immobel.com/albeach*

Hector Rivera
American Dream Investment Realty, Inc.
6447 Miami Lakes Drive East, Suite 200-G
Miami Lakes, FL 33014
Phone: 305.373.2648 Fax: 305.826.8666
Email: *hector@americandream4u.com*
URL: *www.americandream4u.com*

Magaly Rubio
Coldwell Banker Residential Real Estate, Inc.
15100 N.W. 67th Avenue, Suite 110
Miami Lakes, FL 33014
Phone: 305.821.0203 Fax: 305.821.2277
Email: *mrubiore@bellsouth.net*
URL: *www.magalyrubio.com*

Juan Selaya
J.A.S. Properties Marketing Corporation
601 E. Chaminade Drive
Hollywood, FL 33021
Phone: 954.966.5529 Fax: 954.962.1524
Email: *propiedadesjuanselaya@realtor.com*
URL: *www.juanselaya.realtor.com*

Navall Sookdeo
Navall D. Sookdeo Realty
725 South Rainbow Drive
Hollywood, FL 33021
Phone: 954.445.5869 Fax: 954.983.8432
Email: *realestate90@hotmail.com*

Liza Mendez
Pedro Realty International
5031 S.W. 151 Terrace
Mirramar, FL 33027
Phone: 305.558.7676 Fax: 305.556.0343
Email: *liza@pedrorealty.com*
URL: *www.lizamendez.com*

Monica Azpurua
Keller Williams Partners Realty

2000 NW 150th Ave., Suite 2000
Pembroke Pines, FL 33028
Phone: 954.217.3978 **Fax:** 954.237.0401
Email: *monica@monicaa.com*
URL: *www.monicaa.com*

Pilar Moscoso
Keller Williams Partners
2000 NW 150th Ave., Suite 2000
Pembroke Pines, FL 33028
Phone: 954.438.0345 **Fax:** 954.237.0401
Email: *pilarmosc@bellsouth.net*
URL: *www.pilaronline.com*

Luz Ibrahimovic, LLC
Charles Rutenberg Realty
11555 Heron Bay Boulevard, Suite 200
Coral Springs, FL 33076
Phone: 954.650.0712 **Fax:** 954.827.0541
Email: *cpclucy@aol.com*
URL: *www.luzmarinaflorida.com*

Robert Lee Bryant
Robert Lee Bryant REALTOR®
P.O. Box 01-0310
Miami, FL 33101-0310
Phone: 786.514.7325 **Fax:** 305.324.7056
Email: *rbryant@robertleebryant.com*
URL: *www.immobel.com/robertleebryantrealtor*

Wanda Bee
RE/MAX Advance Realty
151 S.E. 15th Road, Suite 1102
Miami, FL 33129
Phone: 305.577.0016 **Fax:** 305.577.0015
Email: *realestate@wandabee.com*
URL: *www.wandabee.com*

Valeria Grunbaum
Vistas International Realty
2840 S.W. Third Avenue
Miami, FL 33129
Phone: 305.854.1900 **Fax:** 305.854.1934
Email: *vgrunbaum@vistasmiami.com*
URL: *www.invertirenmiami.info*

Pablo Langesfeld
Fortune International Realty
2666 Brickell Avenue
Miami, FL 33129
Phone: 305.857.3613 **Fax:** 305.470.7441
Email: *propiedades@aol.com*
URL: *www.businessma.com*

Alicia Ale
The Urban Development Group Realty
1801 S.W. Third Avenue, Suite 500
Miami, FL 33129-1012
Phone: 305.586.4160 **Fax:** 305.704.3854
Email: *info@miamiriviera.com*
URL: *www.miamiriviera.com*

Steven Cantor
Cantor & Webb P.A.
1001 Brickell Bay Drive, Suite 3112
Miami, FL 33131
Phone: 305.374.3886 **Fax:** 305.371.4564
Email: *steve@cantorwebb.com*
URL: *www.cantorwebb.com*

Manuela Janak
International R.E. Services & Investments, Inc.
1221 Brickell Avenue, Ninth Floor
Miami, FL 33131-5015
Phone: 305.968.3350 **Fax:** 425.963.1901
Email: *m_janak@bellsouth.net*
URL: *www.internationalrealestate.net*

John Kinney
World Properties USA, Inc.
1717 North Bayshore Drive, Suite 2256
Miami, FL 33132
Phone: 305.975.1888 **Fax:** 305.577.0065
Email: *johnkinney@usa.net*
URL: *www.worldpropertiesusa.com*

Oscar Resek
Keller Williams Eagle Realty
700 N.E. 90th Street
Miami, FL 33138
Phone: 305.694.5354 **Fax:** 305.759.8991
Email: *oresek@kw.com*
URL: *www.resekhomesalesteam.com*

Fatima Upegui
Fortune House Sofi International Realty
400 Alton Road, #TH 1A
South Beach, FL 33139
Phone: 786.426.5050 **Fax:** 305.531.8399
Email: *fatima@fatimaupegui.com*
URL: *www.fatimaupegui.com*

Robert Maskin, P.A.
Robert Maskin, P.A.
900 Bay Drive, Suite 804
Miami Beach, FL 33141-5632
Phone: 305.868.1810 **Fax:** 305.861.3262
Email: *mrobertmaskin@aol.com*

Betty Mitchell
Mitchell International Realty
7231 S.W. 63rd Avenue, Suite 101
South Miami, FL 33143
Phone: 305.444.7833 **Fax:** 305.444.7828
Email: *bmitchell@miamihome.com*
URL: *www.miamihome.com*

Charlette Seidel
Coldwell Banker Residential Real Estate, Inc.
1501 Sunset Drive
Coral Gables, FL 33143
Phone: 305.666.5922 **Fax:** 305.667.8106
Email: *csseidel@aol.com*

Carol Housen, P.A.
Esslinger-Wooten-Maxwell, Inc., REALTORS®
6150 S.W. 76th Street
South Miami, FL 33143-5002
Phone: 305.992.8163 **Fax:** 305.866.9310
Email: *housen.c@ewm.com*
URL: *www.carolhousen.com*

Martha Pomares
New Image Realty Group
2490 Coral Way, Suite 401
Miami, FL 33145
Phone: 305.298.4978 **Fax:** 305.854.0395
Email: *pomares@mindspring.com*
URL: *www.newimagerealtygroup.com*

Aida Adams
Coldwell Banker Residential Real Estate, Inc.
1500 San Remo Avenue, Suite 110
Coral Gables, FL 33146
Phone: 305.667.4815 **Fax:** 305.667.5531
Email: *aidatadams@aol.com*
URL: *www.floridamoves.com/aidaadams*

Julie Alvarez
The Keyes Company, REALTORS®
634 Crandon Boulevard
Key Biscayne, FL 33149
Phone: 305.361.5401 **Fax:** 305.361.9773
Email: *juliealvarez@keyes.com*
URL: *www.keyes.com*

Richard Hattler
Chesterfield Capital Corporation
6130 S.W. 135th Terrace
Miami, FL 33156
Phone: 305.669.1279 **Fax:** 305.669.1283
Email: *rhattler@sprintmail.com*

Armando Montero
MGI Realty, LLC
9130 S. Dadeland Blvd.
Two Datran Tower, Suite 1902
Miami, FL 33156
Phone: 305.670.0367 **Fax:** 305.661.5364
Email: *Amontero@mgi-realty.com*
URL: *www.mgi-realty.com*

Francesca Nieto
Century 21 Fine Homes and Estates
Premier Elite Realty
7875 SW 104th Street, Suite 101
Miami, FL 33156
Phone: 305.279.8814 **Fax:** 305.279.8827
Email: *francescanieto@century21.com*
URL: *www.fnietorealestate.com*

Ana Roque
Coldwell Banker Premier Realty
International
7875 S.W. 104th Street, Suite 101
Miami, FL 33156
Phone: 305.279.8814 **Fax:** 305.279.8827
Email: *anamroque@aol.com*
URL: *www.anamariaroque.com*

Marie Story
Coldwell Banker Residential Real Estate, Inc.
12155 South Dixie Hwy (US1)
Miami, FL 33156
Phone: 305.776.0010 **Fax:** 305.253.0554
Email: *mstory@bellsouth.net*
URL: *www.mariestory.com*

Ana Ordonez
Acol Realty, Inc.
"The International Service Group"
15321 South Dixie Highway, Suite 308
Miami, FL 33157
Phone: 305.969.4444 **Fax:** 305.969.8828
Email: *ana@acolrealty.com*
URL: *www.acolrealty.com*

Fausto Gomez
Universal Realty Corporation
18335 Collins Avenue
Sunny Isles Beach, FL 33160
Phone: 305.466.9344 **Fax:** 305.466.9345
Email: *gomezuniversal@msn.com*
URL: *www.miamibeachcondominios.com*

Jose Nunes
Algebra Investments & Realty Corporation
17008 Collins Avenue
Miami Beach, FL 33160
Phone: 305.956.5900 **Fax:** 305.956.7800
Email: *algebra@algebra.net*
URL: *www.joseaugusto.net*

Gustavo Lumer
Lumer Real Estate
16300 N.E. 19th Avenue, Suite A
North Miami Beach, FL 33162
Phone: 305.948.9480 **Fax:** 305.948.9755
Email: *gustavo@lumer.com*
URL: *www.lumer.com*

Leon Srebrenik
Lumer Real Estate
16300 N.E. 19th Avenue, Suite A
North Miami Beach, FL 33162
Phone: 305.948.9480 **Fax:** 305.948.9755
Email: *info@leonsrebrenik.com*
URL: *www.lumer.com*

Elizabeth Alvarez
Pan Florida Realty, Inc.
9731 S.W. 20th Street
Miami, FL 33165
Phone: 305.554.1059 **Fax:** 305.220.6423
Email: *elizabeth@miamihomesales.com*
URL: *www.miamihomesales.com*

Teresa King Kinney
REALTOR® Association of Greater
Miami & The Beaches, Inc.
700 So Royal Poinciana Blvd., Suite 400
Miami, FL 33166-6600
Phone: 305.468.7010 **Fax:** 305.468.7070
Email: *tkinney@miamire.com*
URL: *www.miamire.com*

Sonia Roa
Andsof Realty, Inc.
9495 SW 72nd Street, B-285
Miami, FL 33173
Phone: 305.396.0100 **Fax:** 305.596.0105
Email: *soniaroa@bellsouth.net*
URL: *www.andsofrealty.com*

Dorita Fernandez
Delco Realty, Inc.
8798 S.W. Eighth Street
Miami, FL 33174

Phone: 305.553.8904 **Fax:** 305.553.5701
Email: *dorita@doritaanddaniel.com*
URL: *www.doritaanddaniel.com*

Jennie Jimenez
Global Connection Realty, Inc.
941 S.W. 87th Avenue, Suite A
Miami, FL 33176
Phone: 305.265.1100 **Fax:** 305.265.1992
Email: *global_realty@bellsouth.net*
URL: *www.realtor.com/southeastflorida/
jenniejimenez*

Mirta Bussey
Keller Williams Elite Properties
20801 Biscayne Blvd., Suite 101
Aventura, FL 33180
Phone: 954.816.7529 **Fax:** 305.931.8155
Email: *invest@mirtabussey.com*
URL: *www.investmentmb.com*

Fatima Gonzalez-Triana
Prudential Florida WCI Realty
19056 NE 29th Avenue
Aventura, FL 33180
Phone: 305.469.8337 **Fax:** 305.940.2199
Email: *fgfatima1014@aol.com*
URL: *www.fatimagonzalez.com*

Licia Leal
Prudential Florida WCI Realty
19056 NE 29th Avenue
Aventura, FL 33180
Phone: 305.749.1510 **Fax:** 305.932.6355
Email: *finehomes@licialeal.com*
URL: *www.licialeal.com*

Ana Ordaz
Coldwell Banker Residential Real Estate, Inc.
20803 Biscayne Boulevard, Suite 102
Aventura, FL 33180-1534
Phone: 305.613.6751 **Fax:** 305.937.0235
Email: *anaordaz@comcast.net*
URL: *www.anaordaz.com*

Victoria Zambrano
Coldwell Banker Continental
8240 Mills Drive
Miami, FL 33183
Phone: 305.978.3566 **Fax:** 305.596.0081
Email: *zambranoteam@hotmail.com*
URL: *www.zambranoteam.com*

Frank Pulles
Coldwell Banker
8240 Mills Drive
Miami, FL 33183-4805
Phone: 305.962.6683 Fax: 305.779.7735
Email: *frank@pulles.com*
URL: *www.pulles.com*

Yvonne Hartshorn
Alpha & Omega International Realty
and Consultants
P.O. Box 571011
Miami, FL 33257-1011
Phone: 305.234.8887 Fax: 305.252.6464
Email: *yvonnehartshorn@hotmail.com*
URL: *www.fl.living.net/firm/1006069*

Drew Cashmere
Cashmere & Associates Realty, Inc.
2881 E. Oakland Park Boulevard, Suite 201
Fort Lauderdale, FL 33304
Phone: 954.315.1759 Fax: 305.675.2324
Email: *drew@drewcashmere.com*
URL: *www.drewcashmere.com*

Toni Napolitano
The Keyes Company
1520 Foot Sunrise Blvd.
Fort Lauderdale, FL 33304
Phone: 954.463.8664 Fax: 954.467.2722
Email: *toni@performancenotpromises.com*
URL: *www.performancenotpromises.com*

Susanne Girlich
Century 21 Hansen Realty, Inc.
3010 E. Commercial Boulevard
Fort Lauderdale, FL 33308
Phone: 954.776.5400 Fax: 954.776.5532
Email: *susanne@susannegirlich.com*

Hilda Prigge, P.A.
Coldwell Banker Residential Real Estate, Inc.
4757 N. Ocean Boulevard
Fort Lauderdale, FL 33308-2914
Phone: 954.781.9393 Fax: 954.781.4334
Email: *priggeone@bellsouth.net*

George Traikos
Florida Home Realty, Inc.
10200 States Road 84, Suite 107
Davie, FL 33324
Phone: 954.815.1541 Fax: 954.635.6602
Email: *george@georgetraikos.com*
URL: *www.georgetraikos.com*

Cesar Osorio
Keller Williams
1625 North Commerce Parkway, Suite 105
Weston, FL 33326
Phone: 305.725.7305 Fax: 954.358.6518
Email: *kwinvest@aol.com*
URL: *www.cesarosorio.com*

Maria Taticchi
Keller Williams Properties
1625 N. Commerce Parkway, Suite 105
Weston, FL 33326
Phone: 954.609.8828 Fax: 954.452.9282
Email: *borgia@aol.com*
URL: *www.mariamtaticchi.realtor.com*

Vincenzo Anzellini
Century 21 United Properties
2625 Executive Park Drive, Suite 5
Weston, FL 33331
Phone: 954.802.2802 Fax: 954.349.3392
Email: *vanzellini@verizon.net*
URL: *www.enzoanzellini.com*

Francisco Estremon
Century 21 United Properties, Inc.
2625 Executive Park Dr, Suite 5
Weston, FL 33331
Phone: 954.326.7020 Fax: 954.389.3086
Email: *info@franciscoestremera.com*
URL: *www.franciscoestremera.com*

Ulla Siekmann
Singer Island Realty
2655 N. Ocean Drive, Ste 100
Singer Island, FL 33404
Phone: 561.262.8585 Fax: 561.658.6380
Email: *ulla@ullasiekmann.com*
URL: *www.ullasiekmann.com*

Tony Macaluso
Portside Properties
9492 Bloomfield Drive
Palm Beach Gardens, FL 33410
Phone: 561.622.8498 Fax: 561.626.5411
Email: *portsidefl@aol.com*
URL: *www.tonymacaluso.com*

Kevin Kent
Coldwell Banker Residential Real Estate, Inc.
6716 Forest Hill Boulevard
West Palm Beach, FL 33413
Phone: 561.642.1900 Fax: 561.641.1342
Email: *kevin.kent@floridamoves.com*

Paulo Oliveira
Coldwell Banker Residential, Inc.
6716 Forest Hill Boulevard
West Palm Beach, FL 33413
Phone: 561.632.8428 **Fax:** 561.641.1342
Email: *pro@floridahomesbypaulo.com*
URL: *www.cipsnet.org*

Grissel "Missey" Fernandez
RE/MAX Direct
11924 Forest Hill Boulevard, Suite 4
Wellington, FL 33414
Phone: 561.301.1945 **Fax:** 561.798.6690
Email: *misseyf@remax.net*
URL: *www.worldwiderelo.com*

Jay Colman
RE/MAX Direct
11924 Forest Hill Boulevard, Suite 4
Wellington, FL 33414-6298
Phone: 800.940.0602 **Fax:** 561.798.3432
Email: *jay@flrelo.com*
URL: *www.flrelo.com*

Arthur Colligan
Realty World - Gold Coast
11379A W. Palmetto Park Road
Boca Raton, FL 33428
Phone: 561.483.5368 **Fax:** 561.852.7420
Email: *goldrealty@aol.com*

Nena Rivas-McCaughey
RE/MAX Select Boca, Inc.
P.O. Box 1096
Boca Raton, FL 33429
Phone: 561.702.4232 **Fax:** 561.852.3003
Email: *nena-boca@worldnet.att.net*
URL: *www.nenaboca.com*

Fred DeFalco, P.A.
DeFalco Real Estate Group
3299 NW Boca Raton Boulevard
Boca Raton, FL 33431
Phone: 561.391.4141 **Fax:** 561.391.3911
Email: *fred@defalco.com*
URL: *www.defalco.com*

Robert Reiter
Grand Floridian Estate Realty
151 N. Ocean Blvd.
Boca Raton, FL 33432
Phone: 561.483.5555 **Fax:** 561.483.6986
Email: *info@bbreiter.com*
URL: *www.barbaraandbobreiter.com*

Sonia Dehesa
Coldwell Banker Residential Real Estate
7763 Glades Road
Boca Raton, FL 33434
Phone: 561.479.5951 **Fax:** 561.479.5999
Email: *sonia@soniadehesa.com*
URL: *www.soniadehesa.com*

Bard Wechsler
RE/MAX Innovations
7410 Boynton Beach Boulevard, Suite A-1
Boynton Beach, FL 33437
Phone: 561.945.5713 **Fax:** 561.737.3557
Email: *bardw@bellsouth.net*
URL: *www.bewechsler.com*

Ruth Sheffy
Joe Fearnley Real Estate, Inc.
1203 North Dixie Highway
Lake Worth, FL 33460
Phone: 561.582.9037 **Fax:** 561.582.8041
Email: *ruthann@ruthannsheffy.com*
URL: *www.ruthannsheffy.com*

Rosa Simmons-Klein
RE/MAX Southeast
9804 S. Military Trail, Suite E-10
Boynton Beach, FL 33467
Phone: 561.364.8600 **Fax:** 561.364.7677
Email: *rosas1@remax.net*
URL: *www.iwantmyownroom.com*

Dalys "Didi" Rogers
Prudential Florida WCI Realty
1150 US Highway One
Jupiter, FL 33477
Phone: 561.354.1727 **Fax:** 561.354.1701
Email: *dialdidi@aol.com*
URL: *www.dialdidi.com*

Aida Turbow
Prudential Florida WCI Realty
1555 South Federal Highway, Apt. 204
Delray Beach, FL 33483
Phone: 561.265.0802 **Fax:** 561.265.0803
Email: *turbow@gate.net*

Marianella Monsalve de Velarde
Thomas W. Melba Realty
612 Atlantic Avenue
Delray Beach, FL 33484
Phone: 561.792.9441 **Fax:** 561.276.5487
Email: *mmonsalve@adelphia.net*

Carlos Fuentes
VET Realty
23738 Peace Pipe Ct.
Lutz, FL 33559
Phone: 813.598.4224 **Fax:** 813.948.0535
Email: *cfuentes@ccim.net*
URL: *www.commercialrealtorglobal.com*

Connie Carberry
RE/MAX Action First
8855 Dr. M.L.K. Street N.
St. Petersburg, FL 33702
Phone: 727.522.4122 **Fax:** 727.527.1697
Email: *connie@conniecarberry.com*
URL: *www.conniecarberry.com*

Michael Avey
Avey Realty
410 150th Avenue, Suite A
Madeira Beach, FL 33708
Phone: 727.490.3441 **Fax:** 727.490.3795
Email: *michaelavey@atlantic.net*
URL: *www.aveyrealestate.com*

Frank Kowal
Coldwell Banker Residential Real Estate, Inc.
315 Indian Rocks Road North
Belleair, FL 33770
Phone: 727.581.9411 **Fax:** 727.585.0482
Email: *fkowal@tampabay.rr.com*
URL: *www.floridamoves.com/frank.kowal*

Michael Davis
Davis Suncoast Realty
2113 Gulf Boulevard
Indian Rocks Beach, FL 33785
Phone: 727.595.7592 **Fax:** 727.596.3064
Email: *mwdavisco@earthlink.net*
URL: *www.davissuncoastrealty.com*

Richard Howard
Howard Properties, Inc.
596 US 27 North
Avon Park, FL 33825
Phone: 863.453.4655 **Fax:** 863.453.6676
Email: *rhoward@strato.net*

Maria Guevara-Gatley
RE/MAX Downtown
1902 S.E. 39th Terrace
Cape Coral, FL 33904
Phone: 239.945.8500 **Fax:** 239.945.8501
Email: *info@davidggatley.com*
URL: *www.davidgatley.com*

Amelia Barreto
SellState Achievers Realty Network, Inc.
7431 College Parkway
Fort Myers, FL 33907
Phone: 239.253.9274 **Fax:** 239.947.0245
Email: *amelia@ameliabarreto.com*
URL: *www.ameliabarreto.com*

Eric Matthews
Gulf Coast Realty International
4409 Sweetbay Street
Port Charlotte, FL 33948
Phone: 941.766.7091 **Fax:** 941.766.8102
Email: *matthewsgulfcoast@comcast.net*
URL: *www.matthewsgulfcoast.com*

Robert Lapietro
Century 21 Aztec & Associates
P.O. Box 495583
Port Charlotte, FL 33949
Phone: 941.286.7834 **Fax:** 877.860.8079
Email: *boblc21@earthlink.net*
URL: *www.livebythegulf.com*

Noreen McCarthy
Remax State Properties, Inc.
25001 Harborside Boulevard
Punta Gorda, FL 33955
Phone: 941.637.7779 **Fax:** 941.637.8022
Email: *noreen@noreensells.com*
URL: *www.noreensells.com*

Linda Loomis, P.A.
Prudential Florida WCI Realty
4130 Tamiami Trail North
Naples, FL 34103
Phone: 239.451.0769 **Fax:** 239.659.3392
Email: *lindaloomisnaples@yahoo.com*
URL: *www.4naplesrealestate.com*

Gabriela Saad
Sun Realty, Inc.
3757 Tamiami Trail North
Naples, FL 34103
Phone: 239.649.1990 **Fax:** 239.649.1980
Email: *gsaad@patagoniadevelopment.com*
URL: *www.patagoniadevelopment.com*

Sebastianus Hermans
Thalassa Realty Group International, LLC
840 111th Avenue North, Suite 11
Naples, FL 34108
Phone: 239.596.1131 **Fax:** 239.596.1159

Email: *sebastian@thalassarealty.com*
URL: *www.thalassarealty.com*

Hilda Diaz-Perera
Golden Coast-Costa Dorada Realty, Inc.
5630 Copper Leaf Lane
Naples, FL 34116
Phone: 239.354.1110 **Fax:** 866.844.0495
Email: *brokerhilda@gccd.us*
URL: *www.gccd.us*

Nelson Zuleta
Golden Coast-Costa Dorada Realty, Inc.
5630 Copper Leaf Lane
Naples, FL 34116
Phone: 239.354.1110 **Fax:** 866.844.0495
Email: *nelsonjzuleta@gccd.us*
URL: *www.gccd.us*

Eduardo Hirsch
John R. Wood, Inc. REALTORS®
26269 S. Tamiami Trail
Bonita Springs, FL 34134
Phone: 239.949.7447 **Fax:** 239.498.9250
Email: *realaide@comcast.com*
URL: *www.realaide.com*

Benita Ray
Downing-Frye Realty, Inc.
27180 Bay Landing Drive, Suite 5
Bonita Springs, FL 34135
Phone: 239.992.8711 **Fax:** 239.948.7910
Email: *info@globalpropertysource.net*
URL: *www.globalpropertysource.net*

Rimma Halperin
Rimma Smull Lic. Real Estate Broker
11207 Marigold Drive
Bradenton, FL 34202
Phone: 941.756.2124 **Fax:** 941.756.2124
Email: *rmrealty@msn.com*
URL: *www.sarasotahome4you.net*

Louis Wery
Coldwell Banker Residential Real Estate, Inc.
201 Gulf of Mexico Drive, Suite One
Longboat Key, FL 34228-0000
Phone: 941.232.3001 **Fax:** 941.358.1752
Email: *louiswery@comcast.net*
URL: *www.louiswery.com*

Margo MacKenzie
Capital Properties & Services, Inc.

4956 S. Tamiami Trail
Sarasota, FL 34231
Phone: 941.921.1000 **Fax:** 941.921.1111
Email: *margo@margomackenzie.com*
URL: *www.floridasunshineliving.com*

Charlotte Hedge
Michael Saunders & Company
1801 Main Street
Sarasota, FL 34236
Phone: 941.951.6600 **Fax:** 941.951.6667
Email: *hedgeteam@aol.com*
URL: *www.hedgeteam.com*

Selma Dyer
Sarasota Realty Properties
8488 South Tamiami Trail
Sarasota, FL 34238
Phone: 941.966.0037
Email: *selmadyer@aol.com*
URL: *www.sarasotarealtyproperties.com*

Judith Pittman
Mapp Realty & Investment Company
3120 Southgate Circle
Sarasota, FL 34239
Phone: 941.302.1720 **Fax:** 941.379.5720
Email: *jspitt97@comcast.net*
URL: *www.judithpittman.com*

Felix Power
Coldwell Banker Residential Real Estate, Inc.
5145 Ocean Boulevard
Sarasota, FL 34242
Phone: 941.924.9000 **Fax:** 941.349.8090
Email: *felix@sarasotaflhomes.com*
URL: *www.sarasotaflhomes.com*

Steve Diller
Paradise West Realty, Inc.
12515 Spring Hill Drive
Spring Hill, FL 34609
Phone: 888.863.1500 **Fax:** 352.688.0430
Email: *paradise@cusave.com*
URL: *www.paradisewestrealty.com*

Christian BonJorn
BonJorn Real Estate
516 W. Hwy 50
Clermont, FL 34711
Phone: 352.267.6476 **Fax:** 352.394.6907
Email: *cbonjorn@aol.com*
URL: *www.bonjorn.com*

Frank Gay, III, P.A.
RE/MAX Executive Group
9310 W. Hwy. 192
Clermont, FL 34714
Phone: 863.424.8802 Fax: 863.424.8803
Email: *frankgay@remax.net*
URL: *www.frankgaypa.com*

William McCombs
Florida Real Estate Unlimited, Inc.
140 Honeywood Drive
Kissimmee, FL 34743
Phone: 407.518.9860 Fax: 407.344.9843
Email: *bill@floridarealestateunlimited.com*
URL: *www.floridarealestateunlimited.com*

Truette Wyman, II
La Primera, Inc.
705 N. Main Street
Kissimmee, FL 34744-4520
Phone: 407.847.8170 Fax: 407.847.3103
Email: *laprimerainc@earthlink.net*
URL: *www.laprimerarealty.com*

Kathryne Lenox
Regent International Realty, Inc
7801 W Lake Bronson
Mem. Highway, Suite B
Kissimmee, FL 34747-1760
Phone: 407.397.9868 Fax: 407.397.7881
Email: *klenox@regentint.com*
URL: *www.regentint.com*

Edgardo Arvelo, P.A.
RE/MAX Achievers
463 Tamarind Park Lane
Kissimmee, FL 34758
Phone: 407.518.9193 Fax: 407.628.1119
Email: *arvelore@aol.com*

Robert Lowe
Lowes International Realty Plus, Inc.
2901 N. A1A
North Hutchinson Island, FL 34949
Phone: 772.467.6500 Fax: 772.467.6535
Email: *c21lowe@aol.com*
URL: *www.lowesinternationalrealtyplus.com*

Joan Miller
Joan S. Miller Real Estate, Inc.
3266 Lake Shore Drive
North Hutchinson Island, FL 34949-8711

Phone: 772.467.2646 Fax: 772.465.2791
Email: *joan@joan-s-miller.com*
URL: *joan-s-miller.com*

Carmen Pappa
Coldwell Banker Residential
1973 S.W. Savage Boulevard
Port St. Lucie, FL 34953
Phone: 772.344.7279 Fax: 772.344.7271
Email: *slwcc@msn.com*

Eugene Gibbins
Gibbins Real Estate & Consulting
P.O. Box 7835
Port St. Lucie, FL 34985-7835
Phone: 772.971.7134 Fax: 877.723.3987
Email: *cips@gibbins.com*
URL: *www.the-dreamteam.com*

James Hayes
Hayes Realty & Investment Co.
1655 N.W. Fork Road
Stuart, FL 34994
Phone: 772.692.3823 Fax: 772.402.4534
Email: *rei7@adelphia.net*
URL: *www.yinvest.com*

Georgia

Julieta Issa
RE/MAX Realty Group
2615 Sandy Plains Road
Atlanta, GA 30066
Phone: 770.973.5000 Fax: 770.578.9112
Email: *jjissa@bellsouth.net*
URL: *www.julietaissa.com*

Oscar Melara
RE/MAX Action Realty
5387 Fairburn Road
Douglasville, GA 30135
Phone: 770.265.6804
Email: *oscar@oscarmelara.com*
URL: *www.oscarmelara.com*

Renee Hutchinson
Harry Norman, REALTORS®
2660 Peachtree Road, Suite 23-H
Atlanta, GA 30305
Phone: 404.816.5141 Fax: 404.365.0026
Email: *reneehut@bellsouth.net*

Julia Song
RE/MAX Greater Atlanta

3510 Shallowford Road
Atlanta, GA 30341
Phone: 770.290.0100 **Fax:** 770.290.0101
Email: *juliasong@gmail.com*
URL: *www.juliasong.com*

Van Yon
RE/MAX Commercial Atlanta, LLC
5600 Roswell Road, Suite E-275
Atlanta, GA 30342-1135
Phone: 404.978.2288 **Fax:** 404.978.2288
Email: *van@vansells.com*
URL: *www.vansells.com*

Wanda Stephens
Wanda G. Stephens & Associates
Prime Properties
125 River Bend Road
Dawsonville, GA 30534
Phone: 706.265.0625 **Fax:** 706.216.4282
Email: *wandagstephens@alltel.net*

Hawaii

Brian Berry
RE/MAX Brokers
75-5995 Kuakini Hwy., Suite P
Kailua Kona, HI 96740
Phone: 808.327.3475 **Fax:** 808.327.3280
Email: *bjberry@aloha.net*
URL: *www.berryhawaii.com*

Robert Cheesbrough
Prestige World Properties
65-1235 Opelo Road
Opelo Cottage #2
Kamuela, HI 96743
Phone: 808.885.8787 **Fax:** 808.885.8778
Email: *robert@prestigeworldproperties.com*
URL: *www.prestigeworldproperties.com*

Illinois

Michael Mileykovsky
Admiral Realty, Inc.
2743 Wilshire Lane
Northbrook, IL 60062
Phone: 847.412.0411 **Fax:** 847.412.0169
Email: *michael7007@earthlink.net*

Vanessa Falcon
Century 21 Classic Properties
1146 West Chicago Avenue
Oak Park, IL 60302
Phone: 708.955.1171 **Fax:** 708.524.8450

Email: *vanessa.forry@century21.com*
URL: *www.c21homeseller.com*

Sylvia Rivera
Coldwell Banker Residential Brokerage
321 N. Weber Road
Bolingbrook, IL 60490-1569
Phone: 630.759.3100 **Fax:** 630.759.3354
Email: *sylvia.rivera@cbexchange.com*
URL: *www.sylviarivera.com*

Dianne Black Robinson
Coldwell Banker Commercial NRT
133 E. Ogden Avenue
Hinsdale, IL 60521
Phone: 630.887.8900 **Fax:** 630.887.7995
Email: *dianne.blackrobinson@cbexchange.com*
URL: *www.coldwellbankercommercialnrt.com*

Han Wang
Prospect Equities, Inc.
5980 S. Route 53, Suite F
Lisle, IL 60532
Phone: 630.663.4000 **Fax:** 630.663.0143
Email: *hanwang21@yahoo.com*
URL: *www.prospectequities.com*

Debbie Maue McNally
Rubloff Residential Properties
2663 N. Halsted
Chicago, IL 60614
Phone: 773.572.6522 **Fax:** 773.572.6572
Email: *dmaue@rubloff.com*
URL: *www.debbiemaue.com*

Terry Watson
Watson World
1341 W. Fullerton Avenue, Suite 303
Chicago, IL 60614
Phone: 773.404.7721 **Fax:** 773.880.6550
Email: *terry@terrywatson.com*
URL: *www.getwatson.com*

Ari Matsoukas
RE/MAX Signature
2329 W. Belmont Avenue
Chicago, IL 60618
Phone: 773.404.3833 **Fax:** 773.348.8519
Email: *arimatsoukas@hakkinen.com*

Mark Chruscinski
Century 21 McMullen
6400 N. Harlem Avenue
Chicago, IL 60631

Phone: 800.848.0387 Fax: 773.631.8702
Email: *mark@jaske.net*
URL: *www.markch.com*

Raymond Covyeau
Troy Realty Ltd.
5420 North Harlem Avenue
Chicago, IL 60656
Phone: 773.704.0600 Fax: 773.625.1824
Email: *raycovyeau@aol.com*

Kansas

Paul Daemen
Plaza Real Estate, Inc.
8442 W. 13th, Suite 102
Wichita, KS 67212
Phone: 316.722.0030 Fax: 316.722.1809
Email: *daemen@sbcglobal.net*
URL: *www.plazare.com*

Louisiana

Barbara Hall
Prudential Gardner REALTORS®, Inc.
1300 Gause Boulevard
Slidell, LA 70458
Phone: 985.649.7779 Fax: 985.645.9937
Email: *bhall@prudentialgardner.com*
URL: *www.bobbiehall.prugardner.com*

Maryland

Lawrence Weiner
Executive Realty Services
4305 Rosedale Avenue
Bethesda, MD 20814-4750
Phone: 301.656.2366 Fax: 301.656.2367
Email: *larryweiner@mris.com*

Silvia Rodriguez
Silvia International Realty
1010 Rockville Pike, Suite 400
Rockville, MD 20852
Phone: 301.309.1919 Fax: 301.309.1929
Email: *silviainternationalrealty@starpower.net*

Massachusetts

Jose Esmeral
Polo Realty Group
313 Littleton Road #7
Chelmsford, MA 01824
Phone: 978.244.0220 Fax: 978.455.0826

Email: *joineenterprises@aol.com*
URL: *www.polorealty.net*

Rosemary Matthews
Century 21 Hughes & Carey
2277 State Road, Suite K
Plymouth, MA 02360
Phone: 508.642.5010 Fax: 508.888.5778
Email: *rosemary02360@hotmail.com*
URL: *www.c21hughesandcarey.com*

Patrick Crowley
Crowley/Marquis REALTORS® GMAC
3193 Cranberry Highway
East Wareham, MA 02538
Phone: 508.759.4430 Fax: 508.759.6922
Email: *pcrowley@capecod.net*
URL: *www.crowleyre.com*

Laura Usher
Kinlin Grover GMAC Real Estate
1990 Main Street
P.O. Box 2000
Brewster, MA 02631
Phone: 508.896.7000 Fax: 508.896.9845
Email: *lusher@kinlingrover.com*
URL: *www.kinlingrover.com/laurausher*

Wendy Ustach
Coldwell Banker Atlantic Realty
1 Villages Drive
Brewster, MA 02631
Phone: 508.896.5701 Fax: 508.896.4633
Email: *wendy.ustach@coldwellbanker.com*
URL: *www.wendyustach.com*

Nancy Griffin
Kinlin Grover GMAC Real Estate
193 Cranberry Highway
Orleans, MA 02653
Phone: 508.255.3001 Fax: 508.255.1489
Email: *ngriffin@kinlingrover.com*
URL: *www.kinlingrover.com*

Michigan

Anthony Peterson
Coldwell Banker Schmidt
402 E. Front Street
Traverse City, MI 49686
Phone: 231.995.7647 Fax: 231.922.2374
Email: *ampeterson@coldwellbanker.com*

Minnesota

Todd Shipman
Great Minneapolis Real Estate
357 Penn Avenue South
Minneapolis, MN 55419
Phone: 612.925.5990 **Fax:** 612.925.9117
Email: *tashipman@aol.com*
URL: *www.greatminneapolis.com*

Mississippi

John Dean
Landmart/Dean Land & Realty Co.
303 N. Broad Street
P.O. Drawer 272
Leland, MS 38756
Phone: 662.686.7807 **Fax:** 662.686.7890
Email: *jdean@deanlandmart.com*
URL: *www.deanlandmart.com*

New Jersey

Elizabeth Makatura
Coldwell Banker
One Campus Drive
Parsippany, NJ 07054
Phone: 973.496.7707 **Fax:** 973.496.7720
Email: *elizabeth.makatura@cendant.com*

Deborah Madey
Peninsula Realty Group, Inc.
621 Shrewsbury Avenue
Shrewsbury, NJ 07702
Phone: 732.530.7755 **Fax:** 732.559.8256
Email: *deborah@peninsulafirst.com*
URL: *www.peninsulafirst.com*

Thomas Stephens
Deborah Madey REALTORS®
621 Shrewsbury Avenue
Shrewsbury, NJ 07702
Phone: 732.530.7755 **Fax:** 732.559.8256
Email: *tom@peninsularealtygroup.com*
URL: *www.peninsulafirst.com*

Missouri

Judith Foster
Prudential Alliance, REALTORS®
1000 Schnucks Woods Mill Plaza
Chesterfield, MO 63017
Phone: 636.386.2900 **Fax:** 636.386.3335
Email: *jfoster@prudentialalliance.com*

Nevada

B. Monique Wilson
Realty Executives of Nevada
1389 Galeria Drive, Suite 100
Henderson, NV 89014
Phone: 702.795.4500 **Fax:** 702.795.8718
Email: *moniquewn@aol.com*
URL: *www.moniquewilsonrealtor.com*

Debbie Drummond-Thompson
RE/MAX One
5580 W. Flamingo Road, Suite 101
Las Vegas, NV 89103
Phone: 702.873.5900 **Fax:** 702.873.5910
Email: *debbie@lasvegas-luxury-homes.com*
URL: *www.lasvegas-luxury-homes.com*

Robert West
Prime Properties of Las Vegas
6787 W. Tropicana Avenue, Suite 274
Las Vegas, NV 89103
Phone: 702.525.6763 **Fax:** 702.233.6678
Email: *bobwest.1@netzero.net*

Mina Farah
Real Estate of Las Vegas, Ltd.
2620 Regatta Drive, Suite 102
Las Vegas, NV 89128
Phone: 702.365.1193 **Fax:** 702.364.2135
Email: *minafarah@minafarah.com*

Leslie Trayer
Century 21 Advantage Gold
9436 W. Lake Mead Blvd, Ste 9
Las Vegas, NV 89134
Phone: 702.862.8500 **Fax:** 702.862.8410
Email: *ltrayer@cox.net*
URL: *www.aadvantagegold.com*

Michael Ornelas
Dickson Realty
P.O. Box 11685, Zephyr Cove
Lake Tahoe, NV 89448
Phone: 800.861.9082 **Fax:** 775.588.2224
Email: *mikentahoe@aol.com*
URL: *www.globalalternatives.com*

New Mexico

Maria Van Gelder
New Mexico Homes
4200 Montgomery Boulevard NE, Suite 122
Albuquerque, NM 87109

Phone: 505.920.0000 Fax: 505.920.0000
Email: *newmexicohomes@aol.com*
URL: *www.n-e-w-mexico-homes.com*

Philip Valaika
RE/MAX of Taos
723 Paseo del Pueblo Sur
Taos, NM 87571
Phone: 505.758.5400 Fax: 505.758.0925
Email: *remax@taos.newmex.com*
URL: *www.remax-taos-nm.com*

Ernest Romero
Taos Management Co., Inc.
5522 NDCBU 829 Paseo Sur
Taos, NM 87571-5522
Phone: 505.758.0080 Fax: 505.758.5677
Email: *eromero@c21success.com*
URL: *www.c21success.com*

New York

Francisca Tayag
FMT International Properties, LLC
131 Barrow Street, Suite 2B
New York, NY 10014-6313
Phone: 212.243.5594 Fax: 212.243.5776
Email: *fmt.realestate@verizon.net*
   fmtre@yahoo.com
URL: *www.fmt-ip.com*

Dr. Anka Manitiu
Weichert REALTORS® – Peters Associates
110 East 42nd Street
New York, NY 10017
Phone: 212.461.4242 Fax: 212.461.4279
Email: *ankam@weichertpeters.com*
URL: *www.weichertpeters.com*

Eugenia Foxworth
Coldwell Banker Hunt Kennedy
1200 Lexington Avenue
New York, NY 10028
Phone: 212.327.1200 Fax: 212.327.1361
Email: *eugenia.foxworth@cbhk.com*
URL: *www.eugeniafoxworth.com*

Robin Servidio
Houlihan Lawrence, Inc.
32 Popham Road
Scarsdale, NY 10583
Phone: 914.723.8877 Fax: 914.723.3548

Email: *robser@msn.com*
URL: *www.houlihanlawrence.com/ robinservidio*

Myriam Ramos
Coldwell Banker Residential Brokerage
366 Underhill Avenue
Yorktown Heights, NY 10598-4546
Phone: 914.424.7156 Fax: 914.245.8602
Email: *myriamramos@optonline.net*
URL: *www.myriamramos.com*

Eydie Lopez
RE/MAX Benchmark Realty Group
95-1 Maher Lane
Harriman, NY 10926
Phone: 845.783.0004 Fax: 845.783.0005
Email: *elopez@remax.net*
URL: *www.benchmark-properties.com*

Ana Castro
RE/MAX Five Star Realty
1733 Flatbush Avenue
Brooklyn, NY 11210
Phone: 718.253.0777 Fax: 718.253.4828
Email: *acastro@remax.net*

Alan Berger
Breslin Realty Inc.
500 Old Country Road, Suite 200
Garden City, NY 11530
Phone: 516.741.7400 Fax: 516.741.5621
Email: *aberger@breslinrealty.com*
URL: *www.nyliving.net/realtor/10425768*

Nino Perdomo
Espanol Realty, Ltd.
4 Clowes Avenue
Hempstead, NY 11550-1616
Phone: 516.565.3146 Fax: 516.565.0408
Email: *espanolinc@aol.com*

Joseph Canfora
Century 21 Selmar Realty
96 E. Main Street
East Islip, NY 11730
Phone: 631.277.0900 Fax: 631.277.1901
Email: *jlcanfora@c21selmar.com*
URL: *www.c21selmar.com*

Maria Quirk
Coldwell Banker Residential Brokerage
82 Main Street
Huntington, NY 11743

Phone: 631.944.8918 **Fax:** 631.425.2399
Email: *mariateresa.quirk@cbmoves.com*
URL: *coldwellbankermoves.com/maria_
teresa.quirk*

Maria Palmar
Jolie Powell Realty, Inc.
406 Main Street
Port Jefferson, NY 11777
Phone: 631.473.0420 **Fax:** 631.473.7959
Email: *maria@jprealtor.com*
URL: *www.mariapalmar.com*

Jolie Powell
Jolie Powell Realty, Inc.
406 Main Street
Port Jefferson, NY 11777
Phone: 631.473.0420 **Fax:** 631.473.7959
Email: *jolie@jprealtor.com*
URL: *www.jprealtor.com*

John Wallace
The Gray Rider Real Estate Company
143 Longview Drive
Chatham, NY 12037
Phone: 518.382.7062 **Fax:** 877.875.5704
Email: *john@grayrider.com*
URL: *www.worldrealtynews.com*

North Carolina

Mariana Fiorentino
Terra Nova Global Properties, Inc.
304 Weaver Street, Suite 203
Carrboro, NC 27510
Phone: 919.929.2005 **Fax:** 919.969.8553
Email: *mariana@terranovaglobal.com*
URL: *www.terranovaglobal.com*

Nancy Wiggins
Nancy Wiggins LLC
and Property Consultants
6611 Gaywind Drive
Charlotte, NC 28226
Phone: 704.998.0040 **Fax:** 704.998.0041
Email: *nbwiggins@ccim.net*
URL: *www.nwcre.com*

Gloria Valdez
145 West W.T. Harris Boulevard
Charlotte, NC 28262
Phone: 704.547.8900 **Fax:** 704.549.9544

Email: *glovalre@bellsouth.net*
URL: *www.glovalpr.com*

Deborah Cook
Segrest International REALTORS®
P.O. Box 1956
Wilmington, NC 28402
Phone: 910.470.4800 **Fax:** 910.762.6568
Email: *deb@segrestrealty.com*
URL: *www.deborahcook.com*

Ohio

Diane Eplin
RE/MAX Affiliates, Inc., REALTORS®
7239 Sawmill Road, Suite 210
Dublin, OH 43016
Phone: 614.766.5330 **Fax:** 614.766.0153
Email: *blues1_singer@yahoo.com*

Robert Stewart
Columbus Real Estate Brokers
1386 E. Dublin-Granville Road
Columbus, OH 43229-3306
Phone: 614.436.0484 **Fax:** 614.436.0485
Email: *creb43229@hotmail.com*

Lawrence Kell
Colliers Ostendore-Morris
1100 Superior Avenue, Suite 800
Cleveland, OH 44114
Phone: 216.861.5573 **Fax:** 216.861.4672
Email: *lfkell@colliers.com*
URL: *www.colliers.com*

Morris Goins
Trimerica Real Estate Corporation
P.O. Box 1201
Cincinnati, OH 45201
Phone: 513.241.4100 **Fax:** 513.825.5580
Email: *globalrealestate@earthlink.net*

Oklahoma

A. Earnest Gilder
Interstate Properties, Inc.
218 W. Okmulgee
P.O. Box 2519
Muskogee, OK 74402-2519
Phone: 918.682.1119 **Fax:** 918.687.7200
Email: *interstate@interstateproperties.com*
URL: *www.interstateproperties.com*

Oregon

Janie Brown
City of Roses Realty, LLC
P.O. Box 1681
Hillsboro, OR 97123
Phone: 503.313.8005 Fax: 503.648.6743
Email: *janie@cityofrosesrealty.com*
URL: *www.cityofrosesrealty.com*

Susan Estes
RE/MAX Signature Properties
2717 N.E. Broadway
Portland, OR 97232
Phone: 503.282.4000 Fax: 503.282.8558
Email: *susan@susanestes.com*
URL: *www.yournewnwhome.com*

Pennsylvania

Ann Ashton
RE/MAX Main Line
49 East Lancaster Avenue
Paoli, PA 19301
Phone: 610.640.9330 Fax: 610.640.9322
Email: *ashton@aol.com*
URL: *www.annashton.com*

Tennessee

L. Roscoe Kasior
Crye-Leike Roslin Realty
P. O. Box 888
Decatur, TN 37322
Phone: 423.334.2606 Fax: 423.334.2608
Email: *lrkasior@yahoo.com*
URL: *www.tennhomes.com*

Cindy Holt
Realty Executives Associates
190 N. Purdue Avenue
Oak Ridge, TN 37830
Phone: 865.482.3232 Fax: 865.482.0203
Email: *cindy@cindyholt.com*
URL: *www.cindyholt.com*

Joyce Nussbaum
Coldwell Banker Wallace & Wallace
124 N. Winston Road
Knoxville, TN 37919
Phone: 865.385.3455 Fax: 865.692.8467
Email: *joycenussbaum@comcast.net*
URL: *www.cbww.com/agent/joycenussbaum*

Texas

Audree Mevellec
Coldwell Banker Apex
2105 Waterview Pkwy
Richardson/North Dallas, TX 75080
Phone: 972.423.5772 Fax: 972.578.9699
Email: *mevellec@msn.com*
URL: *www.viphomechateaux.com*

John Stone
John M. Stone Company
6060 N. Central Expressway, Suite 512
Dallas, TX 75206-5206
Phone: 214.368.7133 Fax: 214.265.8100
Email: *jmstone@johnmstone.com*
URL: *www.johnmstone.com*

Brian Smith
Ellen Terry REALTORS®
6025 Luther Lane
Dallas, TX 75225
Phone: 972.588.8300 Fax: 214.522.8644
Email: *brian@countryconnection.com*
URL: *www.countryconnection.com*

Charlene Clements
RE/MAX Associates of Dallas
9090-C Skillman, Suite 120
Dallas, TX 75243
Phone: 214.349.9900 Fax: 214.341.7282
Email: *charclem@airmail.net*
URL: *www.charleneclements.com*

Ghitta Torrico
Ebby Halliday REALTORS®
7601 Campbell Road, Suite 700
Dallas, TX 75248
Phone: 972.248.8800 Fax: 972.248.6872
Email: *ghitta@ebby.com*
URL: *www.ghitta.com*

Bruce Binkley
Houston Community College System
3100 Main, MC 1748
Houston, TX 77002
Phone: 713.718.5240 Fax: 713.718.5336
Email: *alex.binkley@hccs.edu*

Luther "Luke" Romero
Cameron & Tate Properties
3229 Houston Avenue
Houston, TX 77009
Phone: 713.426.3200 Fax: 713.426.3201

Email: *luke.romero@cameronrate.com*
URL: *www.cameronrate.com*

Carmen Nadolney
Nadolney Enterprises
P.O. Box 24457
14015 Nimitz Street
Houston, TX 77015-5138
Phone: 713.455.2286 **Fax:** 713.455.2780
Email: *cnadolney@houston.rr.com*

Marilyn Edwards
Keller Williams Realty
550 Post Oak Boulevard, Suite 350
Houston, TX 77027
Phone: 713.825.5951 **Fax:** 713.467.2932
Email: *mmedwards@kw.com*
URL: *www.marilynedwards.com*

Cynthia Montero
Stewart Title
1990 Post Oak Boulevard, Suite 100
Houston, TX 77056
Phone: 713.625.8661 **Fax:** 713.629.2321
Email: *cmontero@stewart.com*
URL: *www.stewart.com*

Adelle Shaw
Shaw Interests
1 Riverway, Suite 1700
Houston, TX 77056
Phone: 713.795.0484 **Fax:** 713.840.6324
Email: *shaw_int@swbell.net*

Edna Corona
RE/MAX Alliance
5629 FM1960, Suite 121
Houston, TX 77069
Phone: 281.444.4848 **Fax:** 281.655.0367
Email: *ednacorona@sbcglobal.net*

Margie Kaplan
RE/MAX Professional Group
9234 FM 1960 West
Houston, TX 77070
Phone: 281.463.6365 **Fax:** 281.463.4773
Email: *margie@margiekaplanhomes.com*
URL: *www.margiekaplanhomes.com*

Richard Miranda
Keller Williams Realty
8300 FM 1960 West, Suite 310
Houston, TX 77070
Phone: 281.807.1874 **Fax:** 281.894.1302

Email: *richardmiranda@kw.com*
URL: *www.kw.com*

Wayne Stroman
Stroman Realty, Inc.
14500 Highway 105 West
Conroe, TX 77304
Phone: 936.648.4400 **Fax:** 936.588.4884
Email: *wayne@stroman.com*
URL: *www.timesharelink.com*

Sabrina Didier
Keller Williams Realty
20665 West Lake Houston Parkway
Houston, TX 77346
Phone: 281.358.4545 **Fax:** 281.812.0640
Email: *sdidier@kingwoodcable.net*
URL: *www.4sabrina.com*

Consuelo Zubizarreta
Prudential Gary Greene REALTORS®
2323 Town Center Drive
Sugar Land, TX 77478
Phone: 281.980.5050 **Fax:** 281.980.5426
Email: *zubic@garygreene.com*
URL: *www.garygreene.com*

Kathleen Owen
McKENZIE-OWEN
4653 Bear Springs Road
Pipe Creek, TX 78063-5303
Phone: 800.684.1220 **Fax:** 830.535.4769
Email: *kakiowen@gte.net*
URL: *www.texland.com*

Jean Ann Lindley
Century 21 Best of the Best
6802 Saratoga
Corpus Christi, TX 78414
Phone: 361.739.5936 **Fax:** 361.949.1961
Email: *idoj1@msn.com*
URL: *www.corpuschristiathome.com*

Alston Boyd
Boyd & Boyd Properties, LLC
14607 Bear Creek Pass
Austin, TX 78737-8933
Phone: 512.306.9966 **Fax:** 512.301.8382
Email: *alston@boyd2.com*
URL: *www.boyd2.com*

Philip Schoewe
HomeIndex, Real Estate
P.O. Box 53123

Lubbock, TX 79453
Phone: 806.794.5557 **Fax:** 806.797.0090
Email: *pschoewe@flash.net*
URL: *www.homeindexrealestate.com*

Utah

Maire Rosol
Lewis, Wolcott & Dornbush Real Estate, Inc.
1283 Deer Valley Drive
P.O. Box 2370
Park City, UT 84060
Phone: 435.649.1884 **Fax:** 435.615.7141
Email: *mrosol@lwdparkcity.com*
URL: *www.topmtnproperties.com*

Virginia

James Robinson
Weichert REALTORS®
6715 Little River Turnpike
Annandale, VA 22003
Phone: 703.941.0100 **Fax:** 703.941.1516
Email: *jrcares@yahoo.com*

Sandra Crews
RE/MAX Allegiance
4157 Chain Bridge Road
Fairfax, VA 22030-4102
Phone: 703.899.7629 **Fax:** 866.315.2039
Email: *sandracrews@cox.net*
URL: *www.sandracrews.com*

Michael Lorenzo
First Lady Realty Corp.
3126 Shadeland Drive
Falls Church, VA 22044-1726
Phone: 703.534.7920 **Fax:** 703.534.7927
Email: *mikelor@mris.com*

Lupe Chandler
Laughlin REALTORS®
6824 Elm Street
McLean, VA 22101-3866
Phone: 703.356.0100 **Fax:** 703.448.1893
Email: *lupechandler@realtor.com*
URL: *www.lupechandler.realtor.com*

Sharon Wasz
RE/MAX Allegiance
440 Belmont Bay Drive, Suite 101
Woodbridge, VA 22191
Phone: 703.494.9774 **Fax:** 703.494.9766

Email: *sharon@wasz.net*
URL: *www.wasz.net*

B. Bruce Wasz
RE/MAX Allegiance
440 Belmont Bay Drive, Suite 101
Woodbridge, VA 22191
Phone: 703.494.9774 **Fax:** 703.494.9766
Email: *bwasz@wasz.net*
URL: *www.wasz.net*

Kurt Soester
KCS Associates
1609 N. Jackson Street
Arlington, VA 22201
Phone: 703.875.3334 **Fax:** 703.875.3334
Email: *csoester@kcscips.com*
URL: *www.kcscips.com*

Phyllis Willoughby
William E. Wood & Associates
222 Mustang Trail
Virginia Beach, VA 23452
Phone: 757.486.2410 **Fax:** 757.486.2705
Email: *info@internationalchoice.com*
URL: *www.internationalchoice.com*

Washington

Melba Miller
Windermere Real Estate
13901 N.E. 175th Street, Suite 100

Woodinville, WA 98072
Phone: 425.483.5100 **Fax:** 425.486.1665
Email: *melba.miller@mindspring.com*
URL: *www.windermere.com*

Wisconsin

Stephen Beers
Keefe Real Estate, Inc.
751 Geneva Pkwy, P.O. Box 460
Lake Geneva, WI 53147-1824
Phone: 414.248.4492 **Fax:** 414.248.9539
Email: *sbeers@keeferealestate.com*
URL: *www.keeferealestate.com*

Official Embassies and Consular Offices

Belize

Embassy of Belize
2535 Massachusetts Avenue NW
Washington DC 20008
Phone: 202.332.9636
Fax: 202.332.6888
Email: *belize@oas.org*

The Belize Consulate
5825 Sunset Boulevard, Suite 206
Hollywood, CA 90028
Phone: 213.469.7343/4
Fax: 213.469.7346
Email: *belizeconsul@earthlink.net*

U.S. Embassy in Belize City, Belize
29 Gabourel Lane
P.O. Box 286
Belize City, Belize
Phone: 501.227.7161

Consulate of Belize in Ontario, Canada
c/o McMillan Binch
Suite 3800 South Tower, Royal Bank Plaza
Toronto, Ontario, M5J 2JP, Canada
Phone: 416.865.7000
Fax: 416.864.7048

Consulate of Belize in Quebec, Canada
1800 McGill College, Suite 2480
Montreal, Quebec H3A 3J6, Canada
Phone: 514.288.1687
Fax: 514.288.4998
Email: *dbellemare@cmmtl.com*

Consulate of Belize in Vancouver, Canada
2321 Trafalgar Street
Vancouver, British Columbia V6K 3T1, Canada
Email: *dwsmiling@hotmail.com*

Costa Rica

Embassy of Costa Rica

2114 S Street, NW
Washington, DC 20008
Phone: 202.234.2945 and 202.234.2946
Fax: 202.265.4795
URL: *www.costarica-embassy.org*

U.S. Embassy in San Jose, Costa Rica
Apartado 920-1200 Pavas
San Jose, Costa Rica
Phone: 506.220.3939

Consulate of Costa Rica in Atlanta, GA
1870 The Exchange, Suite 100
Atlanta, GA 30339
Phone: 770.951.7025
Fax: 770.951.7073

Consulate of Costa Rica in Boston, MA
175 McClellan Highway East
Phone: 617.561.2444
Fax: 617.561.2461

Consulate of Costa Rica in Chicago, IL
203 N. Wabash Ave. Suite 1312
Chicago, IL 60601
Phone: 312.263.2772
Fax: 312.263.5807

Consulate of Costa Rica in Dallas, TX
7777 Forest Lane Building C, Suite 204
Dallas, TX 75230
Phone: 972.566.7020
Fax: 972.566.7943

Consulate of Costa Rica in Denver, CO
3356 South Xenia Street
Denver, CO 80231
Phone: 303.696.8211
Fax: 303.696.1110

Consulate of Costa Rica in Houston, TX
3000 Wilcrest, Suite 112
Houston, TX 77042
Phone: 713.266.0484
Fax: 713.266.1527

Consulate of Costa Rica in Los Angeles, CA
1605 West Olympic Blvd., Suite 400
Los Angeles, CA 90015
Phone: 213.380.6031 **Fax:** 213.380.5639

Consulate of Costa Rica in New Orleans, LA
World Trade Center Bldg., 2 Canal St.
Suite 2334

New Orleans, LA 70130
Phone: 504.581.6800
Fax: 504.581.6850

Consulate of Costa Rica in New York, NY
80 Wall Street, Suite 718
New York, NY 10005
Phone: 212.509.3066
Fax: 212.509.3068

Consulate of Costa Rica in Phoenix, AZ
7373 E. Doubletree Ranch Road, Suite 200
Scottsdale, AZ 85258
Phone: 480.951.2264
Fax: 480.951.1204

Consulate of Costa Rica in Saint Paul, MN
2424 Territorial Road
Saint Paul, MN 55114
Phone: 651.645.4103
Fax: 651.645.4684

Consulate of Costa Rica in San Antonio, TX
6836 San Pedro Street, Suite 116
San Antonio, TX 78216
Phone: 210.824.8474
Fax: 210.824.8489

Consulate of Costa Rica in San Francisco, CA
P.O. Box 7643
Fremont, CA 94536
Phone: 510.790.0785
Fax: 510.792.5249

Consulate of Costa Rica in Tampa, FL
17633 Gunn Hwy, Box 178
Odessa, FL 33556
Phone: 813.842.0744

Consulate of Costa Rica in Tucson, AZ
3567 E. Sunrise Drive, Suite 235
Tucson, AZ 85718
Phone: 520.529.7068
Fax: 520.577.6781

El Salvador

1400 16th Street, NW, Suite 100
Washington, DC 20036
Phone: 202.265.9671/72
Fax: 202.232.3763
Email: *correo@elsalvador.org*

U.S. Embassy in San Salvador, El Salvador
Embajada de Los Estados Unidos
Boulevard Santa Elena Final
Antiguo Cuscatlán, La Libertad
El Salvador
Phone: 503.278.6020

Consulate of El Salvador in Boston, MA
222 Third St., Suite 1221
Cambridge, MA 02139

*General Consulate of El Salvador
in Chicago, IL*
104 S. Michigan Ave., Suite 707
Chicago, IL 60603
Phone: 312.332.1393
Fax: 312.332.1393

*General Consulate of El Salvador
in Dallas, TX*
Oakbrook Plaza
1555 W. Mockingbird La., Suite 216
Dallas, TX 75235

*General Consulate of El Salvador in
Houston, TX*
6420 Hillcroft St., Suite 100
Houston, TX 77081
Phone: 713.270.6239

*General Consulate of El Salvador
in Los Angeles, CA*
3450 Wilshire Bl., Suite 250
Los Angeles, CA 90010
Phone: 213.383.8580

*General Consulate of El Salvador
in New Orleans, LA*
World Trade Center, 2 Canal St.
Suite 2310
New Orleans, LA 70130
Phone: 504.522.4266

*General Consulate of El Salvador
in New York, NY*
46 Park Ave.
New York, NY 10016
Phone: 212.889.3608

*Honorary Consulate of El Salvador
in Phoenix, AZ*
4521 E. Charles Dr., Paradise Valley
P.O. Box 2979
Phoenix, AZ 85253
Phone: 602.948.4899

*Honorary Consulate of El Salvador
in Philadelphia, PA*
119 Bleddyn Rd.
Ardmore, PA 19003

*General Consulate of El Salvador
in San Francisco, CA*
870 Market St., Suite 508
San Francisco, CA 94102
Phone: 415.781.7924

*Honorary Consulate of El Salvador
in St. Louis, MO*
7730 Forsyth, Suite 150
St. Louis, MO 63105
Phone: 314.862.0300

*Consular Affairs Office
in Washington, DC*
1424 16th St., N.W., Suite 200
Washington, DC 20036
Phone: 202.331.4032

*Vice Consulate of El Salvador
in Santa Ana, CA*
1212 N. Broadway Ave., Suite 100
Santa Ana, CA 92701

*Permanent Mission of El Salvador
to the United Nations in New York, NY*
46 Park Avenue
New York, NY 10016
Phone: 212.679.1616
Fax: 212.725.7831
Email: *elsalvador@un.int*

Guatemala

*Embassy of the United States of America
in Guatemala City, Guatemala*
Avenida de la Reforma 7-01
Zona 10, Guatemala
Phone: 502.331.1541

*General Consulate of Guatemala
in New York, NY*
57 Park Ave.
New York, NY 10016
Phone: 212.686.3837
Fax: 212.889.5470
Email: *conguatny@aol.com*

Honorary Consulate of Guatemala
in Pittsburgh, PA
709 Washington Dr.
Pittsburgh, PA 15229
Phone: 412.366.7715

Honorary Consulate of Guatemala
in Philadelphia, PA
1245 Highland Ave., Suite 301
Abington, PA 19001
Phone: 215.885.5551

Honorary Consulate of Guatemala
in Portland, OR
921 S.W. Sixth Ave.
Portland, OR 97204
Phone: 503.499.4200

Honorary Consulate of Guatemala
in San Antonio, TX
4840 Whirlwind
San Antonio, TX 78217

Honorary Consulate of Guatemala
in San Diego, CA
10405 San Diego Mission Rd., Suite 205
San Diego, CA 92108
Ph: 619.282.8127

General Consulate of Guatemala
in San Francisco, CA
870 Market St. #667
San Francisco, CA 94102
Phone: 415.788.5651
Fax: 415.788.5653
Email: *guate-sf@pacbell.net*

Honorary Consulate of Guatemala
in San Juan, Puerto Rico
Garden Hills, A-22 Serrania St.
Guaynabo, 00966
Phone: 809.782.7409

Honorary Consulate of Guatemala
in Atlanta, GA
4772 E. Conway Dr., N.W.
Atlanta, GA 30327
Phone: 404.255.7019

General Consulate of Guatemala
in Chicago, IL
200 N. Michigan Ave., Sixth Floor
Chicago, IL 60601

Phone: 312.332.1587
Fax: 312.332.4256
Email: *conguatch@aol.com*

Honorary Consulate of Guatemala
in Ft. Lauderdale, FL
2200 S. Ocean La., Apartment 1705
Ft. Lauderdale, FL 33316
Phone: 305.467.1700

General Consulate of Guatemala
in Houston, TX
3600 S. Gessner Rd. #200
Houston, TX 77063
Phone: 713.953.9531
Fax: 713.953.9383

Honorary Consulate of Guatemala
in Lafayette, IN
735 Rue Jefferson
Lafayette, IN 70501
Phone: 318.268.5474

Honorary Consulate of Guatemala
in Leavenworth, KS
419 Delaware St.
Leavenworth, KS 66048
Phone: 913.682.0342

Consulate of Guatemala in Los Angeles, CA
1605 W. Olympic Blvd. #422
Los Angeles, CA 90015
Phone: 213.365.9245
Email: *consulgualax@aol.com*

Honorary Consulate of Guatemala
in Memphis, TN
Jefferson Plaza
147 Jefferson Ave., Unit 900
Memphis, TN 38103
Phone: 901.527.8466

General Consulate of Guatemala
in Miami, FL
1101 Brickell Ave. #1003S
Miami, FL 33131
Phone: 305.679.9945/48
Fax: 305.679.9983
Email: *cgguamia@bellsouth.net*

Honorary Consulate of Guatemala
in Minneapolis, MN
2105 First Ave., S.
Minneapolis, MN 55404
Phone: 612.870.3459

APPENDIX B

*Honorary Consulate of Guatemala
in Montgomery, AL*
2153 Meadow Lane Dr.
Montgomery, AL 36106
Phone: 205.269.2756

*Honorary Consulate of Guatemala
in New Orleans, LA*
Plaza Tower
1001 Howard Ave., Suite 2504
New Orleans, LA 70113
Phone: 504.558.3777

Honduras

Embassy of Honduras
3007 Tilden Street Northwest, 4M
Washington, DC 20008
Phone: 202.966.7702
Fax: 202.966.9751
Email: *embassy@hondurasemb.org*

American Embassy
Apartado Postal 3453
Avenida La Paz
Tegucigalpa, M.D.C.
Honduras, C.A.

*Honorary Consulate of Honduras
in Baltimore, MD*
5803 Loch Raven Bl.
Baltimore, MD 21239
Phone: 301.435.6233

*Honorary Consulate of Honduras
in Baton Rouge, LA*
11017 N. Oak Hills Pw.
Baton Rouge, LA 70810

Consulate of Honduras in Boston, MA
486 Beacon St., Suite 2
Newton, MA 02115
Phone: 617.247.2007

*General Consulate of Honduras
in Chicago, IL*
4506 West Fullerton Avenue
Chicago, IL 60639
Phone: 773.342.8281/8289
Fax: 773.342.8293

*Honorary Consulate of Honduras
in Honolulu, HI*
1734 Malanai St., Apartment B

Honolulu, HI 96826
Phone: 808.944.2811

*General Consulate of Honduras
in Houston, TX*
4151 Southwest Freeway, Suite 700
Houston, TX 77027
Phone: 713.622.7911
Fax: 713.622.3540
Email: *honduras@ix.netcom.com*

Consulate of Honduras in Jacksonville, FL
1914 Beachway Rd., Suite 3-0
Jacksonville, FL 33207
Phone: 904.348.3550

*General Consulate of Honduras
in Los Angeles, CA*
3450 Wilshire Boulevard, Suite 230
Los Angeles, CA 90010
Phone: 213.383.9244
Fax: 213.383.9309
Email: *Consulla@aol.com*

*General Consulate of Honduras
in Miami, FL*
300 Sevilla Avenue, Suite 201
Coral Gables, FL 33134
Phone: 305.447.9036/8927/6375
Fax: 305.447.9036
Email: *honmiami@bridge.net*

*Honorary Consulate of Honduras
in Minneapolis, MN*
20 Cygnet Pl.
Long Lake, MN 55356
Phone: 612.473.5376

*General Consulate of Honduras
in New Orleans, LA*
World Trade Center, 2 Canal Street
Suite 1641
New Orleans, LA 70130
Phone: 504.522.3118/3119
Fax: 504.523.0544

*General Consulate of Honduras
in New York, NY*
80 Wall Street, Suite 915
New York, NY 10005
Phone: 212.269.3611
Email: *consuladonyc@msn.com*

Nicaragua

Embassy of Nicaragua in Washington, DC
1627 New Hampshire Avenue NW
Washington, DC 20009
Phone: 202.939.6570 or 202.939.6531
Fax: 202.939.6532
Email: *faguirresacasa@ibm.net*

U.S. Embassy in Managua, Nicaragua
KM. 4 1/2 Carretera Sur
Managua, Nicaragua
Phone: 505.266.6010

*Honorary Consulate of Nicaragua
in Atlanta, GA*
3161 Lemons Ridge Dr.
Atlanta, GA 30339
Phone: 770.319.1673

*General Consulate of Nicaragua
in Houston, TX*
6300 Hillcrof, Suite 250
Houston, TX 77081
Phone: 713.272.9628 or 713.272.9629
Fax: 713.272.7131

*General Consulate of Nicaragua
in Los Angeles, CA*
3303 Wilshire Boulevard, Suite 410
Los Angeles, CA 90010
Phone: 213.252.1179
Email: *agapeconsul@aol.com*

*General Consulate of Nicaragua
in Miami, FL*
8370 W. Flagler Street., Suite 220
Miami, FL 33144
Phone: 305.220.0214 or 305.220.6900
Fax: 305.220.8794
Email: *consulnic@aol.com*

*General Consulate of Nicaragua
in Milwaukee, WI*
Hispanic Medical Center
3521 W. National Ave.
Milwaukee, WI 53215

*General Consulate of Nicaragua
in New Orleans, LA*
World Trade Center, 2 Canal Street
Suite 1937
New Orleans, LA 70130

Phone: 504.523.1507
Fax: 504.523.2359

*General Consulate of Nicaragua
in New York, NY*
820 Second Avenue, Eighth Floor, Suite 802
New York, NY 10017
Phone: 212.983.1981
Email: *eliseonum@aol.com*

*Honorary Consulate of Nicaragua
in Philadelphia, PA*
1201 North Second St.
Philadelphia, PA 19122-4501
Phone: 215.627.9414
Fax: 215.627.0734

*General Consulate of Nicaragua
in San Francisco, CA*
870 Market St., Suite 1050
San Francisco, CA 94102
Phone: 415.765.6821
Fax: 415.765.6826

*Honorary Consulate of Nicaragua
in San Juan, PR*
B1 Palma Sola Bl.
Guaynabo, Puerto Rico 00966
Phone: 787.781.6530

*Permanent Mission of Nicaragua
to the United Nations in New York, NY*
820 Second Avenue, Eighth Floor, Suite 801
New York, NY 10017
Phone: 212.490.7997
Fax: 212.286.0815
Email: *nicun@nygate.undp.org*

Panama

U.S. Embassy in Panama City, Panama
Embajada de Estados Unidos
Sección Informativa y Cultural
Apartado 6959
Panamá 5, República de Panamá

General Consulate of Panama in Atlanta, GA
Cain Tower
Peachtree Center, 229 Peachtree St. NE
Suite 1209
Atlanta, GA 30303
Phone: 404.522.4114

*Honorary Consulate of Panama
in Cleveland, OH*
31300 Tuttle Dr.
Bay Village, OH 44140

*General Consulate of Panama
in Houston, TX*
24 Guenway Plaza, Suite 1307
Houston, TX 77046
Phone: 713.622.4451
Fax: 713.622.4468

*Honorary Consulate of Panama
in Los Angeles, CA*
3137 W. Ball Rd., Suite 104
Anaheim, CA 92804
Phone: 714.816.1809

Consulate of Panama in Miami, FL
444 Brickel Avenue, Suite 729
Miami, FL 33131
Phone: 305.371.7031
Fax: 305.371.2907

*Honorary Consulate of Panama
in Mobile, AL*
551 Church St.
Mobile, AL 36602
Phone: 334.432.4424

*General Consulate of Panama
in New Orleans, LA*
1324 World Trade Center
2 Canal Street
New Orleans, LA 70130
Phone: 504.525.3458
Fax: 504.524.8960

*General Consulate of Panama
in Philadelphia, PA*
124 Chestnut St.
Philadelphia, PA 19106
Phone: 215.574.2994
Fax: 215.625.4876

*Honorary Consulate of Panama
in San Diego, CA*
2552 Chatsworth Bl.
San Diego, CA 92106
Phone: 619.225.8144

*Honorary Consulate of Panama
in San Juan, Puerto Rico*
Marginal Kennedy Ave.
San Juan, PR 00920
Phone: 787.792.1050

*General Consulate of Panama
in Tampa, FL*
Galleria Office Building
4326 El Prado Bl., Suite 4
Tampa, FL 33629
Phone: 813.251.0316

Ministry of the Foreign Affairs of Panama
2201 Wisconsin Avenue N.W., Suite 240
Washington, DC 20007
Phone: 202.965.4826 or 202.965.4819
Fax: 202.965.4836
Email: *eaa@emba-Cdccmail.compuserv.com*

*Panamanian Institute of Foreign Trade
Regional Office*
1477 South Miami Avenue
Miami, FL 33130
Phone: 305.374.8823
Fax: 305.374.7822

*Permanent Mission of Panama
to the United Nations in New York, NY*
866 United Nations Plaza, Room 4030
New York, NY 10017
Phone: 212.421.5420/5421
Fax: 212.421.2694
Email: *panun@un.int*

Index

*America's Emigrants—U.S. Retirement
Migration to Mexico and Panama*
(Migration Policy Institute), 12
amortization of rental property, 212–13
ANABIR *see* Honduras National Real Estate
Association
Antigua (Guatemala), xix, 141, 144, 145,
153–54
"apostilling" of documents, 247
appliances, 28–29, 136, 204, 210, 235
appreciation of property value, 199, 200,
201, 249, 253, 254, 257, 262, 283, 285
capital appreciation, 101, 120, 121,
131, 239
in Central America, xvii, 197, 247, 266,
281, 285
in Costa Rica, xii, 43, 50, 54
as a factor in selecting property, 198,
213–14, 225
in Nicaragua, 101, 103, 106, 120, 121,
131
in Panama, 16, 31, 32, 34, 41
archeology, 145
Arco Seco see Dry Arc of Panama
*Asociacion Nacional de Agencias de Bienes
Raices de Honduras see* Honduras
National Real Estate Association
asset method for determining discretionary
income, 207–9
assurance of ownership *see* title insurance
Atitlan *see* Lake Atitlan (Guatemala)
attorneys
documents needed by in Guatemala,
150
documents needed by in Nicaragua,
117–18
finding and choosing, 85, 111
importance of, 67, 168
as Notaries, 112
and rental property, 237
used instead of Notaries in Belize, 246
automobiles, duty free availability
in Belize, 176
in Honduras, 92
Autonomous Regions of the North and
South (Nicaragua), 107
Ayales, Omar, 58

— B —

baby boomers *see* boomer generation
background checks, 175
Bainbridge-Ometepe Sister Islands
Association, 127–28
bujareques (showers), 23
Balboa Avenue (Panama City), 18
balboas, 6
Ballena National Marine Park
(Costa Rica), 50
BAMER, 83
banana capital *see* Golfito (Costa Rica)
"banana republics," disappearance of, xix
Banco Banex, 73
Banco B.G.A., 79
Banco de Occidente, 83
Banco Internacional, 151
Banco Mercantil *see* BAMER
banks and banking, 202, 258
bank financing in Central America
just beginning, 257–58
in Belize, 171, 173, 175
in Costa Rica, 45, 53, 54
in El Salvador, 185, 186, 187, 188,
191, 192–93
in Guatemala, 151, 152
in Honduras, 78–79, 87
and IRAs, 254, 255
in Nicaragua, 114
in Panama, 29, 40
and rental property, 239, 282
see also financing; lenders
Barcelo (company), 105
Barra de Santiago (El Savador), 183
Barrier Reef of Roatán (Honduras), 77
Barrio Dent (Costa Rica), 55–56
Barva (development in Costa Rica), 56
Bastimentos National Marine Park
(Panama), 26
Bay Islands (Honduras), xix, 75, **76**, 77, 80,
81, 90
Bay of Panama, 15, 19
beaches *see* under names of individual
countries
beachfront property, xviii

INDEX

Order Form

Crabman Publishing

Online Orders:	*www.crabmanpublishing.com*
Fax Orders:	206-855-0605
Telephone Orders:	206-842-0877
E-mail Orders:	*orders@tomkelly.com*
Postal Orders:	Crabman Publishing
	P.O. Box 4719
	Rolling Bay, WA 98061

	Price	Quantity	Subtotal
Cashing In on a Second Home in Central America	$19.95	_____	_____
Cashing In on a Second Home in Mexico	$19.95	_____	_____

Sales Tax: Please add 8% for books shipped to Washington state addresses: $_____

Shipping: In the U.S., please add $5 for first book, $3 for each additional book. Outside the U.S., please add $10 for first book, $6 for each additional book. $_____

TOTAL: $_____

Shipping Address:

Name: _____

Address: _____

City: _____State: _____ Zip:_____

Telephone: _____

E-mail address: _____

Payment: ❏ Check enclosed   ❏ VISA   ❏ MasterCard

Card number:_____ Exp. Date: _____

Signature: _____

Name on card: _____